COOKING FOR
FAMILY & FRIENDS

Margaret Fulton

Angus&Robertson
An imprint of HarperCollins*Publishers*

*Jacket: Grilled Lemon Chicken (p. 278) served with
Spanish Orange Salad (p. 147) and garnished with
watercress. The chicken breast is first marinated in
lemon juice, onion and garlic before cooking on a ribbed
pan. Pears in Citrus Sauce (p. 356) is on the back
jacket. These fresh-tasting, translucent pears are among
the loveliest of fresh fruit desserts.*

An Angus & Robertson Publication

Angus&Robertson, an imprint of
HarperCollins*Publishers*
25 Ryde Road, Pymble, Sydney, NSW 2073, Australia
31 View Road, Glenfield, Auckland 10, New Zealand
Distributed in the United States of America by
HarperCollins*Publishers*
10 East 53rd Street, New York NY 10022, USA

First published in Australia in 1993 under title of
Margaret Fulton's New Cookbook

ISBN 0 207 18340 6

Produced in association with
Barbara Beckett Publishing
14 Hargrave Street, Paddington, Sydney, Australia 2021

Food by Margaret Fulton and Suzanne Gibbs
Photography by Rodney Weidland
Designed by Amanda McPaul
Jacket design by Clare Forte
Typeset by Graphicraft Typesetters Limited, Hong Kong
Printed in Australia by Griffin Press, Adelaide

9 8 7 6 5 4 3 2 1
97 96 95 94 93

Contents

Introduction   8

Breakfast   16

Herbs   26

Snacks   44

Soups   64

Vegetables and Salads   96

Vegetarian Dishes   158

Sauces   180

Fish   194

Meat   218

Poultry   268

Luncheons and Suppers   292

Home Baking   318

Desserts   342

Cook it Light   364

Index   396

Weights and Measures

*T*he recipes in this book are given in metric measures, using standard measuring cups and spoons. In brackets are the imperial equivalents. These translations are not exact equivalents but brought to the nearest round figure; however, they still preserve the correct balance of ingredients. To retain that balance, follow either metric or imperial, never a mixture.

All Good Cooks Need

• A nest of four graduated measuring cups for measuring dry ingredients. These come in $1/4$, $1/2$, $1/3$ and 1 cup size.

• A standard measuring cup for measuring liquids.

• A 1-litre or 4-cup measuring jug for measuring large quantities of liquid. These jugs usually show both cup and metric measures and are marked in cups and millilitres, others in imperial fluid ounces.

• A set of graduated measuring spoons. The set includes a tablespoon, teaspoon, half-teaspoon and quarter-teaspoon. Level spoon measures are used.

• Scales. Usually marked nowadays in both metric and imperial measurements. Scales are needed for weighing meat, vegetables and bulky items.

Spoon and Cup Measurements

	Australia	*New Zealand*	*United Kingdom*	*United States*
1 tablespoon	20 ml	15 ml	$1/2$ fl oz (14 ml)	$1/2$ fl oz (14 ml)
1 cup	250 ml	250 ml	8 fl oz (237 ml)	8 fl oz (237 ml)

All countries use the same teaspoon measurements.

Preheat the Oven

Always preheat an oven, unless you are reheating food. The time this takes varies with the oven. As so many cookery procedures vary, like chilling pastry for an hour or folding in egg whites for a soufflé in 3 minutes, it is not practical to include instructions to preheat the oven at the beginning of each recipe. Keep this in mind when using the oven and make sure it is at the required temperature by the time you are ready to put the dish in the oven. The usual time to reach a required oven temperature varies from 15 to 20 minutes. Check with the instruction book of your oven.

The correct oven temperature is essential to the success of a dish. It makes pastry crisp, a soufflé or cake rise. Only a high heat will seal in meat juices—too low a heat draws the juices out. Sometimes oven temperatures are changed during cooking, high heat for a crispy topping, then low to cook the filling.

Bright red freshwater shellfish, when alive, are bright blue, black or green, or even yellowish pink. Crayfish, crawfish, yabbies and marron turn bright red when dropped into boiling water.

Acknowledgements

Cooking is my life. It is both my work and my hobby. It is what makes my life a good life. Imagine the added pleasure of working on this book when the three musketeers who went into action with me had a lot in common.

First Barbara Beckett, a friend of twenty-five years, book publisher and lover of fine food, wine and people. It was Barbara who sold me on the idea of writing this new book. Perhaps not unexpectedly, I called on my daughter Suzanne Gibbs for help and support. Suzanne inherited my love of food and polished her natural talents at the Cordon Bleu School of Cookery in London, graduating with its prestigious Diploma; this was followed by a year as the head of the pastry and dessert kitchen of the Cordon Bleu restaurant in Marylebone Lane, London. The third member of the team was Rodney Weidland, a brilliant photographer, whose enthusiasm and mastery of his craft and his love of the subject brought sheer magic to each dish we prepared. What you see in these pages is the result of a wonderful year spent together—shopping, cooking and creating, writing it all down and recording it with superb photography.

In all the photographs you see my own favourite china, glassware and silver, collected over many years and used from day to day in my own home. You see glimpses of Suzanne's lovely garden and home. You see some of Barbara's treasures, her precious heirloom table linen and china. You see Rodney's sensitive and skilful interpretation of my food and the way I like to show it, with Barbara's artistic direction and Suzanne's fine cooking all contributing inimitable style.

I have been able to include a few special recipes that have appeared in the pages of *New Idea*, with the permission of my chief and friend, Dulcie Boling.

I would like to add a sincere word of appreciation to Iris Silva and Amber Keller, who kept law and order in our busy kitchens.

The recipes in this book express the way I cook for today's healthy lifestyle. It is the food I enjoy with Suzanne and her family, with Barbara and my friends.

Introduction

This is a book about the food we cook and enjoy today.
It is about the way we approach breakfast, the way we
make a snack or prepare a light lunch or dinner, the
special biscuits we bake for a wedding, the pastry
discovered in France and the pleasure of making it at
home. The recipes chosen for family meals, celebrations,
picnics, luncheons with friends all reflect my love of
cooking and eating, more so when enjoyed in good
company.

I keep in mind the advice of nutritionists and health
bodies—from them we can learn much about developing
recipes for healthy food that tastes good. The changes
in our eating habits have also been taken into
consideration. We are learning to use different foods,
appreciating grains and pulses, vegetables and fruits,
and turning them into nourishing and delicious meals.
The keyword is variety: dolmeh from Iran, couscous
from North Africa, lentil and vegetable curries from
India, Thai dishes, Vietnamese dishes—all increase our
awareness of what's good.

In this book are the dishes that have made life for my
family, my friends and myself one long, continuous
source of pleasure with the added bonus of good health.

*A glass of crisp white wine helps a busy cook relax in a peaceful garden—
whether it be while writing recipes, shelling peas, trimming artichokes,
listening to birds, watching fish in the pond or just reflecting.*

It All Starts with Shopping

*W*hen I go shopping I look for the freshest vegetables, herbs and fruit, always at their best and cheapest when in season. The new meat cuts and the variety of seafood and poultry mean we can get exactly what we want, be it one or twenty chicken breasts or a hundred wings. The lovely oils, vinegars, butters, cheeses, fresh eggs of any size, the pastas, grains, dried legumes, pickles, jams and other delicacies make cooking a joy.

Eat Fresh Vegetables Every Day

I take my hat off to the vegetable growers, who take such an interest in the varieties of vegetables they grow and make sure they are picked and packed with care and rushed to the markets while still at their peak. How they cope with floods, droughts, heat and frost I don't know, but I appreciate what they accomplish and do my bit by purchasing, storing, cooking and serving vegetables with the same love and attention. I am repaid with good eating and good health.

The modern healthy way to cook vegetables is in as little water as possible with very little salt; you may even wean yourself right off salt. You need a heavy saucepan with a tight-fitting lid. Vegetables will then retain maximum vitamins and minerals, which are often thrown down the sink in the old 'water' method. Consider also the microwave cooking of vegetables; nutritionists say this method gives major health benefit.

Storing vegetables. Certain fruit and vegetables should not be stored together. For example, apples give off an ethylene gas that makes carrots bitter, and onions hasten the spoilage of potatoes. Do not wash vegetables until you are ready to use them, and do not soak them unless that is indicated in the recipe, because moisture tends to leach out the water-soluble vitamins. A good general rule for leaf vegetables, peas and beans is to store them in the refrigerator in plastic bags; there are ones made especially for vegetables. Look also for the brown all-purpose bags. There is enough moisture within the vegetables to keep them fresh this way.

When buying vegetables, shop on the days when supplies reach your store and buy so that you can hold them the least possible time before use. If you can, buy vegetables in season when they are at their best and cheapest.

If the vegetables are mature, dress them up with seasoned butter, herbs, spices and sauces. If young, toss in just a touch of butter or olive oil or a little lemon juice and season very lightly, so that their own flavour prevails. You will find that while young vegetables have an abundance of natural sugars, older ones often profit by an added pinch of sugar in cooking. Whether you cook vegetables whole or sliced, see that pieces are uniform in size, so that they will all be done and tender simultaneously.

A Word about Salads

Don't neglect the possibility of using a salad as a first course—and there are some salads that are a meal in themselves. When including a salad as part of a meal, make sure that it is one that provides the right balance to the meal. A large main dish needs only the lightest of salads, while a richer, fuller salad may be just right after a poached or grilled fish or an omelette. A rich dish needs a tart salad; slaws go well with casual meals. Elaborate, beautifully arranged salads look good on a buffet table; at suppers and luncheons, consider individual salads, carefully arranged on individual plates.

Use your imagination with dressings, but at the same time don't go overboard with experimenting. I've tasted some salads so strong with garlic that they have been positively unpleasant. Your salad dressing should enhance, not overpower, the flavour of your salad.

Chinese cabbage, savoy, sugarloaf, the large, green, white and red cabbages, although winter vegetables, are around for the early summer months and are popular for coleslaw and other salads.

The beautiful corello pear is a lovely addition to the cheese board.

Mini Lamb Topside Roast, one of the new cuts suitable for pan roasting, serves 2.

Among the cresses and tiny leaves, we can now get watercress and also green and peppery corn salad (lamb's lettuce), shaped like a lamb's tongue and called *mache* in France, which has a delicious nutty taste. Mustard and cress, sold in little punnets, bring their warm, sharp taste to salads and sandwiches.

Unusual, but becoming less so, is the bright, colourful radicchio, sometimes marbled red, pink and white, adding beauty to salads. There is arugula (sometimes called rocket), a favourite Italian green with a distinctive peppery taste, which is wonderful mixed with other greens or used as a base for light meals, cheese or fish starters.

Don't forget sorrel and tender young spinach or silver beet (Swiss chard), lightly steamed or crisped and torn into salads. Both are particularly good as a base for salad made with a hot dressing of vinegar and crisp bacon.

Herbs are their shining best in salads: basil, curly and flat-leafed parsley, mint, coriander (Chinese parsley), salad burnet and dill all liven salad and other foods with their light, fresh and aromatic qualities.

Make Good Use of Herbs

Strew mixed herbs over all salads, vegetables and grills. Use them in savoury breads and muffins. Learn what goes with what: basil with tomato; tarragon with chicken; chives with eggs, potato or cheese dishes; coriander with South-East Asian dishes; dill with cucumbers, fish, or new potatoes; bay leaf with soups, stews and, yes, custard. A little marjoram or oregano with avocados, mushrooms, veal, fish and stuffings works wonders. Sage is vital for sausages, stews, trout, veal and bread stuffings, savoury dumplings and biscuits. The combinations are endless and add interest to daily meals.

If you don't have access to fresh herbs, try at least to grow parsley. By chopping dried herbs together with parsley you will get the flavour of the herb with that of the fresh parsley.

It is important to store fresh herbs correctly. Wash, then spin them dry in a salad basket. Wrap each herb loosely in kitchen paper and store in the refrigerator in an airtight container or plastic bags. Stand coriander, still with its roots, in a jug of water, then put a plastic bag over the top and store in the refrigerator. Check the stored herbs from time to time, shaking them and refreshing paper or water as necessary.

The Birds We Buy

Modern poultry farming has put chicken on everyone's table at a reasonable price. Some growers are proud of their champion breeds with more breast and less fat. Not only whole birds are available, but also breasts, whole or halved, fillets cut from the breast, minced chicken, drumsticks or thighs, with or without the skin and bone, wings—all have their uses. While these jointed birds are mostly battery fed and lacking in that old-time flavour, with a little imagination a lot can be done with them.

Learn to French-roast poultry. By cooking it on a rack over stock, wine or water and frequently basting it with the liquid underneath, it is kept beautifully moist and still plumps to a golden crispy skin. Look, too, at the Chinese way of steeping a bird—they call it white cooked chicken—then finish it off with Asian oils and seasonings. Thai chicken, with its unusual spices, is different. Every nationality can take pride in their skills at cooking poultry.

A grilled (broiled) chicken is one of the most delicious foods at any time. Choose a small bird, size 5–9 (500 g to 1 kg/1–2 lb), split it and grill it, skin side up, for 5 minutes, turn and grill for another 5 minutes, then finish skin side up for about 4 minutes, basting well during the whole procedure. Various joints may also be grilled using the same technique. Also make use of one of those useful ribbed grills.

There are many flavourings that will give jointed birds and those small birds flavour: tarragon, slices of orange or lemon, herbs. When on a weight-loss program, remove the skin and protect the flesh from drying out with a marinade very lightly brushed over. Marinate chicken in a good olive oil, an unusual vinegar (sherry, balsamic or a herby one) before grilling or frying.

Fish Is Important in Our Diet

Most of us eat fish simply because we enjoy it, but there are other good reasons for serving it regularly. Fish is a good source of the proteins needed for growth and repair of our bodies. Fish is easy to digest, and it is an ideal food for people who are watching or reducing their weight.

Fish is rich in vitamins A and D and contains beneficial minerals such as iodine, which some scientists consider benefits the brain. Fish is also an important food for those with heart and circulation problems, because its oils (long-chain highly polyunsaturated omega-3 fatty acids) are effective in reducing blood cholesterol.

Fish is so delicious when cooked well, and so comparatively inexpensive, it seems a pity not to make more use of it.

Know how much to buy? Appetites vary, of course, but there's a rule to guide you. If you're buying your fish whole (head, bones and all), allow 500 g (1 lb) per person. On the other hand, 500 g (1 lb) of fillets will give you two large or three average servings. Combined with other foods, such as rice, pasta or vegetables, it will serve more.

Meat—Know What You Buy

You can judge meat to some degree by its appearance, but many of us rely on the skill and integrity of our butcher. While eating is the final test, there are some points you could bear in mind:

Beef should be a bright cherry red when freshly cut, and finely grained. There should be flecks of fat (marbling) through it. The fat should be firm, smooth and creamy white. Lamb should be a light reddish-pink and have an even edging of firm white fat. Pork should have pale pink, finely grained flesh, pearly white fat and thin, smooth skin. Veal should be very pale, pinkish, finely grained and smooth. There should only be a thin edge of white satiny fat. The bones are large in proportion to the size and should be bluish-white.

To store meat. As a general rule the larger the piece of meat the longer it will store. Minced meat, sausages and variety meats should be cooked within 24 hours of purchase; diced meats within 48 hours. Steaks and chops will keep for 2 to 4 days, roasts for 3 to 5 days. Store meat in the coldest part of the refrigerator, loosely covered with foil. Never leave meat in its plastic wrap if that's how it has been bought—supermarkets often sell meat this way.

Learn to Master the Basic Sauces

Anyone interested in cooking should learn to master the basic sauces. For many of us, a simple salad dressing of oil and vinegar, a fine buttery hollandaise for new-season asparagus, beurre blanc for fish and seafood, and a classic mayonnaise have become part of life. Whether simple or intricate, all good sauces have one thing in common: they must be made with the freshest and choicest ingredients available. Don't be put off by the richness of some sauces like beurre blanc and hollandaise; they are served so rarely and in such small quantities that they should be relished as the first fragrant fruits of summer.

A sauce should have so pleasant a flavour and be so discreetly blended that you feel you could eat it by itself. Although sauces can lift any dish, it is a mistake to use too much sauce. As a rule of thumb, about two tablespoons per serve is a suitable allowance.

A sauce may be an essential part of a dish, as when the liquid from meat or fish forms part of its composition. Fricassees and casseroles are examples of this. Poached salmon with the rich butter sauce known by the French as *beurre blanc* is another example of blending flavours. Mussels are often steamed in wine and aromatics and the juices used as a soup-sauce. This precious liquid turns mussels into a dish fit for a king.

It may be the coating of a dish, such as when béchamel masks vegetables, fish or poultry to prevent the food from drying out while it is being 'gilded' under a grill for those delicious gratins. Béchamel is a most useful sauce when made correctly, and this is easy. It moistens food, it adds lightness and delicacy, and is one of the great classics of the sauce world as well as being a traditional stand-by of the home cook.

Vinaigrette sauce (oil, lemon, herbs) can be varied in a multitude of ways, by changing the herbs used or using different oils and vinegars. Olive oil comes in many grades from the expensive extra virgin to the regular, and now there are light oils perfect for frying. There's a wide choice of nut oils, including walnut, macadamia and hazelnut oil, and oils made from seeds—sunflower, safflower, sesame—and all have their uses. As with wine, it's worth shopping around for the one that really suits your palate.

Vinegars, too, should be explored. A harsh vinegar will taste harsh in a dressing. Look for the different flavours: tarragon, wine, cider, raspberry, sherry and the lovely aged balsamic are just a few. The best quality oil and vinegar you can afford, the freshest butter and eggs you can find, and garden herbs freshly picked will make a world of difference to the quality of the sauces and dressings you make.

Bucatini with Pesto. Allow 125 g (4 oz) pasta for each person, cook it in boiling salted water, strain and place in heated bowls, then mix in a generous lump of butter and 2 tablespoons of pesto. Grated Parmesan is served separately.

Breakfast

Breakfast is a very personal meal. Some of us treasure the time we spend with the family before we go our separate ways to face each day. Such families look forward to muffins warm from the oven, flapjacks (pancakes, griddle cakes) hot from the pan or perhaps a treat of mushrooms on toast or a large bowl of steaming porridge. There will be freshly squeezed orange juice and huge mugs of piping hot coffee.

For others, staying in bed seems awfully attractive. Once you have succumbed, starting the day becomes a hectic scramble and breakfast suffers.

If you're convinced that breakfast is important, yet the reality of providing it seems daunting, there are ways to be sure you get off to a good start. First, learn to make a basic muesli. This can be made in advance and stored in an airtight container. It is important to add one piece of fresh fruit to the muesli when serving. An apple, grated skin and all, is a favourite. With a serving of milk you have a complete meal and one that will stand the family in good stead for the rest of the day. Look also at the pep drinks—a meal in a glass is something that will get you going when you are on the run.

A bowl of homemade toasted muesli with grated apple, fresh hot Blueberry Bran and Orange Pecan Muffins, fresh orange juice and tea or piping hot coffee —a great way to start the day.

Fruit for Breakfast

Tip

Poached rhubarb should be just that—washed and cut into short lengths, the stalks are poached in a syrup of ¹/₂ cup (4¹/₂ fl oz) of water and ¹/₂ cup (4 oz) of sugar with the rind and juice of 1 orange. Don't allow it to boil; just bring it to the simmer, covered. By this time the rhubarb should be tender but whole. When cold, slide the contents into a bowl.

$\mathcal{M}$any of us like to start the day with fresh fruit juice—a good way to make sure we get vitamin C. Freshly squeezed citrus juice is, of course, the best, but if you haven't time to squeeze oranges every morning, the next best thing is to buy large containers of juice, preferably vitamin-fortified. Buttermilk and fresh orange juice, half and half, are a particularly good combination.

Others start the day with fruit. Easily digestible, light and energy-giving, fruit can make a good breakfast. Try these ideas:

Coarsely grate an unpeeled apple, sprinkle it with lemon juice and combine with 1 tablespoon of chopped nuts, 1 tablespoon of honey and 2–3 tablespoons of natural (plain) yoghurt. Serve with fresh strawberries, sliced peaches, alone or with other fruits.

Summer fruit salad. Combine chunks of peach, apricot and plum, and sprinkle with a little lemon juice. Best made just before eating.

Fruit with yoghurt. Try fresh or stewed fruit with either natural or fruit-flavoured yoghurt. Stewed rhubarb or apricots and yoghurt is delicious. Some people like yoghurt with fresh orange segments or sliced banana.

Fresh rockmelon (cantaloupe) or honeydew melon make a refreshing start to a hot summer day. Cubes of fresh pawpaw (papaya), lightly sweetened if necessary, can be served sprinkled with a little lemon juice.

Dried fruit (apricots, peaches, prunes, figs), soaked in water for a few hours or overnight, lightly sweetened and cooked until just tender, is delicious served either warm or chilled, by itself or with yoghurt.

For those who enjoy fruit for breakfast: just-squeezed orange juice, refreshing rockmelon, muesli with a pile of freshly grated unpeeled apple and a dollop of natural (plain) yoghurt, and stewed fruit, this time poached rhubarb and a few strawberries.

Pep Drinks

$\mathcal{T}$here are people who just can't get out of bed in the morning; they fly out of the house without breakfast or a moment to spare. Catch them on the run with one of these pep drinks recommended for health and vitality. Some are pick-me-ups after a late or heavy night; others will keep you going through a full and busy day. An electric blender or food processor is a great help in preparing these quick meals, but failing them, a good egg whisk or one of those practical electric wands will do the job. (In the United States, where health reports advise against using raw eggs because of endemic contamination by salmonella of the US egg and chicken supply, it may be better to stick to the drinks that don't call for a raw egg.)

Orange and buttermilk. Combine $^1/_2$ cup ($4^1/_2$ fl oz) of cold buttermilk, $^1/_2$ cup ($4^1/_2$ fl oz) of orange juice, 1 tablespoon of lemon juice, 1 ice cube and 1 teaspoon of honey. Mix well with a whisk or an electric blender. Serve cold in a glass. Serves 1.

Yoghurt shake. Put in a blender $^2/_3$ cup of crushed pineapple, 1 thin slice of lemon, 1 teaspoon of honey and $^2/_3$ cup (6 fl oz) of natural (plain) yoghurt, and blend at maximum speed for 30 seconds. Buttermilk can be used instead of yoghurt, and fresh fruits such as a banana, a few strawberries or a peach can be added for extra flavour. Serves 1.

Meal in a glass. Put the following ingredients in a blender container and blend at maximum speed for 30 seconds: 1 egg, 1 cup (9 fl oz) orange juice, 1 tablespoon honey, 1 tablespoon lemon juice, 1 tablespoon wheat germ. Serves 1.

Vitality cocktail. Warm 1 cup (9 fl oz) of orange juice just enough to take the chill off, place in an electric blender with 1 tablespoon of lemon juice, 2 teaspoons of honey and 1 egg yolk and blend for 30 seconds. Add an ice cube and serve chilled. Serves 1.

Quick pep juice. In an electric blender, combine 1 fresh egg and 1 cup (9 fl oz) of unsweetened orange, pineapple or mango juice. Mix well. This makes an ideal protein breakfast. Fresh eggs are considered to be one of the richest sources of lecithin (good for the nerves). Serves 1.

German egg tonic. This drink is not for children, but it is a great tonic for a quick pick-up: Beat a fresh egg yolk into half a glass of sherry. Sip slowly.

Basic Muesli

3 cups (14 oz) quick-cooking oats
$^1/_2$ cup (2 oz) dried apricots, finely chopped
$^1/_2$ cup (3 oz) sultanas (golden raisins)
$^3/_4$ cup (2 oz) wheat germ
$^1/_2$ cup (4 oz) raw sugar
FOR SERVING
Fresh apples
Milk or cream

oast the oats in a moderate oven (180°C/350°F) for 8–10 minutes. Place the apricots in a bowl and combine with the sultanas, oats, wheat germ and sugar. Cool. Store in a tightly covered container at room temperature. Serve 3–4 tablespoons of muesli in individual cereal bowls. Grate 1 apple over each serving and add milk or cream.

Almond muesli. Increase the apricots to 1 cup (4 oz) and add ¹/₂ cup (2 oz) chopped almonds toasted under a hot grill (broiler) or in the oven.

Hazelnut muesli. Toast 125 g (4 oz) of hazelnuts the same way as almonds. Rub them in a towel to remove as much brown skin as possible. Chop them coarsely and add them to the basic muesli mixture.

Muesli with dried fruit. Chop finely 1 cup (4 oz) of dried apples or pears and add them to the basic muesli mixture. The apricots may be omitted.

Bran muesli. To the basic muesli mixture add 1 cup of bran cereal.

Muesli with honey. If you like to use honey instead of sugar, omit the raw sugar from the mixture and drizzle honey over each serving to taste.

Apple muesli with yoghurt. Blend 3 tablespoons of natural (plain) yoghurt with 1 teaspoon of lemon juice and 1 tablespoon of honey. Pour over the apple-topped muesli mixture and serve.

Sweet Corn Fritters

Canned sweet corn kernels are convenient and good, but when it's the season for corn I like to use it fresh. Cook on the cob in fast-boiling water about 8 minutes, then scrape off the kernels ready for making fritters.

> *310 g (10 oz) can of whole-kernel corn, drained*
> *2 tablespoons chopped onion or chopped chives*
> *2 eggs, lightly beaten*
> *¹/₄ teaspoon salt*
> *Freshly ground black pepper*
> *1 teaspoon sugar*
> *3 tablespoons self-raising four, sifted*
> *60 g (2 oz) butter*

ix all the ingredients except the butter in a bowl and beat until well blended. Heat the butter in a heavy frying pan (skillet). When the foam subsides, drop in the batter in large spoonfuls. Fry over a moderate heat until golden brown on both sides. Drain on rumpled kitchen paper towels and serve hot with grilled (broiled) bacon, tomatoes and plenty of toast. Makes 8–10.

Griddle Cakes

Also called flapjacks, these are a great American breakfast favourite. The name *griddle* comes from the circular flat metal surface which originally was suspended over the fire. Serve these thick pancakes piping hot with melted butter and maple syrup. Grilled bacon is often served on the side.

> *2 cups (8 oz) plain (all-purpose) flour*
> *2 teaspoons baking powder*
> *1 tablespoon sugar*
> *$^1/_2$ teaspoon salt*
> *3 eggs, lightly beaten*
> *2 cups (18 fl oz) milk*
> *60 g (2 oz) butter, melted*
> *A little oil for cooking*

OPPOSITE PAGE
Griddle Cakes—a great pile, piping hot, tender and light, served with butter that melts along with sweet maple syrup.

Sift the flour with the baking powder, sugar and salt into a large bowl. Make a well in the centre and add the eggs and milk. With a large spoon mix the centre ingredients, incorporating the dry ingredients just enough to blend. Stir in the melted butter. The batter will still be lumpy. It is important not to overmix or the griddle cakes will toughen.

Heat a griddle or frying pan (skillet) over a moderate heat until a drop of water flicked on it evaporates instantly. Brush lightly with a little oil, and pour the batter from a jug or use a small ladle to form pancakes about 10 cm (4 in) in diameter. This size is right for stacking American style; smaller ones are best for individual eating. Cook for about 3 minutes or until small bubbles have formed on the surface; the pancakes should be turned before these bubbles break. Cook for a minute on the other side until golden brown. Stack on a heated plate and serve with butter and maple syrup. Makes 10–12.

Fruit griddle cakes. A few slices of fresh peach or other soft fruit or a spoonful of blueberries (bilberries) or sliced strawberries may be added to the batter as it is spooned onto the griddle.

LEFT
A modern griddle, based on the centuries-old 'girdle' of Scotland, cooks griddle cakes, pikelets (drop scones) and other treats.

Orange Pecan Muffins

An unusual method, but to my mind these are just as muffins should be—light, moist, and fresh-tasting.

> *2 large oranges*
> *2 large eggs*
> *¹/₃ cup (3 oz) sugar*
> *125 g (4 oz) unsalted (sweet) butter, melted*
> *2 cups (8 oz) plain (all purpose) flour*
> *2 teaspoons baking powder*
> *¹/₂ teaspoon each bicarbonate of soda (baking soda) and salt*
> *¹/₂ cup (2 oz) pecans, roughly chopped*
> *1 tablespoon sugar mixed with 1 teaspoon ground cinnamon*

*P*reheat the oven to hot (200°C/400°F). Butter 16 muffin tins (deep patty tins), ¹/₃ or ¹/₂ cup size.

Grate the rind off the oranges. Carefully cut away and discard the white pith. Quarter the flesh and chop finely in a food processor or by hand, reserving all the juice that comes from them. In a large bowl whisk the eggs until foamy and add the sugar and melted butter, whisking until the mixture is thick and well combined. Add the chopped oranges, rind and juice, stirring.

Sift in the flour with the baking powder, bicarbonate of soda and salt and fold the mixture lightly until it is just combined. Lastly fold in the chopped pecans. Divide the batter among 12–16 muffin tins, depending on size, three-quarters filling them; sprinkle each with the cinnamon sugar. Bake in the centre of the oven for 15 to 20 minutes or until golden and risen. Turn out onto wire racks to cool slightly. Makes 16.

Blueberry Bran Muffins

90 g (3 oz) unsalted (sweet) butter, melted and cooled

1/2 cup (4 1/2 fl oz) milk

2 large eggs

1 1/2 cups (6 oz) plain (all-purpose) flour

2/3 cup (5 oz) sugar

2 teaspoons baking powder

A large pinch of salt

5 tablespoons processed bran

1 1/2 cups blueberries

1 tablespoon sugar mixed with 1 teaspoon ground cinnamon

Preheat the oven to hot (220°C/425°F). Butter 12 muffin tins (deep patty tins), 1/3 cup size. In a bowl lightly whisk together the melted butter, milk and eggs. Sift the flour, sugar, baking powder and salt over the liquid mixture and add the bran. Stir the batter until it is just combined—it should still be lumpy—then fold in the blueberries lightly.

Spoon the mixture into the muffin tins. Sprinkle with the cinnamon sugar and bake for 20–25 minutes until the muffins are risen and golden. Makes 12.

Tip
You can use either fresh blueberries or the free-flowing packaged frozen blueberries for these simple-to-mix, healthy muffins. Serve them warm or at room temperature, with or without butter.

Creamed Mushrooms

500 g (1 lb) mushrooms

2 tablespoons butter

2 tablespoons plain (all-purpose) flour

Salt and freshly ground pepper

1 cup (9 fl oz) milk

1/4 cup (2 1/4 fl oz) cream (single, light)

2 teaspoons grated onion or juice of onion (optional)

Slice the caps and tender stems of the mushrooms. Simmer stems in their own juices in a covered pan for about 10 minutes. Strain the liquid into a cup. Heat the butter in a heavy frying pan and sauté the sliced mushrooms for 3 minutes, stirring constantly. Sprinkle over the flour and season well with salt and freshly ground pepper. Stir until well blended. Add the mushroom liquid, milk, cream and onion, and stir the mixture until it is very hot but not boiling. Serve on freshly buttered toast. Serves 3–4.

Herbs

A generous use of fresh garden herbs to enliven dishes is one of the simplest ways of bringing a spirit of adventure into cooking. A judicious scattering or addition of herbs can lift a good dish into a great one, and with the new awareness of reducing salt and fat in our diet, using a few well-chosen fresh herbs is one of the best ways of adding interest and flavour.

Most herbs have a special affinity with certain foods. Mixtures can be used, and sometimes should be, and often one herb can be substituted for another.

Fresh herbs are a delight to use and can be fun to grow, even if you don't have a garden. You can grow herbs in a one-room apartment in the middle of a city; most thrive in a window box or in a flower pot by a sunny window. When the growing season is over, the greener, annual herbs like parsley, basil, dill and coriander (Chinese parsley) can be preserved by puréeing the leaves with a little olive oil and freezing in cubes for later use.

The joy of using fresh herbs is not for the gardener alone. More and more greengrocers are selling bunches of herbs which they keep fresh and green in their coolroom, as they have become an essential part of our cooking style.

A knowledge and use of herbs is essential to good cooking. We learn to use them with both discretion and gay abandon, depending on the mood and occasion. A serving of goat's cheese subtly flavoured with herbs and some fresh tomatoes with basil make a delicious simple starter.

BASIL

A fragrant herb with an aromatic, minty flavour, basil is used frequently in Italian cooking. Italians call it the tomato herb because it goes so well with that robust red fruit.

In the past, basil was considered a royal plant and only the sovereign could cut it, supposedly with a golden sickle. Basil is easy to grow, but being an annual it is available fresh only during summer months. However, it can be stored in oil very successfully for use in cooking throughout winter.

Use fresh basil leaves in all salads, particularly when tomato is included, to flavour salad dressing, to blend into creamed butter for sandwiches, in cheese sauces, scrambled eggs and other egg dishes, to sprinkle on pizzas before baking and over pasta dishes, to go with liver, chicken, meat and fish. Sprinkle lamb chops with chopped basil before grilling. Dress tomato slices with a little salt, olive oil and chopped basil.

When adding basil to dishes as a garnish, cut thin slivers of basil leaves (you can roll a stack of leaves like a cigar) and add them at the very last moment, as they discolour quickly.

Pesto

This famous speciality from Genoa can be made successfully only with the fresh herb (see recipe, page 187).

Lunch roll

Split a bread roll, fill with sliced tomatoes, salt, olive oil and a few leaves of fresh basil (no butter). Squash the roll gently to make the oil and juice impregnate the bread. Leave with a light weight on it to press the roll for at least 30 minutes.

BAY LEAF

N o kitchen should be without bay leaves. A hint of this aromatic leaf is often found in French stews, sauces and soups and in the dishes of other Mediterranean countries. When used with discretion it can make an ordinary dish quite splendid—but too much will often spoil what could have been a lovely dish.

Bay trees (*Laurus nobilis*) grow very well in any climate. A large tub in a shaded position near the kitchen door is ideal for this attractive ornamental tree—it makes a great gift. Fresh bay leaves should be picked and kept for a day or two to allow them to lose their bitterness. They are more often used dried: cut

a small twig or branch and hang it for a week or two in a cool, dry, airy place, then pick off the leaves and pack them into an airtight jar. Bay leaves are mostly sold in packets, but watch for very old, dried, brown-looking leaves which have little flavour. You'll sometimes find branches of bay leaves for sale by greengrocers.

The bay leaf is the foundation of the bouquet garni, which is used to flavour marinades, stocks, soups and many other dishes. Just half a bay leaf is all that most dishes require. Place a small leaf on top of a terrine or meat loaf; when making kebabs, secure small pieces of bay leaf between the meat cubes; add it to the liquid when cooking ham, sheep or ox tongue, corned beef or other boiled meats. It improves many braised dishes—oxtail, kidneys, beef or veal: just place a leaf on top of the meat before cooking. When making vegetable or fish soups, add a leaf too.

Bay leaves improve rice dishes and also vegetables. Try adding a piece when cooking eggplant (aubergine), carrots or beetroot (beets). It is especially good with tomatoes, onions and asparagus . . . just see what a bay leaf can do for asparagus! Heat the drained asparagus in a little butter with a piece of bay leaf— the heat will bring out the aroma. An infusion of bay leaf and milk transforms sweet custards and rice puddings, too.

Generally a dish is often better for using only half a bay leaf; certainly take care with very large ones, and don't overdo it.

Basil is often called the tomato herb. The simplest of salads is made from thick slices of tomato, arranged overlapping, a grinding of pepper, a drizzle of good olive oil and shredded basil leaves scattered over. One of the best snacks is sourdough bread filled with this combination. When basil is young, use the leaves whole.

29

CHIVES

hives are a well-known member of the onion family and, because of their delicate flavour and bright green colour, are used frequently as a garnish. They grow easily in clumps in the garden or in pots, and the more you cut chives the thicker and better they seem to grow. When adding chives to food, it is easier to snip them with scissors straight into or over the food.

Chives go well with all kinds of salads—tossed green, tomato, potato, rice and macaroni—in egg and cheese dishes (especially with cream and cottage cheese), with fish and vegetable dishes and snipped over soups. Mix snipped chives with soft butter and spread on loaves of bread, like garlic bread. Try adding snipped chives to beaten eggs for an omelette and cook in the usual way. Try baby beetroot (beets) served hot with butter and chives.

Garlic Cheese

The French have always found lovely ways of using the freshest ingredients, in all kinds of dishes. Crushed garlic flavours a cottage, cream or curd cheese that is used as a dip or spread for crusty bread. Sometimes a more robust cheese is made with the addition of a mixture of fresh garden herbs and chopped spring onions.

> *250 g (8 oz) Neufchâtel or cream cheese*
> *250 g (8 oz) plain cottage cheese or ricotta*
> *2 garlic cloves, crushed*
> *Snipped chives*

Fresh Herbed Cheese is made with a fresh curd cheese such as ricotta, to which is added a tablespoon of finely chopped green shallots (spring onions, scallions), a crushed clove of garlic, a few spoons of chopped parsley with either chopped fresh thyme or oregano, a squeeze of lemon juice and a good grinding of pepper.

eat the Neufchâtel cheese until creamy. Add the cottage cheese and crushed garlic. Beat well, pile into a serving bowl and top with plenty of chives. Serve with crusty bread or water biscuits (crackers). Makes about 2 cups (16 oz).
Variations:
Fresh Herbed Cheese: To the garlic cheese add 1 tablespoon of finely chopped green shallots (spring onions, scallions), 2 tablespoons of chopped parsley with either chopped fresh thyme, oregano, chervil—whatever you have in the garden—a squeeze of lemon juice and a good grinding of black or white pepper.
Fresh Herbed Cheese in Nasturtium Leaves: Pick 24 fresh nasturtium leaves, wash and pat them dry, trim the stems. With the smooth side down, fill the leaves with a teaspoon of Fresh Herbed Cheese; lift up the sides of the leaves to make a cradle for the cheese. Arrange on a platter and serve as an appetiser with drinks.

FINES HERBES (MIXED HERBS)

*T*raditionally, *fines herbes* are a mixture of equal parts of chopped parsley, chives, tarragon and chervil, but they can be used in any combination. A mixture of herbs is used in many dishes. There are some herbs that combine particularly well. Thyme and marjoram team well; parsley goes with most herbs; thyme, marjoram and sage are the favourite herbs to blend into crumbs for stuffings for poultry; and a bouquet garni (or bunch of herbs and flavourings) is essential to many stews, braises, casseroles and soups.

Bouquet Garni

The herbs in a bouquet garni are generally thyme, parsley and bay leaf, but the thyme and parsley can be alternated with other herbs according to the nature of the dish. Tarragon or rosemary go well with chicken; basil is ideal when tomatoes are used; rosemary or thyme team with lamb.

To make a bouquet garni, place about 5 black peppercorns inside a short piece of celery and secure them in place with a small carrot; add a sprig or two of thyme, a few sprigs or stalks of parsley and a bay leaf. Tie with a long piece of string so that the end can be tied to the handle of the pot. A few bouquets garnis can be made up and stored, sealed in plastic wrap (cling film), in the crisper.

Herb Bread

Beat 125 g (4 oz) of butter until softened and blend in 3 tablespoons of chopped mixed herbs (parsley, mint, thyme, sage and chives or a combination of your choice). Slash a loaf of French bread at 1 cm (1/2 in) intervals, leaving the base attached. Spread the herb butter between slices and smear the remainder on top. Wrap the bread in aluminium foil and bake in a moderately hot oven (190°C/375°F) 15 minutes, then open the foil and leave in the oven a further 5 minutes.

Herb Vinegars and Oils

*F*resh herbs steeped in oil or vinegar give the most delightful flavours. Together they produce a superlative salad dressing. Basil-flavoured oil is especially delicious; it can be added to spaghetti or other pasta before it is served or even in the cooking water. Herb-flavoured oils are good for basting roasts, spooning over stuffed tomatoes and other vegetables to be cooked in the oven, over fish, over meats to be grilled (broiled)—thyme-flavoured oil for steaks, rosemary oil for lamb.

Herb Vinegars

Select freshly picked herbs. Strip the leaves from the stalk, wash and dry. Place 3–4 tablespoons in a jar and add 1 cup (9 fl oz) of wine vinegar, red or white as you prefer. Cover the jar tightly and leave for 2 weeks, shaking it each day. Strain the vinegar into a screw-top jar. A herb sprig may be added to give the vinegar a decorative appearance. For garlic lovers, garlic vinegar makes the basis of an excellent vinaigrette. Just place 4 peeled garlic cloves into 2 cups (18 fl oz) of vinegar and leave for 2 days, then strain.

Herb Oils

Oil is a preservative and enables you to have the flavour of fresh basil all through the winter. Just pack the clean leaves into a wide-mouthed jar and cover with olive oil. The leaves may be chopped first and then covered with oil, making it very easy to add to dishes by the spoonful. Other herbs which are particularly good for flavouring oil are rosemary, tarragon and lemon thyme. All should be crushed first to release their own pungent oils. Rosemary should be picked and left a few days before using, to prevent it clouding the oil. Use 2 tablespoons of herbs for each cup of oil. Place on a window sill in strong sunlight for 2–3 weeks and then strain, pressing all the oils from the herbs. I use olive oil for herbs, a regular olive oil for most uses, extra virgin for table use.

Oils and vinegars come in a great range of quality and flavours. You can make your own flavoured oils and vinegars, a good idea if the oil is not a particularly interesting one. The top oils should be left alone; they already have a superb flavour.

Tomatoes with Mixed Herbs

Such a simple dish, but tomatoes with herbs topped with crunchy golden breadcrumbs are very good indeed.

> *2 tablespoons olive oil*
> *4 large ripe tomatoes, cut into thick slices*
> *Salt and freshly ground pepper*
> *¹/₂ cup mixed chopped fresh herbs, such as parsley, marjoram,*
> *   oregano, basil, tarragon*
> *2 cups (4 oz) fresh breadcrumbs*

*H*eat 1 tablespoon of the oil in a large frying pan (skillet) over fairly high heat, and quickly sauté the slices of tomato, a few at a time, for about 2 minutes on each side. Transfer them to a hot serving dish and keep them warm until all of the tomatoes have been sautéed. Season them with salt and pepper, sprinkle with the chopped herbs, and then spoon over them the fresh breadcrumbs which have been fried for a few seconds in the remaining oil. Serves 4–6.

Tip
This is one recipe where fresh herbs are essential. A choice of marjoram, oregano, thyme or basil can be used, but mix these with parsley in the proportion of 2 parts of parsley to 1 part of the other herb.

Chicken Provençale

> *1.5 kg (3 lb) chicken, jointed, or chicken pieces (portions)*
> *60 g (2 oz) butter*
> *4 garlic cloves, unpeeled*
> *A wine glass of sherry or brandy*
> *4 tomatoes, peeled, seeded and chopped (see page 130)*
> *1 teaspoon tomato paste (concentrate)*
> *Salt and pepper*
> *2 heaped tablespoons chopped mixed herbs*

This pot of herbs includes parsley, chives and thyme. The sweet william, such a dainty flower, just grew there—don't add it to the soup!

*D*ry the chicken and, in a large frying pan (skillet), gently fry, skin side down, in the butter with the garlic, for about 15 minutes. Turn the chicken over, remove the garlic and add the sherry or brandy to the pan. Ignite it. When the flames subside, simmer until all liquid evaporates.

Add the tomatoes and tomato paste, and salt and pepper to taste. Cook for a further 15 minutes, until the chicken is tender. Remove the chicken and cook the tomatoes until very thick, then pour them over the chicken and sprinkle with the herbs. Serve with rice and a green salad. Serves 4.

Herbed Cheese

2 cups (8 oz) grated Cheddar cheese
2 tablespoons cream sherry or dry sherry
90 g (3 oz) butter
2 teaspoons each finely chopped parsley and chives
1/2 teaspoon each finely chopped tarragon, chervil and thyme
A pinch of salt and pepper

*P*lace all ingredients into the top of a double boiler and stir constantly over hot water until creamy. Turn into pots, cool and cover with clarified butter. Serve with water biscuits (crackers) or crusty bread. Makes about 3 cups.

MARJORAM

*T*his strongly perfumed herb is one of the most important of all kitchen herbs. There are three types of marjoram—sweet, pot and wild (known as oregano)—but sweet marjoram is the one found growing in most gardens and it is the most delicate of the three.

Marjoram and thyme team exceptionally well together, and marjoram can be used in almost any dish that is flavoured with thyme. Marjoram, thyme and sage are the favourite combination for old-fashioned poultry seasoning. There are many more dishes in which marjoram is a good flavouring. It goes particularly well with veal, poultry, pork or beef; for flavouring meat loaves and sausages; in liver dishes; and in most stews. Some fish dishes, such as baked fish, salmon croquettes and creamed shellfish, are enhanced by the addition of marjoram.

Many vegetables are complemented by the flavour of marjoram. Try it added to mushroom dishes, green beans and peas, potato dishes, broccoli, Brussels sprouts, eggplant (aubergine), asparagus, carrots, spinach, zucchini (courgettes) or onions. In salads, try adding freshly chopped marjoram to tossed greens in vinaigrette dressing; with sliced green capsicums (sweet peppers); coleslaw; stirred through cottage cheese and cream cheese. A little chopped fresh marjoram gives piquancy to tomato juice, consommé à la madrilène, chicken noodle soup or onion soups.

Green Beans with Herb Crumb Topping

250 g (8 oz) green beans
30 g (1 oz) butter
3 tablespoons fresh white breadcrumbs
1 tablespoon chopped fresh marjoram

Trim and wash the beans but leave them whole. Cook in a pan of boiling salted water until tender but not soft. Drain. Heat the butter in a saucepan and stir in the breadcrumbs. Continue stirring over low heat until golden. Add the marjoram and spoon over beans. Serves 4.

Marinade for Chicken

Combine 4 tablespoons of salad oil, the juice of half a lemon, a crushed clove of garlic (optional), a good pinch of salt and a good grinding of black pepper. Add a tablespoon of chopped marjoram and thyme. Mix well. Chicken pieces (portions) may be marinated in this mixture, covered, for several hours or overnight in the refrigerator. Drain the chicken pieces before cooking. Makes about 1/2 cup (4 1/2 fl oz).

MINT

In most countries of the Old World, mint is one of the most commonly used herbs. It goes into soups and sauces, omelettes and salads, lentil purées and even tea. In India it is used in some curries (particularly potato or lamb curry), both at the beginning and end of cooking. It's also used in the cooling chutneys that accompany hot, spicy dishes.

Mint is a clean-tasting herb which gives a tangy freshness to all dishes it's used in. It doesn't go well with other herbs or with garlic (although a notable exception is tabbouleh, the lovely parsley and mint salad made with burghul wheat). It does go well with orange—try it in duck à l'orange or in orange salad—and with lamb and mutton, particularly the fatty cuts. It is good with vegetables like beans, peas, potatoes, lentils, tomatoes, eggplant (aubergine), carrots and mushrooms. Add finely chopped mint to potato salad, then dress with mayonnaise.

It is one herb that can be used in sweet dishes as well—many fruit salads are better for the addition of finely chopped mint. Pineapple, mint and Kirsch make a delightful combination. Garnish drinks with leaves of mint and drop them into iced tea. Pea soup is superb with mint.

Mint Tea. Place fresh or dried mint leaves in a teapot and pour boiling water over. Leave to infuse 4–5 minutes. Serve with lemon and sugar to taste.

Mint Butter. Add finely chopped mint to softened butter with lemon juice, then chill. Serve in place of parsley butter.

Baked Apples with Mint

6 apples
12 mint leaves
6 tablespoons honey
6 mint leaves, chopped
Butter

Wash the apples, remove the cores and split the skins around the middle with a knife. Lay the mint leaves in a baking dish, place the apples on top and fill each apple with a mixture of 1 tablespoon honey, 1 chopped mint leaf, a tiny nut of butter and about 1 teaspoon of water. Bake, covered with aluminium foil, in a moderately hot oven (190°C/375°F) until almost cooked, then remove the foil, baste with the juice in the dish and bake until tender. Serves 6.

PARSLEY

*T*o cook without parsley is almost unthinkable. However, it is not used nearly enough. The stalks of the parsley contain the most flavour, and these should be used in almost all your savoury dishes, making up, with thyme and bay leaf, a bouquet garni or the most important basic seasoning. The curly, attractive, bright green leaves, chopped finely, can be sprinkled over dishes before serving to give both colour and flavour interest; the youngest, tightly packed leaves can be used whole to decorate platters of food. The flatter, longer leaves of Italian parsley are preferred by some, who like its fresh taste.

Parsley is not limited just to background seasoning. It is very important and prominent in such sauces as tartare, vinaigrette, ravigote, verde and meunière. It is also the basis of Maître d'Hôtel Butter (page 40), which goes with all grilled (broiled) meats and fish. Many good cooks add chopped parsley to dishes as instinctively as most add salt, so it's convenient to have a ready supply of chopped parsley handy. First wash it, then shake it or pat dry on kitchen paper towels, as it's harder to chop if wet. A sharp knife is the best implement, as the parsley chopping gadgets tend to bruise the leaf. Chop more than you will need at one time and store the remainder in an airtight container in the refrigerator.

To store parsley you've just bought or picked from the garden, wash it and shake it very well to remove moisture, wrap it in kitchen paper towels, place it in a plastic (polythene) bag and squeeze out all the air before sealing with a wire tie. Stored in a crisper, parsley will keep fresh for quite a long time.

Tips

Parsley sandwiches are particularly good—full of vitamin C, iron and chlorophyll. Chop the leaves roughly or just break off the stems and season well.

Chew a handful of parsley to freshen the breath—a good tip, especially after you have been eating garlic.

Tomatoes Provençale

Tomatoes Provençale is prepared with halved tomatoes (or, if small, with tops removed), garlic, parsley and breadcrumbs and a drizzle of olive oil. Serve as a starter, part of an antipasto selection or as a separate course.

1 garlic clove, peeled and crushed
3 tablespoons chopped parsley
$^1/_4$ cup (2$^1/_4$ fl oz) olive oil
1 cup (2 oz) fresh white breadcrumbs
4 large tomatoes

*M*ix the garlic with the parsley, oil and breadcrumbs. Cut the tomatoes into halves or cut off the tops of whole tomatoes, and top each half with some of the breadcrumb mixture. Grill (broil) about 15 minutes under medium heat. Serve with grills or as an entrée. Serves 4.

Parsley Butter (Maître d'Hôtel)

90 g (3 oz) butter
2 tablespoons finely chopped parsley
1 tablespoon lemon juice
Pepper and salt

Beat the butter with the parsley and lemon juice. Season well with pepper and salt. Roll into a small log, wrap in aluminium foil and chill. Cut off small pats of the butter to serve with grills as you need it.

Fried Parsley

To go with fish. Wash and dry parsley sprigs thoroughly, then drop them into a small saucepan of deep, hot oil for 1 minute or until they rise to surface. Drain and sprinkle with salt.

The herb garden supplies me with parsley, borage, rosemary, arugula (rocket) and coriander (Chinese parsley), complete with its useful roots. I did not grow the Japanese green on the left but will seek out the seeds.

SAGE

Sage is one of the strongest-flavoured of the familiar herbs; a favourite, but its use is often abused. Its powerful fragrance and pleasantly bitter flavour can do so much for strong-flavoured meats, cutting the fatty taste—as in the case of pork or goose—but it must be used in small quantities.

Sage is one herb that comes across better if picked fresh for use. It grows all year round, so this is quite easy. Use parsley in conjunction with sage—it seems to tone down the strident sage flavour.

Sage and Onion Tart

1 quantity shortcrust pastry (see Flan Case, page 294)
3 onions, sliced
30 g (1 oz) butter
2 rashers (slices) bacon, chopped
1¼ cups (11 fl oz) cream
2 eggs
1 tablespoon chopped fresh sage
1 tablespoon chopped fresh parsley
Pepper and salt

Prepare the shortcrust pastry and roll it out to fit a 20 cm (8 in) fluted flan tin (pan). Chill while preparing the filling.

Sauté the onions in the butter over low heat until soft; remove to plate. Add the chopped bacon and fry until crisp. Mix the cream, eggs, sage and parsley, and season with pepper and salt. Stir in the onion and bacon, then pour the mixture into the prepared pastry shell. Bake in a hot oven (200°C/400°F) for 10 minutes, then reduce the heat to moderate (180°C/350°F) and bake a further 30 minutes. Serve warm. Serves 6.

Sage Cheese

Grate some full-flavoured Cheddar, and cream it with a little mayonnaise. Add finely chopped fresh sage to taste—be sparing! Chill the cheese for 12 hours to allow it to mature before serving.

THYME

Thyme is one of the great culinary herbs. With bay leaf and parsley it provides the subtle background flavouring to innumerable dishes—casseroles, soups, stews, sauces, etc. It dries well and doesn't have the 'hay' smell that some other herbs develop on drying. Thyme and wine are great cooking partners, especially in slowly cooked dishes.

Thyme goes well with vegetables—use it to season tomatoes, potatoes, zucchini (courgettes), eggplant (aubergine) and capsicums (sweet peppers). Preserved olives are better for the addition of thyme—just store black olives in a bottle with good olive oil and add a spring of fresh thyme.

Lemon thyme is a mild, citrus-flavoured variety of common thyme. It goes particularly well with fish. Both thymes like to be partnered with marjoram.

Fresh Cheese and Herbs in Oil

250 g (8 oz) fresh Neufchâtel, feta, or goat's cheese
Sprigs of thyme
2 garlic cloves
A few peppercorns
1 bay leaf
Olive oil to cover

Either scoop the cheese into small egg shapes using two small spoons or cut it into large cubes. Arrange the pieces of cheese in a sterilised glass jar with the thyme leaves, garlic, peppercorns and bay leaf. Cover with the oil, seal, and keep in the refrigerator. Use the oil for salads or cooking. Serves 6.

Marinated Pork Chops

Pork chops, trimmed of fat
Thyme and marjoram, chopped
Freshly ground pepper
Oil and lemon juice

Chop plenty of thyme and marjoram and strew over the pork chops, seasoning well with plenty of pepper. Pour over a little oil and lemon juice and leave to marinate for 1–2 hours.

Grill (broil) the chops under a preheated grill (broiler) or on a ribbed grill pan, using a moderate heat; baste with the marinade. Cook for 12–14 minutes, turning them several times during cooking. Serve with lettuce dressed with the hot juices and marinade from the grilling pan.

WHEN TO ADD HERBS

Although there is a considerable difference of opinion concerning the best time to add seasonings to food, many experienced cooks recommend the following system:

Long-cooking foods. Add a bouquet garni or selected herbs during the last 60 minutes of the cooking time.

Quickly cooked foods. Mix fresh herbs right in with the other ingredients, but

soak dried herbs in a little milk before blending them in foods that are cooked in a few minutes—such as omelettes.

Mint, basil, chives. Mint is added to peas and new potatoes at the beginning of cooking. However, adding a few sprigs for the last few minutes gives a fresh, fragrant mint flavour. Basil should only ever be added towards the end of cooking time. Chives are almost always added just before serving—scattered over hot dishes, mixed into salads.

STORING HERBS

*D*rying herbs. The faster herbs are dried the better the flavour they will have. Spread them on a sheet of kitchen paper or aluminium foil on a baking tray (sheet) and place in an oven set on the lowest heat for 12 hours. As soon as the leaves are brittle, remove the herbs, allow them to cool and then strip the leaves from the stalks. Place in jars and seal. In the country you can dry herbs by allowing them to hang a week or more in a cool, dry and airy position. However, the dust and general pollution in the city make this method unwise.

Goat's cheese, feta or any other fresh cheese is quite superb after standing in herb-flavoured oil. Serve the cheese with toasted bruschetta or with a sliced tomato salad. Use some of the oil to drizzle over a small salad. Olives, too, benefit from an oil-and-vinegar bath. You may add herbs of your own choice.

Snacks

When the Fourth Earl of Sandwich, Lord Montagu, called for his slab of meat to be put between two slices of bread so that he could continue his luck at the gaming table, he freed mankind from the hot lunch, according to Woody Allen in Getting Even. Woody added, 'We owe him so much'; and indeed we do, because the sandwich, by its convenience and adaptability, has delighted snack eaters ever since.

Most of us enjoy casual meals and have taken to 'snacking'. New Yorkers are experts at sandwiches and all kinds of snacks. 'Hold the mayo', 'Hold the mustard', and 'With a shot', can be heard ringing out at any New York deli, together with definite preferences for the type of bread. Of course, New York has no monopoly on sandwiches. The Brits love a bacon butty, France gave us the lovely croques monsieur, golden on the outside, ham and melting cheese within, and there is bruschetta from Italy, the ultimate garlic bread, to say nothing of 'po' boys' from New Orleans.

Snacks with drinks are a part of life, as are pizzas, pissaladières, muffulettas, frittatas. We enjoy them when picnicking, relaxing, at play. We even take a break from work to snack. Where would we be without them?

Pissaladière is the French answer to Italy's pizza. What makes this so good is the very thick layer of gently cooked onions, better when the onions are the sweet Spanish or Vidalia onions. Tomatoes and the regulation criss-cross of anchovies and scattering of black olives are the final touch.

Basic Yeast Dough

2¹/₃ cups (9 oz) plain (all-purpose) flour
1 teaspoon salt
1 teaspoon sugar
7 g (¹/₄ oz) dried yeast or 15 g (¹/₂ oz) compressed yeast
²/₃ cup (6 fl oz) milk, lukewarm
1 large egg
60 g (2 oz) butter, softened

Sift the flour into a large bowl with the salt and stir in the sugar and yeast. Make a well in the centre and add the milk, egg and butter. Mix to a dough, then turn out onto a well-floured board. Knead lightly for 4–5 minutes until smooth and elastic. Put the dough in a buttered bowl, turn it to coat with butter, and let it rise until doubled in bulk, in a warm place, for about 1 hour.
To make a pizza: Turn the dough out on to a floured board and roll it out to fit a Swiss roll tin about 35 × 25 cm (15 × 10 in) or a 30 cm (12 in) pizza pan. Cover and leave to rise in a warm place for 15 minutes. Spread topping over evenly and bake in a preheated hot oven (200°C/400°F) for 20–30 minutes.

Pizza with Fresh Tomatoes

1 sheet frozen shortcrust pastry or 1 frozen pizza base
*   or 1 quantity basic yeast dough (above)*
1 tablespoon olive oil
¹/₂ cup (4¹/₂ fl oz) tomato paste (concentrate)
6 tablespoons freshly grated Parmesan cheese
1 cup, about 125 g (4 oz), coarsely grated mozzarella
1–2 onions, thinly sliced
3 tomatoes, sliced
8 slices salami, or 4–6 slices ham, cut into ribbons
1 teaspoon chopped oregano or ¹/₂ teaspoon dried
Freshly ground pepper

Tip
Pizzas are easy to make using either frozen rolled pastry or prepared frozen bases—look for them in supermarket freezer shelves. Or you can make your own pastry, using the basic yeast dough recipe on this page.

Preheat the oven to moderately hot (190°C/375°F). Brush a baking tray (sheet) lightly with a little oil, lay the sheet of pastry on it and brush it with oil. Smear with tomato paste. Sprinkle with the Parmesan, reserving 2 tablespoons for later. Sprinkle with the mozzarella, scatter the onion evenly on top, arrange the tomatoes in one layer over the onion. Strew with the salami or ham. Sprinkle the pizza with the reserved grated Parmesan and oregano. Season with pepper to taste and bake in the middle of the preheated oven for 30–35 minutes or until the edges are golden. With a pizza wheel or sharp knife, cut the pizza into squares or slim wedges. Serves 6 as a first course or snack.

Pissaladière

The French version of the pizza, sometimes made with melted onions, anchovies, and black olives, at other times with a thick sauce of melted onions and tomatoes topped with anchovies and black olives. Here is the latter.

> *1 quantity of Basic Yeast Dough (opposite page)*
> *1 kg (2 lb) onions, peeled and thinly sliced*
> *3 large garlic cloves*
> *6 tablespoons olive oil*
> *2 400 g (14 oz) cans peeled tomatoes or 1 kg (2 lb) ripe*
>   *tomatoes, peeled, seeded and diced (see page 130)*
> *1 teaspoon sugar*
> *1 small bay leaf*
> *A sprig of marjoram or thyme*
> *2 tablespoons tomato paste (concentrate)*
> *Freshly ground pepper*
> *6 anchovy fillets, well drained and halved lengthwise*
> *1/2 cup (3 oz) black olives, halved and pitted*

*H*ave the dough made and risen until it has doubled in bulk. Meanwhile, prepare the filling. Slowly cook the onions with the garlic in the oil over a gentle heat for about 15 minutes, until they are a soft pulp without browning. Add the tomatoes, sugar, herbs and tomato paste and continue cooking until the mixture is reduced to a thick pulp. Remove the herbs and season with pepper.

Now turn the dough out onto a floured board and roll or shape it into a large disc or square about 6 mm (1/4 in) thick on a pizza baking tray or stone, a jelly roll pan or a plain baking tray (sheet). Cover and leave to rise in a warm place for 15 minutes. Spread the tomato mixture evenly over the dough. Arrange the anchovy fillets in a lattice over the filling. Put an olive in the centre of each diamond. Brush lightly with extra olive oil and bake in a preheated hot oven (200°C/400°F) for about 25 minutes, until the crust is golden. Serve hot or warm. Serves 8.

Huevos Rancheros

Ranch-style eggs, a famous Latin American dish which makes a great weekend lunch or brunch dish. Serve 1 or 2 eggs per person.

3 tablespoons olive oil
1 small onion, chopped
1 garlic clove, crushed
*1 red capsicum (sweet pepper), halved, seeded and
    shredded*
2 ripe tomatoes, peeled, seeded and diced (see page 130)
Salt and freshly ground pepper
1 dash of Tabasco sauce
1 tablespoon chopped fresh coriander (Chinese parsley)
4 eggs
4–8 tortillas
Coriander (Chinese parsley) sprigs to garnish

*Huevos Rancheros has
to be one of the great
breakfast/lunch/
brunch—any time of
the day—snacks. It
can be Mexican fiery
or mild, but it always
gets top marks for
flavour.*

*H*eat half the oil in a frying pan (skillet) and cook the onion, garlic and capsicum gently until soft. Add the tomatoes and simmer until thick. Season with salt, pepper, Tabasco and chopped coriander. Make 4 depressions in the sauce, break each egg first into a cup, then transfer it gently into a depression. Cover the pan and cook 3–4 minutes or until the eggs are set.

Meanwhile, heat the remaining oil and fry the tortillas 30 seconds on each side or until crisp. Place 1 or 2 tortillas on each plate. Using an egg slice (lifter), lift an egg and its surrounding sauce onto each tortilla. Scatter with coriander sprigs. Serves 2–4.

Bruschetta

The Italian version of garlic bread bears no resemblance to the soggy hot bread served at most barbecues and some restaurants. Now that we can buy good Italian bread and such superb extra virgin olive oils to drizzle on the toast, we can enjoy this simple snack as it is served in Italy.

6 thick slices of Italian or French crusty bread
3 or 4 cloves of garlic, peeled and cut in two
Salt and freshly ground pepper
3 tablespoons extra virgin olive oil

*G*rill or toast the bread on both sides. A char-grill gives the ideal smoky taste, and a ribbed grill gives those decorative toasted bars. While still hot from the grill, rub one side of each slice with garlic, add a sprinkling of salt and grinding of pepper and drizzle with the oil. Serve at once, as is, or offer a bowl of sun-dried tomatoes or sliced fresh tomatoes scattered with shredded basil leaves.

Bruschetta with herbs and sun-dried tomatoes. Toast the bread as above on one side only. Combine 3–6 tablespoons of good olive oil with 3 or 4 cloves of garlic, roughly chopped, and a tablespoon or so of crushed fresh herbs. Arrange the bread, toasted side down, on a baking tray or griller and drizzle with the flavoured oil. Scatter each with a few strips of shredded sun-dried tomatoes. Place under a moderate grill (broiler) or in a hot oven until golden. This goes very well with a green salad.

Bruschetta with olive paste. Toast the bread as above. Combine $1/2$ cup ($4^1/2$ fl oz) of black olive paste, 2 teaspoons each of chopped spring onion (scallion) and capers, a little grated lemon rind, 1 clove of garlic, peeled and crushed, and $1/4$ cup ($2^1/4$ fl oz) of olive oil. Spread or pile this mixture, depending on how much you like it, onto small pieces of bruschetta, and serve as a snack with drinks.

Tapénade

Take your choice: bruschetta, the crisp toasted garlic bread of Italy, topped with basil and tomato; a bowl of Eggplant Mousse, served as a dip or spread; and Tapénade for crisp toasts. A fine olive oil is on hand to top these snacks.

Whether for a picnic, a quick snack or a light lunch, there is nothing nicer than a bowl of this delicious paste. Tapénade is all the better for being made a few days ahead and stored airtight in the refrigerator.

> *125 g (4 oz) black olives, pitted*
> *6 anchovy fillets, drained and rinsed*
> *3 tablespoons capers, drained*
> *95 g (3 oz) drained canned tuna in oil*
> *Juice of 1 lemon*
> *$1/3$ cup (3 fl oz) olive or sunflower oil*
> *A few extra olives to garnish*

*C*rush the olives in a mortar or chop in a food processor. Add the anchovy fillets, capers, tuna and half the lemon juice. Pound or process until the mixture has formed a fairly smooth paste.

Still pounding, or with the motor of the food processor still running, add the oil in a slow, steady stream. Taste and add more lemon juice if you think it's needed. Turn into a small serving bowl and decorate with a few black olives. Serve with halved hard-boiled eggs, some crusty bread and a few crisp vegetables.

Muffuletta

A favourite for any alfresco meal or picnic. It can be made well ahead, wrapped and refrigerated until required. You may vary the meats and cheese used.

1 small to medium-sized eggplant (aubergine)

1 tablespoon salt

$^1/_2$ cup ($4^1/_2$ fl oz) light olive oil

1 cup (6 oz) each stuffed green and black olives, sliced

2 garlic cloves, finely chopped

2 tablespoons capers, drained

1 tablespoon chopped oregano

185 g (6 oz) ricotta

2 tablespoons grated Parmesan cheese

1 tablespoon chopped basil

1 round Italian loaf

1 large red capsicum (sweet pepper), skinned (see page 108),
*   halved, seeded and cut into 8 lengths*

8 thin slices of Italian salami

6 thin slices of fontina cheese (optional)

90 g (3 oz) prosciutto or other ham, thinly sliced

The Muffuletta may have started life as a very filling, very full meal in a bun, but practical cooks have almost turned it into an art form. This muffuletta is party size, full of good things. The round loaf will travel to a picnic or the garden to be sliced in small or giant wedges.

Cut the eggplant into 6 mm ($^1/_4$ in) slices, layer it in a colander with salt between layers, and leave it to drain for 30 minutes. Rinse and pat dry, and brush with some of the measured oil. Grill (broil) or fry it in a dry pan until it is golden on both sides. Remove and set aside.

Combine the olives, garlic, remaining oil, capers and oregano; set aside. Combine the ricotta, Parmesan and basil; set aside.

Split the loaf through, nearer the top than the centre. Remove the inside crumb from both crusts, leaving a 2.5 cm (1 in) layer of bread all round. Save the crumb for another use. Spread half the ricotta mixture over the base of the loaf, and on top of this place half the eggplant, half the capsicum, and half the olive salad in layers. Add a layer of half of the salami, half the fontina cheese slices (if using), then all the prosciutto or ham. Finish now with the layers worked in reverse, ending with ricotta. The filling will be well piled by now. Place the top crust over the filling and press down firmly.

Wrap the loaf in plastic wrap (cling film), then aluminium foil, and place it in the refrigerator until ready to serve. To ensure the muffuletta stays together when cutting to serve, place a 1 kg (2 lb) weight on top for the last hour of chilling.

Tomato Crostini

Have the topping prepared and the oven hot, and this delicious snack will be ready in the time it takes to get out the plates and make a drink.

1 tablespoon olive oil

1 red capsicum (sweet pepper), skinned (see page 108), seeded and diced or 1 canned red pimiento, diced

3 ripe tomatoes, peeled (see page 130), seeded and chopped

8 basil leaves, shredded

Salt and freshly ground pepper

1 or 2 two slabs of focaccia, split in halves, or 2 or 3 slices of long Italian loaf, cut thickly lengthwise

Extra olive oil

Anchovy fillets, small peeled prawns (shrimp), or olive halves to garnish

*H*eat the tablespoon olive oil in a pan and gently cook the capsicum for a few minutes. Add the tomatoes and basil, and cook for a few minutes more. Season with salt and pepper. Set aside in a bowl in the refrigerator until ready to use.

Preheat the oven to very hot (220°C/425°F). Drizzle the bread slices with a little extra olive oil and spread with the tomato topping. Garnish with anchovy fillets or prawns or black olive halves, and bake for 8–10 minutes, until the bread is crispy and light golden. (Alternatively, toast one side of the bread, spread with the topping, garnish, and toast the top side.) Cut into fingers to serve. Serve piping hot with drinks or with soup. Serves 6.

Bacon, Lettuce and Tomato Sandwich (The BLT)

3 or 4 rashers (slices) of bacon, rind removed

2 slices of toast-cut white bread

2 tablespoons mayonnaise

A dash of Worcestershire sauce (optional)

4 large slices of tomato

Salt

1 crisp lettuce leaf

$\mathscr{F}$ry the bacon until crisp; drain on a kitchen paper towel. Toast the bread and spread each slice with mayonnaise. Pile the tomatoes on one slice, salt, and top with the bacon, lettuce and the second slice of toast, mayonnaise side down. Cut, if desired. Serve immediately. Serves 1.

Monte Cristos

These pan-fried chicken and Swiss cheese sandwiches make a great snack for an easy lunch or supper. A good rye bread is called for, although any grainy country-style bread can be used.

> *3 tablespoons mayonnaise*
> *1 tablespoon tomato sauce (ketchup)*
> *A few dashes of Tabasco sauce*
> *4 slices of rye bread*
> *1 boned poached half chicken breast, thinly sliced*
> *4 slices of Swiss cheese*
> *2 pickled gherkins, sliced*
> *$^1/_2$ small salad onion, thinly sliced*
> *1 large egg*
> *2 tablespoons milk*
> *15 g ($^1/_2$ oz) butter*
> *1 tablespoon oil*

$\mathscr{M}$ix the mayonnaise with the ketchup and Tabasco and spread it on the 4 bread slices. Lay the sliced chicken, Swiss cheese, gherkins and onion on 2 of the bread slices. Top with the remaining bread. Press down well.

Beat the egg with the milk in a shallow bowl and dip the sandwiches in carefully, turning to coat thoroughly. All the egg should be absorbed. Have ready a frying pan (skillet) heated with the butter and oil; when hot, lower the sandwiches in and fry them over a moderate heat for about 4 minutes on each side. Transfer the sandwiches to plates and cut them in half. Serves 2.

French Baton Pizzas.
Crusty French bread is
a great base for snacks
topped with ham,
cheese, tomatoes—
indeed, anything
savoury. When toasted
they may be eaten as
a sandwich or open as
a pizza.

French Baton Pizzas

Young family members can make this for themselves and friends—a great snack.

1 French bread baton or ficelle
3 tablespoons tomato paste (concentrate)
1–2 garlic cloves, crushed or finely chopped
2 teaspoons chopped fresh oregano
2 tomatoes, sliced
12 slices of salami
1 cup (4 oz) grated Gruyère or Cheddar cheese, or 6 thin slices
1 tablespoon capers

Preheat the oven to hot (200°C/400°F). Cut the bread in half lengthwise and spread the tomato paste with the crushed garlic over the cut surfaces. Sprinkle with the oregano.

   Arrange the sliced tomatoes and salami on each half of bread. Lay the cheese on top, sprinkle with the capers. Cut each piece of bread into two. Place on lightly oiled baking trays (sheets) and bake for 15 minutes. Serve hot. Serves 4.

Croques Monsieur

A visit to Paris calls for sitting on the boulevard in one of the fashionable cafés, ordering a snack, a coffee, a beer or a Dubonnet and settling down to watching the world go by. After tasting the popular French fried sandwich snack, *croques monsieur*, most of us are sold on them. They make a super lunch or supper dish.

> *2 slices of boiled ham*
> *2 slices of Gruyère or other Swiss-style cheese*
> *4 slices of French bread, cut on the bias*
> *French mustard*
> *Butter*

Cut the ham and cheese the same size as the bread or a little larger. Butter 2 slices of bread, lay a slice of ham on each, then a slice of cheese. Spread with a little mustard. Top with a slice of bread and press down well. Fry in a pan of sizzling butter on both sides, until golden. Serve immediately. Serves 2.

Po' Boys

> *4 oval bread rolls*
> *90 g (3 oz) butter, melted*
> *24 fresh oysters*
> *3 tablespoons plain (all-purpose) flour*
> *1 egg, beaten with 2 tablespoons water*
> *1 cup fresh or dried breadcrumbs*
> *Salt and freshly ground black pepper*
> *Tabasco and Worcestershire sauce*
> *Lemon wedges to serve*

In New Orleans a 'po' boy' is something anyone can afford and enjoy, even a poor boy. A po' boy is simply a filled roll. It comes in a variety of fillings. Popular in Louisiana, though, is a prawn or crawfish po' boy, or one filled with fried oysters, like this one. A snack for some; for others, a weekend lunch with a difference.

Cut the tops off each roll. Scoop out the centres and set aside. Brush the inside of the rolls with melted butter, place them on a baking tray (sheet) and toast them lightly under a griller (broiler).

Meanwhile, coat each oyster with a little flour. Dip them in the beaten egg mixture, then roll them in breadcrumbs. Heat the remaining butter in a frying pan and sauté the oysters for 20 seconds only, just until the edges begin to curl. Spoon the oysters into the toasted rolls, sprinkle them with salt, pepper and a little Tabasco and Worcestershire sauce. Cover with the tops of the rolls and serve immediately. Pass lemon wedges separately. Serves 4.

Eggplant Mousse

Serve this as a dip piled in a bowl, with Lebanese bread for dipping. Guests break the bread as they dip. It may also be used to top hot toast or baked croutes as a savoury.

> 2 medium eggplants (aubergines)
> Salt and freshly ground pepper
> 3 tablespoons olive oil
> 2 garlic cloves, crushed
> 1/4 teaspoon ground cinnamon
> 2 tablespoons wine vinegar
> 1 tablespoon lemon juice
> 1/2 cup chopped parsley

Tip
The eggplants can be cooked in the microwave. Prick them with a fork, wrap them in kitchen paper towels and microwave on high for 20 minutes, turning several times. This makes a lighter, green-coloured mousse.

Wash the eggplants and cut them in half lengthwise. Score the cut surfaces diagonally several times, sprinkle generously with salt, and place the halves upside down on a plate. Tilt the plate so that the juices drain away. Leave for 1 hour, then rinse the eggplant in water to remove the excess salt, wipe the halves dry, and arrange them cut side up on a baking tray (sheet). Season with salt and pepper and drizzle with a little olive oil. Bake in a preheated moderate oven (180°C/350°F) for about 45 minutes or until soft.

Remove the eggplants from the oven, allow them to cool slightly, then scoop the flesh from the skin. Finely chop the flesh, then mash it with a fork or purée it in an electric blender or food processor. Add the garlic and beat until smooth. Gradually beat 2 tablespoons of olive oil into the purée until it resembles a thick and mousse-like mayonnaise, adding more oil if necessary. Stir in the remaining ingredients. Mix well, cover and chill.

Parmesan Twists

A very easy pastry morsel, using ready-rolled puff pastry. Serve with drinks or use as an accompaniment with soups.

> 1 sheet of ready-rolled puff pastry
> 1 egg, beaten with 1 tablespoon water
> 1/2 cup (2 oz) grated Parmesan cheese
> A pinch of ground cayenne

Parmesan Twists, found in many French bakeries, are easy to make at home, particularly with the advent of ready-rolled puff pastry.

*P*reheat the oven to very hot (230°C/450°F). Butter several baking trays (sheets) and dust them with flour. Brush the sheet of pastry with the beaten egg and sprinkle liberally with the grated Parmesan cheese mixed with a little ground cayenne. Cut into thin strips about 1 cm ($^1/_2$ in) wide and 10 cm (4 in) long. Pick up each strip with both hands and twist it like a corkscrew before placing it on the prepared baking tray. Press down both ends onto the tray with your thumbs so that the twists will keep their shape. Bake for 5–8 minutes. Serve warm, or cool on wire racks; store in an airtight container. Makes 48 twists.

Herbed Pittas

Pitta bread is brushed with herb butter and grilled (broiled). It can be served with a green salad or used to serve with dips or as a crispbread.

> *2 tablespoons butter, melted*
> *1 teaspoon fresh rosemary or 1 teaspoon dried*
> *2 teaspoons fresh oregano or 1 teaspoon dried*
> *1 tablespoon snipped dill*
> *4 small-sized pitta breads*

*C*ombine the butter with the herbs. Preheat the grill (broiler), split and open each pitta, and brush inside with the herb butter. Cut each piece in half or leave whole and place them on a baking tray (sheet). Grill, turning once, until crisp on both sides.

Artichoke Frittata

Frittatas are as good, if not better, cold as they are hot. This one depends on young tender artichokes with no chokes, which are becoming more and more available when in season. Good preserved artichokes in olive oil may be used instead of cooking the artichokes—it makes this a quick snack to make.

4–6 young fresh artichokes, depending on size, trimmed
(see page 98)
2 tablespoons olive oil
1/2 cup (41/2 fl oz) water
6 large eggs
1/2 cup (2 oz) freshly grated Parmesan cheese
Freshly ground pepper
A little oregano or marjoram, freshly chopped

Cut the artichokes into slim wedges, removing the choke if any. Heat a large frying pan (skillet) and cook the artichoke in the oil for about 15 minutes, uncovered, until golden brown. Add the water, stir and cook, covered, until the artichokes are very tender.

Meanwhile, lightly beat the eggs in a bowl and add the Parmesan, pepper and oregano or marjoram. Add the artichokes, stir quickly and return the mixture to the pan, which has been regreased with a little more oil. Cook over a moderate heat until partially set, slide onto a plate, then place the pan over and flip or turn the uncooked side down to cook just a minute or two more. (Or place the pan underneath a hot griller (broiler) until an even, light golden brown.) Slice into wedges to serve. Serves 4–6.

Scrambled Egg and Smoked Salmon

An easy, delectable quick snack if you keep a supply of smoked salmon on hand.

> *6 eggs*
> *Salt and freshly ground pepper*
> *15 g (¹/₂ oz) butter*
> *125 g (4 oz) smoked salmon, cut in slivers*
> *3 tablespoons cream (single, light)*
> *Hot buttered toast*

*B*eat the eggs, season with a very little salt and pepper and cook gently in the butter, stirring until just set. Fold through the salmon and cream and serve piled on hot buttered toast. Serves 2–3.

Salmon Tartare with Ginger Mayonnaise on Pumpernickel

> *375 g (12 oz) Atlantic salmon or sea trout (raw)*
> *¹/₂ red salad onion or 1 spring onion (scallion), finely sliced*
> *Salt and freshly ground pepper*
> *2 tablespoons vodka or gin*
> *Rounds of pumpernickel or rye bread to serve*
> GINGER MAYONNAISE
> *1 egg yolk*
> *¹/₂ teaspoon Dijon mustard*
> *²/₃ cup (6 fl oz) olive oil*
> *Juice of ¹/₂ lime or lemon*
> *¹/₂ teaspoon chopped fresh ginger*

*S*kin and roughly chop the fish. Put into a ceramic or glass bowl with the onion, salt and a good grinding of pepper and the spirit. Mix lightly, cover and refrigerate for 30 minutes or longer.

Place the marinated fish and onion on a board and chop finely—do not overchop or it becomes soggy.

To serve, butter the pumpernickel rounds to the edge and pile on the prepared salmon tartare, patting down lightly to firm. Top each with a dab of ginger mayonnaise just before serving. Serves 6.

Ginger mayonnaise. In a small bowl beat the egg yolk with the mustard; add some oil, drop by drop, to create a thick emulsion. Add the citrus juice, then more oil and continue beating until thick. Add the ginger just before serving.

Rillettes of Smoked Salmon

This is a great way of making a little smoked salmon stretch out to a very nice first course for a special dinner.

> *185 g (6 oz) smoked salmon*
> *3 tablespoons crème fraîche or (dairy) sour cream*
> *15 g (¹/₂ oz) soft unsalted (sweet) butter*
> *A good pinch of grated lemon rind*
> *4 green shallots (spring onions, scallions), white part only, chopped*
> *1 tablespoon fresh lemon juice*
> *1 tablespoon snipped dill*

Reserve one-third of the smoked salmon. Process the rest in a food processor with the crème fraîche, butter and lemon rind. Transfer to a bowl and mix in the remaining ingredients, including the reserved smoked salmon, diced finely, adding a little pepper to taste. Use two wetted spoons to form the mixture into oval mounds, arranging 2 or 3 mounds on each plate. Garnish with a little dill and salad greens if you wish, and offer with toast. Serves 4.

Smoked Salmon Open Sandwiches

Smoked salmon was always a luxury in the past; but these days, with quality farmed Atlantic salmon, it is something we can afford.

> *Sprigs of fresh dill, cress or lettuce leaves*
> *4 slices of rye or black bread, buttered*
> *4 slices of smoked salmon*
> *4 slices of lemon to garnish*
> *4 tablespoons (dairy) sour cream*
> *2 teaspoons creamed horseradish*

Place the dill, cress or lettuce on the bread. Fold slices of smoked salmon and place them on top. Garnish with lemon slices and top with sour cream and horseradish, lightly combined. Top each with a sprig of dill. Serves 4.

Goat Cheese, Avocado and Smoked Salmon en Ficelle

This is something nice to serve with drinks—made in a trice! Good too on little slices of pumpernickel.

> *200 g (7 oz) soft goat cheese*
> *1 firm ripe avocado, cubed*
> *A few slices of smoked salmon, diced*
> *Freshly ground pepper*
> *A squeeze of lime or lemon juice*
> *1 French bread stick (ficelle)*

*M*ash the goat cheese in a bowl and lightly fold through the avocado, salmon, pepper and lemon juice. Cut the ficelle into 20 slices and pile a little of the goat cheese mixture onto each just before serving. Makes 20 toothsome appetisers.

Goat's Cheese, Avocado and Smoked Salmon en Ficelle may be served as a starter or savoury. It is lovely with drinks. Another favourite is Smoked Salmon Open Sandwiches with a dab of horseradish-flavoured sour cream.

Soups

There's hardly a time of the year when a bowl of soup isn't welcome. When winter comes, those of us who think a good soup is the best part of a meal give a whoop of joy. We look forward to chilly days and nights that seem all the better for a bowl of comforting, nourishing soup.

In summer months a light soup served warm or chilled followed by a grill or salad is one of the best ways of winding down after a busy day. Spring gives us a chance to use the youngest, freshest vegetables, while in autumn we are ready for the bigger flavour of more mature ones.

Don't forget the garnishes in the recipes. They add tremendously to the look of the soup and only take minutes to prepare. Chopped parsley, slivers of lemon, snipped chives and crisp pan-fried croutons all add colour, texture and vitamins.

Whole Chicken Soup calls for a good free-range farm chicken, young carrots, leeks, celery and usually some soup pasta. This is my version of a traditional recipe; it cuts down the fat and shortens the time the vegetables are cooked.

STOCK

lthough soup does not necessarily need to be made from stock, it is good to have stock either in the refrigerator or the freezer ready to turn into soup with fresh ingredients. Stock cubes can be used, but they tend to be rather salty and give a sameness to soups.

Canned consommé, though good, is quite expensive, whereas homemade stock is usually made from ingredients which are very cheap or would otherwise be discarded, and a homemade stock when made correctly is nutritious in itself. In many delicatessens or gourmet shops, homemade stocks are available in beef, chicken or fish. These are usually very good. Look to the packaged stocks as a stand-by.

Although a large amount of stock may be prepared at one time, the soup itself should usually be prepared for one meal. Soups made from dried beans, peas and lentils can be made in larger amounts and they freeze very well.

For making stock, choose a saucepan with a flat base and a well-fitting lid. You don't want your precious liquid to evaporate too quickly and fill the kitchen with steam. In many recipes a particular stock is called for—for example, chicken, meat, fish; where stock only is listed in the ingredients, use your own choice of chicken, beef or vegetable. Stocks keep for a week in the refrigerator, and they can also be frozen.

Stock, known also as broth or bouillon, is the clear, flavourful liquid that remains after various meats and vegetables have been simmered in water and then strained. Stock made from beef is brown or light golden; poultry and veal make a white stock, fish a clear stock. Each stock has its uses.

Beef Stock

1 kg (2 lb) beef bones (shank, marrow bone or rib bones)
500 g (1 lb) shin (shank) of beef, chopped
1 carrot, thickly sliced
1 onion, thickly sliced
2 teaspoons salt
About 12 cups (5 imperial pints) cold water (enough to cover bones)
1 teaspoon black peppercorns
Bouquet garni (page 31)

ut the bones into a large saucepan, then add the other ingredients and the bouquet garni and cover with cold water. Bring slowly to the boil, skim the surface well, then simmer very gently, half-covered, for 4 to 5 hours. (Very slow simmering for a long time is the secret of well-flavoured stock.) Strain through a fine sieve, cool, then chill in the refrigerator. Remove the surface fat before using.

This stock is used in brown sauces and soups; clarified, it is used in clear soups.

To Clarify Stock

Remove all fat from the cold stock and place the stock in a saucepan with 2 egg whites, lightly beaten, and the 2 eggshells. Bring slowly to the boil, whisking occasionally with an egg whisk. Allow the liquid to rise in the pan as it reaches boiling point, then lower the heat, and simmer very gently for 20 minutes.

You will find that as the egg whites cook they attract and hold any remaining particles of fat and residue that might cloud the stock. Strain the stock through a colander lined with butter muslin (cheesecloth), and you have a clear liquid which is the basis of many delicious soups.

Chicken Stock

500 g (1 lb) chicken bones (carcass, backs or wings)
About 6 cups (2½ imperial pints) cold water (enough to cover bones)
1 teaspoon salt
1 carrot, halved
1 teaspoon black peppercorns
Bouquet garni (page 31)

Tip

Use fresh bones for clear, well-flavoured stock. Your poultry supplier often has a bag of bone pieces (carcasses, wing tips, etc.) at a very reasonable price, or you may use necks and backs. Giblets, if available, may also be added to the stock, but avoid the chicken liver, which is inclined to give a bitter taste.

*P*lace the bones in a large, heavy saucepan. Cover with cold water and add the remaining ingredients and the bouquet garni. Bring to the boil and carefully skim the surface. Cover the pan and simmer very slowly for 2–3 hours. Strain through a fine sieve and cool. Refrigerate until needed, then remove the fat which has risen to the top of the stock, leaving the flavoured jelly underneath.

Fish Stock

This stock is used in many fish sauces and soups. It can be frozen or will keep well in the refrigerator for a week.

2 kg (4 lb) bones, heads (without gills) or trimmings of any
*   white, non-oily fish*
5 cups (2¼ imperial pints) cold water
1 cup (9 fl oz) white wine, or the juice of a lemon plus water to
*   make a cup*
1 teaspoon white peppercorns
Bouquet garni (page 31)

Tip

For the best flavour, stock must be simmered, never boiled. Never throw away crab, lobster or prawn (shrimp) heads. Put them in the freezer in plastic (polythene) bags; they will keep there and be ready to toss in the stockpot when you need some fish stock.

*P*lace all the ingredients and the bouquet garni in a large saucepan and bring to the boil. Skim the surface, and simmer very gently for 20 minutes. Strain through a fine sieve or cheesecloth.

Vegetable Stock

As more people opt out of meat eating, there is a call for vegetable stock. Use it in place of meat or chicken stock in soups, sauces and casseroles.

> *1 leek, white part only, chopped*
> *3 celery stalks, chopped*
> *1 parsnip, peeled and chopped*
> *1 white turnip, peeled and chopped*
> *1 head of lettuce, chopped*
> *A piece of ginger (walnut-size), finely chopped*
> *A bouquet garni (page 31)*
> *12 peppercorns*
> *2 teaspoons coarse salt*
> *8 cups (3¹/₂ imperial pints) water*

*P*ut all the ingredients in a large saucepan or stockpot. Bring to the boil, lower heat and simmer, partially covered, for about 1 hour. Pour the soup through a colander set over another container, pressing the vegetables against the sides of the colander to extract the juices; discard the solids. Pour through a strainer, cool and refrigerate.

Zuppa di Verdura

A summer vegetable soup seen on most menus in Italy, Zuppa di Verdura often has dried beans or chickpeas (garbanzo beans) in it. If a favourite vegetable is in season—perhaps asparagus or baby limas—that can be added too.

Italians don't serve chilled soups, even in summer, and though this is hot and has a bounty of vegetables, the simplicity of the dish makes it appropriate for the summer months.

Most soups are finished with a *C* of olive oil 'written' in the soup with the help of an oil-dispensing can. The presence of a good fruity olive oil is always in evidence on Italian tables. The oil may be in a small metal can with a fine spout (see picture, opposite page) or in a small jug, again with a spout. Olive oil is drizzled over salads, pasta, bread, gnocchi and vegetables as well as soups such as Zuppa di Verdura.

Zuppa di Verdura, a soup of choice fresh vegetables, has a characteristic 'C' of oil as a finishing touch. Always have bread on the table with hearty soups—this time it is toasted focaccia.

¹/₄ cup (2¹/₄ fl oz) olive oil

2 carrots, diced

2 medium potatoes, peeled and diced

¹/₂ cauliflower, cut into florets

1 leek, sliced

2 small celery stalks, diced

1 small onion, chopped

250 g (8 oz) green beans, cut into short lengths

125 g (4 oz) tender asparagus, tips and 2 cm (1 in) lengths

1 cup (6 oz) shelled green peas

8 cups (3¹/₂ imperial pints) vegetable stock or water, hot

4 dark lettuce leaves, shredded

*Toasted bread slices, grated Parmesan cheese and extra olive
    oil to serve*

*H*eat the olive oil in a large pan and sauté the vegetables, except the lettuce, gently for a few minutes. Add the hot stock, bring slowly to the boil and simmer very gently for about 20 minutes. (The Italians tend to cook the vegetables longer than this so that the vegetables lose their firmness completely; it is a matter of taste.) Add the shredded lettuce and simmer for a further 5–10 minutes.

Serve very hot ladled over the toasted bread slices or separately. Sprinkle each bowl with plenty of grated Parmesan. Finish off with a trickle of olive oil for that Italian touch. Serves 6.

Potato and Chervil Soup

45 g (1¹/₂ oz) butter
3 potatoes, peeled and diced or cut into small strips
Salt and nutmeg to taste
3 cups (27 fl oz) water
³/₄ cup (6³/₄ fl oz) milk
2 tablespoons fresh chervil, cut with scissors
2 tablespoons cream (single, light) (optional)

Melt the butter in a heavy saucepan. Put in the potatoes and cook very gently in the butter for 10 minutes until they begin to soften—they must not brown. Sprinkle them with a little salt and a grating of nutmeg. Pour in the water, cover the pot and let the potatoes simmer for 20–25 minutes.

Sieve or purée the potatoes in an electric blender or food processor. Return the purée to the rinsed pan. Add the milk, which has been brought to the boil in another pan—this is important. Taste for seasoning, and before serving stir in the chervil and cream. Serves 4–6.

Spiced Coriander Soup

30 g (1 oz) butter
1 teaspoon ground coriander
1 teaspoon ground cumin
2 tablespoons plain (all-purpose) flour
5 cups (2¹/₄ imperial pints) chicken stock (page 68), heated
Juice of ¹/₂ lemon
Salt and freshly ground pepper
¹/₃ cup (3 fl oz) cream (single, light) (optional)
³/₄ cup cooked rice, long or short grain (see tip)
2 tablespoons coriander (Chinese parsley) leaves

Tip
To prepare the rice, bring 1 cup (9 fl oz) of water to the boil, add ¹/₂ teaspoon of salt and 2 tablespoons of rice, bring back to the boil and cook until the water evaporates, about 10–12 minutes. Turn off heat, cover and leave for a further 5 minutes. Fluff up the rice before adding it to the soup.

Heat the butter in a saucepan and stir in the ground coriander and cumin, cooking gently for 1 minute. Add the flour, blend in and return to heat, cook gently 1 minute, then add the stock. Stir until blended and cook a further 3–4 minutes. Add the lemon juice; salt and pepper to taste. Stir in the cream and the cooked rice. When the soup is heated through, add the coriander leaves and let it stand a minute or two before serving. Serves 6.

Borsch

In this version of the famous Russian soup the vegetables are cooked for only a short time: thus they retain most of their vitamins.

500 g (1 lb) shin (shank) of beef or chuck steak, cut into small
cubes
7 cups (3 imperial pints) water
1 teaspoon salt
2 bay leaves
2 tablespoons vegetable or olive oil
3 beetroots (beets), peeled and shredded
2 carrots, peeled and shredded
1 turnip or parsnip, peeled and shredded
1 onion, chopped
1 tablespoon tomato paste (concentrate)
1 tablespoon vinegar
1 teaspoon sugar
1/2 small head cabbage, shredded
Pepper
Light (dairy) sour cream or natural (plain) yoghurt

*P*ut the beef and any bones in a saucepan with the water, salt and bay leaves. Bring to the boil, reduce the heat, cover and simmer until the meat is tender, about 1¹/₂ hours. Remove bones.

Heat the oil in a saucepan, add the beetroots, carrots, turnip and onion, tomato paste, vinegar and sugar, then cover and cook very gently for about 15 minutes. Stir frequently to prevent sticking. Add the cabbage to the saucepan and cook a further 10 minutes. Add the vegetables to the meat and stock. Adjust seasoning and add more vinegar if desired. Simmer for a few minutes. Serve with light sour cream or yoghurt and accompany with sweet and sour or plain rye bread. Serves 8.

Potage Bonne Femme

A well-known and loved French soup. It is worth while making a good stock for this soup with white wine, although canned or packaged beef or chicken stock can be used.

60 g (2 oz) butter
2 onions, finely chopped
3 leeks, washed and sliced (see page 115)
2 medium potatoes, peeled and diced
6 cups (2³/₄ imperial pints) chicken stock (page 68)
³/₄ cup (6³/₄ fl oz) white wine
Salt and freshly ground pepper
A little chopped parsley

Potage Bonne Femme is one of the basic and most versatile soups of France. A chunky soup of potatoes and leeks, it becomes Potage Parmentier when puréed. When this purée is chilled and a cup (9 fl oz) of cream and a sprinkling of chives are added, voila!, you have Vichyssoise.

Melt the butter in a medium saucepan, add the onions, leeks and potatoes and cook covered very gently until the vegetables are soft and pale golden. Add the stock and wine and allow to simmer for 8–10 minutes. Season with salt and pepper and serve in bowls topped with parsley. Serves 4–6.

Potage Parmentier

Prepare Potage Bonne Femme or use any left over. Purée in an electric blender or food processor fitted with the double-sided steel blade (this should be done a few cupfuls at a time), or push through a sieve. Reheat and lighten the soup with 4 tablespoons of cream (light single) and 30 g (1 oz) of butter. Serve hot, sprinkling with parsley or fried croutons.

Fried croutons. Remove the crusts from 3 thick slices of bread and cut the bread into small cubes. Heat some light olive oil or a mixture of butter and oil in a frying pan; when hot, add the bread cubes and fry until golden. Watch them carefully and toss them around for even browning. Remove the croutons with a slotted spoon and drain them on crumpled kitchen paper towels. Sprinkle with salt before serving. A French bread stick may be sliced and fried the same way.

Vichyssoise

Make Potage Parmentier, omitting the cream and butter added at the end of the cooking time. Allow the soup to cool after it is puréed, then stir in 1 cup (9 fl oz) of light (single) cream. Chill and check for seasoning, adding more salt or pepper if necessary. To serve, top with a spoonful of whipped or thick (double or heavy) cream or swirl in a little light (single) cream and sprinkle with snipped chives or parsley. Vichyssoise may also be served hot.

Pumpkin and Saffron Soup

A mellow golden soup fragrant with true saffron. Turmeric is no substitute; look for the saffron threads at good delicatessens or gourmet shops.

30 g (1 oz) unsalted (sweet) butter
1 medium onion, chopped
750 g (1¹/₂ lb) pumpkin (winter squash) or butternut squash,
  peeled and cut into cubes
4 cups (1³/₄ imperial pints) chicken stock (page 68)
A few strands of saffron, soaked in ¹/₄ cup (2¹/₄ fl oz) warm
  water
Salt and freshly ground black pepper
Fried croutons (see page 74) or bread

Pumpkin and Saffron Soup—a brilliant golden soup enhanced by the exquisite flavour and colour of true saffron. These threads, the stigmas of the crocus flower, are expensive, so they are used with discretion. They are first soaked in water to draw out the flavour and colour.

In a large saucepan, melt the butter and gently cook the onion for a few minutes, until softened. Add the pumpkin and cook a further few minutes. Add the chicken stock, bring to the boil, reduce heat and simmer, covered, for 20 minutes. Add the saffron and soaking water for the last 10 minutes of cooking time. In an electric blender or food processor, purée the mixture in batches and return to the pan. Season to taste with salt and freshly ground pepper, then reheat the soup over low heat, stirring. Serve with fried croutons or bread. Serves 6.

Peas and Egg Drop Soup

One of the quick and easy Chinese soups that are light and nourishing. The eggs are very lightly stirred into the hot broth, forming long strands.

6 Chinese dried mushrooms
1 cup (6 oz) fresh or frozen peas
4 cups (1³/₄ imperial pints) chicken stock
2 eggs, lightly beaten

Soak the mushrooms in hot water for 20 minutes. Remove stalks and cut the tops into thin slices. Place the peas, mushrooms and stock in a large saucepan, bring to the boil and simmer for 5 minutes. Remove from heat and add the eggs, stirring until they separate into strands. Serve immediately. Serves 6.

Whole Chicken Soup

1 medium chicken, appoximately 1.5 kg (3 lb)
1 leek, halved and washed well (see page 115), or ¹/₂ onion
4 slices fresh ginger
2 carrots or 8 baby carrots
2 stalks celery
2 leeks, washed well and cut into short lengths
1 cup soup pasta (optional)
Salt to taste
2 tablespoons white wine or dry sherry

*W*ash the chicken inside and out; remove the neck and giblets. Place the chicken, neck and giblets in a large saucepan with enough water to cover. Add the leek or onion and ginger. Bring to the boil, skim the surface, lower heat, and simmer, covered, for 30 minutes. Remove the leek, chicken neck and giblets. Peel the carrots and cut them into matchstick-size pieces (leave baby carrots whole) and cut the celery the same size. Add them to the soup with the cut leeks and pasta, if using. Season with salt. Add the wine and simmer a further 10–15 minutes until tender. Remove the chicken, cut it into large pieces and remove the skin. Each guest is served portions of chicken in the soup bowl with vegetables and broth. Serves 6.

Haricot Bean Soup

Tip
This soup is basically a thick bean purée. Haricot beans are cooked to the stage where they are soft but not disintegrated. The celery, leeks and tomato should also be very soft, so that they can be puréed. An egg-yolk liaison binds the soup.

1 cup (6 oz) haricot beans
5 cups (2¹/₄ imperial pints) water
A bouquet garni (page 31)
1 medium onion
1 garlic clove
4–5 celery stalks, finely chopped
2 leeks (white part only) or 2 onions, finely chopped
3 tablespoons light olive oil
4 large tomatoes, chopped roughly
Salt
2 egg yolks
Bread and garlic-flavoured oil for croutons

$\mathcal{S}$oak the beans overnight in enough water to cover them. Cook the drained beans in the 5 cups of water with the bouquet garni, onion and garlic until tender, about 1 hour. In another saucepan cook the leeks or onions in the oil until soft but not coloured. Add the tomatoes and sauté gently for about 10 minutes.

Remove the onion, garlic and bouquet garni from the beans. Combine the beans and liquid with the vegetables and rub through a sieve or purée in an electric blender or food processor. Season with salt and bring to the boil, stirring. Just before serving, take the pot off the heat and mix in the egg yolks which have been combined with 2 tablespoons of hot soup. Reheat but do not allow the soup to boil. Serve with croutons of bread fried lightly in garlic-flavoured oil (page 74). Serves 6–8.

Spiced Parsnip Soup

Parsnips are popular roasted around a joint or boiled and mashed with butter, but they also make a delicious soup.

> *30 g (1 oz) butter*
> *1 medium onion, chopped*
> *2 medium parsnips, peeled and diced*
> *1 potato, peeled and diced*
> *1 garlic clove, crushed*
> *$^1\!/_2$ teaspoon curry powder*
> *$^1\!/_2$ teaspoon ground cumin*
> *4 cups (1$^3\!/_4$ imperial pints) stock, hot*
> *Salt and pepper to taste*
> *$^1\!/_4$ cup (2$^1\!/_4$ fl oz) cream (single, light)*
> *Chives and parsley, chopped*

$\mathcal{M}$elt the butter in a large, heavy saucepan. Add the onion, parsnips and potato, stir lightly, cover and cook over low heat until the vegetables are slightly soft, shaking the pan occasionally. Add the garlic, curry powder and cumin, cook for a few minutes, then pour in the hot stock. Simmer till the vegetables are tender, then purée in an electric blender on food processor in several batches. Return to the saucepan, season with salt and pepper and if necessary dilute the soup with a little hot water (it should not be too thick). Reheat and ladle into soup bowls. Swirl a little cream into the soup and scatter chives and parsley on top. Serves 4–6.

Tomato and Orange Soup

Who doesn't like tomato soup? It may be chunky and flecked with herbs or puréed, smooth and velvety. Cream is often swirled through it. This recipe calls for the fresh taste of orange—just enough to add interest.

1 kg (2 lb) tomatoes, washed, halved and seeded
1 onion, peeled
1 carrot, sliced
A strip of lemon peel
1 bay leaf
6 peppercorns
30 g (1 oz) butter
3 tablespoons plain (all-purpose) flour
4¹/₂ cups (2 imperial pints) chicken stock (page 68)
Rind and juice of ¹/₂ orange
Salt and pepper to taste
¹/₂ cup (4¹/₂ fl oz) cream (single, light) (optional)

Tomato and Orange Soup. Red, sun-ripened tomatoes give the best results when making this soup. Freshly squeezed orange juice is added just on the point of serving, for that fresh taste.

*P*lace the tomatoes in a saucepan with the onion, carrot, lemon peel, bay leaf and peppercorns. Cover and cook for about 30 minutes until the tomatoes are soft and pulpy. Rub through a sieve or purée in an electric blender or food processor. Rinse out the saucepan, melt the butter and add the flour. Cook over low heat for 1 minute, stirring all the time. Take off the heat and stir in the stock gradually. Add the sieved tomato purée. Return to the heat and bring to the boil. Simmer for 5 minutes.

Meanwhile, cut the orange rind into needle shreds. Drop them into boiling water and drain immediately, rinsing under cold water. Add the strained orange juice to the soup and season with salt and pepper. Pour into bowls, swirl in a little cream if using and sprinkle with the orange rind. Serves 6.

Cream of Sorrel Soup

Tip
You may not find
sorrel at the
greengrocers, but
plants and seeds are
readily available and it
grows easily. It looks a
little like spinach but
loses its wonderful
greenness on cooking.
Sorrel has a strong acid
lemon taste, making it
perfect to be used in a
sauce for fish or veal.
Sorrel soup is
particularly refreshing.

60 g (2 oz) butter
2 leeks, washed and finely sliced (see page 115)
Salt and freshly ground pepper
4 medium potatoes, peeled and diced
3 cups (27 fl oz) chicken stock (page 68)
6–8 sorrel leaves or spinach
3 cups (27 fl oz) milk, hot
A sprinkling of chopped parsley for garnish

*I*n a large pan melt half the butter, add the sliced leeks and cook over a low heat until soft, without colouring. Season with salt and pepper and add the diced potato. Stir in the chicken stock, cover and simmer gently for about 20 minutes.

Wash and shred the sorrel or spinach. Melt the remaining butter in a small saucepan, add the sorrel and cook slowly until most of the moisture has cooked away—about 10 minutes. Add it to the soup, blend in the hot milk and check for seasoning. Reheat and serve sprinkled with chopped parsley. Serves 6.

Sweet Corn Soup

30 g (1 oz) butter
1 onion, chopped
2 potatoes, peeled and diced
2 tablespoons plain (all-purpose) flour
2 cups (18 fl oz) milk
2 cups (18 fl oz) water
1 bay leaf
Salt and white pepper
2 350 g (12 oz) cans of sweet corn kernels, drained
2 tablespoons cream (single, light)
Crumbled fried bacon to garnish

*M*elt the butter in a saucepan, add the onion and cook for 5 minutes, without browning. Add the potatoes and cook for a further 2 minutes. Stir in the flour, then gradually add the milk and water, stirring constantly. Bring to the boil, add the bay leaf and salt and pepper to taste. Add half of the sweet corn, cover and simmer for 15 to 20 minutes. Discard the bay leaf and let the mixture cool slightly.

Sieve or work the soup in an electric blender or food processor until smooth. Return the sieved soup to the saucepan, add the remaining sweet corn and heat through. Stir in the cream, sprinkle over the crumbled bacon and serve immediately. Serves 4–6.

Curried Red Lentil Soup

¹/₂ medium onion, finely chopped
2 tablespoons vegetable oil
1 garlic clove, chopped
1 teaspoon finely grated peeled fresh ginger
1¹/₂ teaspoons curry powder
1 teaspoon ground cumin
1 cup (6 oz) red lentils, picked over and rinsed
1¹/₄ cups (11 fl oz) water
3 cups (27 fl oz) chicken stock (page 68)
2 medium tomatoes, peeled, seeded and diced (see page 130)
Fresh lemon juice to taste
Salt and pepper

*I*n a large, heavy saucepan, cook the onion in the oil over moderate heat, stirring until it is lightly golden. Add the garlic and ginger and cook the mixture, stirring, for 1 minute. Add the curry powder and cumin, and cook the mixture for 30 seconds, stirring all the while. Add the lentils, measured water and stock. Bring the liquid to the boil and simmer, covered, for 25 minutes.

Stir in the tomatoes and simmer the soup, stirring occasionally, for 2 minutes. Season the soup with the lemon juice and salt and pepper to taste. Serves 4.

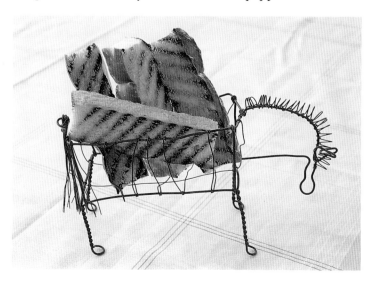

Cream of Carrot Soup

30 g (1 oz) butter
4 medium carrots, washed and sliced
1 onion, sliced
5 cups (2¼ imperial pints) chicken stock or water, hot
1 teaspoon salt
A generous pinch of cayenne pepper
¼–½ cup cream (single, light) or yoghurt (natural, plain)
Chopped parsley or chervil sprigs

Cream of Carrot Soup. Tender young carrots are used whole in clear soups. Mature, bright orange carrots have the best flavour for a soup to be puréed. A rough purée makes a hearty soup; further processing gives a finer, more elegant finish. Each can be right for the occasion.

Melt the butter in a saucepan, add the carrot and onion, and cook gently until softened, about 10 minutes. Add 2 cups of the chicken stock or water and bring to the boil. Reduce the heat, cover, and simmer for 10 minutes. Rub through a sieve or purée in an electric blender or food processor. Add the salt and cayenne. Return the soup to the pan and heat gently with the remaining stock; swirl in the cream or yoghurt. Sprinkle with chopped parsley or chervil before serving. Serves 6.

Oyster Soup Rockefeller

Yon don't have to be as rich as Rockefeller to enjoy this lovely soup.

1 bunch spinach
1 cup (9 fl oz) fish or chicken stock (page 68)
1 small onion, chopped finely
2 cups (18 fl oz) milk
24 oysters, bottled or fresh, 12 of them cut in halves
Salt and freshly ground pepper
2 drops Tabasco sauce
½ cup (4½ fl oz) double (whipping) cream whipped with a
*   pinch of salt*

Wash the spinach well and trim off the stalks; chop roughly. Simmer with the stock and onion for 10 minutes. Purée in an electric blender or food processor or push through a sieve. Heat the milk, add the spinach purée to the saucepan with the halved oysters and heat gently. Season to taste with salt and pepper. Add the Tabasco sauce, place 3 oysters in each bowl, and ladle in the hot soup, garnishing each bowl with a little whipped cream if you like. Serves 4.

Cream of Mushroom Soup is unusual in that the raw mushrooms are sliced, puréed in a blender, then added to the prepared soup and cooked just long enough to be heated through. You get the lovely taste of mushrooms.

Cream of Mushroom Soup

30 g (1 oz) butter

A bunch of spring onions (scallions), washed, trimmed and sliced

1 garlic clove

Salt and pepper

2 tablespoons plain (all-purpose) flour

4 cups (1³/₄ imperial pints) chicken stock (page 68)

250 g (8 oz) mushrooms, sliced

¹/₂ cup (4¹/₂ fl oz) cream (light, single)

A pinch of dried tarragon

*M*elt the butter in a saucepan. Add the spring onions to the pan with the garlic. Toss well, season with salt and pepper, cover and allow to cook over low heat. When the onions are soft, blend in the flour and stir while adding the stock. Bring to the boil and simmer for a few minutes.

Place in an electric blender or food processor with the sliced mushrooms and purée till smooth, or push through a sieve. This is best done in several lots. Return the soup to the saucepan, reheat but do not allow to boil. Pour in the cream and tarragon and stir gently. Serve immediately. Serves 6.

Mussels in Pernod Cream

Select smallish mussels for this dish (not large green ones). The Pernod gives a delicate licorice flavour, but lemon juice is an alternative. A super first course for a relaxed luncheon.

2 kg (4 lb) mussels
³/₄ cup (6³/₄ fl oz) dry white wine
1 tablespoon chopped parsley
A small bouquet garni (see page 31)
90 g (3 oz) butter
2 medium onions, finely chopped
1 garlic clove, chopped
3 cups (27 fl oz) boiling water
³/₄ cup (6³/₄ fl oz) hot milk
2 egg yolks
²/₃ cup (6 fl oz) cream (light, single)
3 tablespoons Pernod or juice of 1 lemon
2 tablespoons chopped parsley
Freshly ground pepper
8 slices French bread
Oil or butter for frying

Scrub the mussels with a scourer and, with a sharp tug toward the rounded opening, remove the beard from each. Place the mussels in a large saucepan with the wine, parsley, and bouquet garni. Cover and cook for about 5 minutes until the mussels open; discard unopened mussels. Strain the resulting broth through a fine sieve. Remove and discard the top shell of the mussels; keep the mussels warm.

Heat the butter in the rinsed-out pan and sauté the onion and garlic gently until pale golden and soft. Add the strained mussel broth, boiling water and milk. Simmer for 5 minutes.

Beat the egg yolks with the cream and the Pernod or lemon juice. Stir in a little of the hot soup, then return this mixture to the pan.

Reheat gently, stirring all the time. Season with freshly ground pepper. Put the mussels in 4 deep, very hot soup plates, pour over the hot broth and strew with the parsley.

Meanwhile, fry the bread in oil or butter until golden on both sides and offer with the mussels. Serves 4.

Fresh Salmon Soup

With successful fish farming throughout the world, those beautiful pink salmon are available most of the year at affordable prices. This lovely soup is great for family meals or entertaining, the soup base being at the ready for the final cooking of the potatoes and peas and the poaching of the fish. I buy two tail ends of Atlantic salmon for this dish and cut two fillets from each. To remove the skin from the fillets, lay them skin side down on a board and with a sharp knife separate the skin from the flesh, pulling the skin gently and easing the flesh with the knife.

Fresh Salmon Soup. The salmon is cut in small steaks and gently poached in some of the prepared soup in a separate pan. A piece of salmon is carefully lifted into the soup bowl and the soup ladled over. This makes for a beautiful presentation.

> *2 salmon tails (or 4 small salmon fillets)*
> *3 tablespoons butter*
> *2 leeks, washed, and finely sliced (see page 115)*
> *1 garlic clove, chopped*
> *1 small bay leaf*
> *6 cups (2¹/₂ imperial pints) fish stock*
> *1 teaspoon salt*
> *Freshly ground pepper*
> *1 medium potato, peeled and diced*
> *1 cup (6 oz) shelled fresh green peas*
> *1 tablespoon plain (all-purpose) flour*
> *¹/₂ cup (4¹/₂ fl oz) cream (optional)*
> *3 tablespoons chopped dill or chervil*

Cut 2 fillets from each salmon tail, remove the skin and set the fillets aside. In a saucepan, melt 2 tablespoons of butter and sweat the leeks with the garlic and bay leaf over gentle heat, shaking the pan occassionally. When the leeks are soft, add the fish stock, salt and pepper to taste, potato and peas. Bring to the boil, reduce heat and simmer, covered, about 10 minutes. Meanwhile, knead together 1 tablespoon of butter and the flour; lightly whisk bits of this into the liquid over a gentle heat to slightly thicken the soup.

Heat 2 cups of the soup in a frying pan (skillet) large enough to take the fish fillets, place the fish in the pan and spoon the soup over them. Bring to the simmer and poach the fish about 4 minutes or until opaque and firm.

To serve: using a slotted spoon, lift the salmon onto 4 heated, flattish soup bowls. Return the liquid from the frying pan to the saucepan and bring the soup just back to the boil. Lightly stir in the cream, if using, and ladle the soup over the salmon in the bowls. Scatter with dill or chervil. Serves 4.

Prawn Bisque

$^1/_8$ teaspoon saffron
$^1/_4$ cup (2$^1/_4$ fl oz) sweet vermouth
1 large carrot, scraped and diced
1 small onion, finely chopped
90 g (3 oz) butter
500 g (1 lb) uncooked prawns (shrimp)
$^3/_4$ cup (6$^3/_4$ fl oz) dry white wine
A bouquet garni (page 31)
6$^1/_2$ cups (3 imperial pints) fish stock (page 68)
4 tablespoons cooked rice
Salt, pepper and ground cayenne
$^1/_2$ cup (4$^1/_2$ fl oz) cream
2 tablespoons brandy
Parsley, chopped

Tip
This bisque can be made with blue swimmer or other crabs or lobster. Buy fresh, uncooked shellfish with heads and tails and follow the directions for prawn bisque. You have to treat each type of seafood accordingly, separating the heads, tails and removing the edible flesh. Heavy shells should be pounded with a heavy metal object to break them up.

Combine the saffron and vermouth in a small bowl and set aside. Shell the prawns, reserving the shells and heads. Devein the prawns and cut them in two; keep them in a small bowl. Sauté the carrot and onion in half the butter until softened without colouring, about 5 minutes. Add the prawn shells and heads, sauté a further minute or so, then add the wine, bouquet garni and stock. Cook gently, crushing the shells with a potato masher every now and then. Simmer about 20 minutes.

Strain this broth through a sieve, pushing it well to extract all the flavours. Wash the saucepan and return the strained liquid to it. Add the rice and cook gently. In a small saucepan, heat the remaining butter and sauté the prawns until they turn pink. When the rice is cooked, add the halved prawns and heat gently. Taste for seasoning, adding the saffron and vermouth, salt, pepper and cayenne, then stir in the cream and brandy. Serve very hot, garnished with parsley. Serves 6.

Many recipes call for a bouquet garni, a little bundle of vegetables and herbs—a small stick of celery, a bay leaf, a sprig of thyme or other herbs, and perhaps a piece of carrot.

Thai Prawn Soup

750 g (1¹/₂ lb) green prawns (shrimp)
1 tablespoon vegetable or olive oil
9 cups (4 imperial pints) water
6 small Kaffir lime or common lime or lemon leaves or strips of
*   rind of the fruit*
1 tablespoon shredded lemon grass
4 coriander (Chinese parsley) roots, finely chopped with a little
*   of the stalks*
2 teaspoons nam pla (fish sauce)
¹/₃ cup (3 fl oz) fresh lime juice
4 tablespoons sliced coriander leaves
3 tablespoons sliced green shallots (spring onions, scallions)
1 red chilli (chili pepper), seeded and sliced into 2.5 cm (1 in) strips

Shell the prawns, reserving the shells and heads, and devein them. Heat the oil in a large wok or saucepan and fry the prawn heads and shells until they turn pink. Add the water, lime leaves, lemon grass and chopped coriander roots and bring to the boil. Simmer for about 20 minutes.

Strain the stock through a colander lined with muslin (cheesecloth) and return it to the saucepan or wok. Add the nam pla and cook for a further 5 minutes. Reduce the heat, add the prawns and lime juice and cook gently until the prawns turn firm and a pale pink. Add the coriander, shallots and red chilli strips just before serving. Serves 6.

Tip
To devein prawns (shrimp), make a slit down the back of each and remove the black intestinal tract with a toothpick or the point of a paring knife or with your fingers and the help of a kitchen paper towel.

Greek Lemon Soup

5 cups (2¹/₂ imperial pints) chicken stock (page 68)
3 tablespoons short-grain rice, washed and drained
2 eggs
Juice of 2 lemons and rind of 1 lemon, finely grated

Bring the stock to the boil, gradually add the rice and cook over a low heat for about 30 minutes. Beat the eggs with the lemon juice and add the grated lemon rind. Slowly stir 1 cup of hot chicken stock into the egg and lemon mixture. Pour this back slowly into the hot stock, stirring rapidly to prevent the soup from curdling. Do not boil. Serve hot. Serves 4–6.

Tip
Wash rice in water to remove excess starch. Drain thoroughly.

Hot and Sour Soup

Tip

Hot and Sour Soup is
one of the best-known
Szechwan recipes. The
vinegar used can be
either malt or, better
still, an oriental
vinegar.

2 tablespoons soy sauce

2 tablespoons plain (all-purpose) flour

Salt and pepper to taste

1 teaspoon grated fresh ginger

125 g (4 oz) pork fillet (tenderloin), sliced thinly

5 Chinese dried mushrooms

1 tablespoon vegetable or olive oil

5 cups (2¹/₄ imperial pints) chicken stock or Chinese style stock

¹/₄ cup bamboo shoots, thinly sliced

2 cakes (squares) bean curd (tofu), cubed

¹/₄ cup rice vermicelli, broken

1 tablespoon vinegar

¹/₄ teaspoon each salt and pepper

3 eggs, lightly beaten

¹/₄ cup (2¹/₂ fl oz) cold water

1 tablespoon cornflour (cornstarch)

1 tablespoon sesame oil

*M*ix the soy sauce, flour, salt and pepper and ginger in a small bowl. Toss
the sliced pork in the mixture. Soak the dried mushrooms in cold water
to cover for 10 minutes. Drain and cook in boiling salted water for 5 minutes.
Heat the oil in a large saucepan or wok and stir-fry the pork for 15 seconds.

Pour in the stock and add the bamboo shoots, bean curd, mushrooms and
vermicelli. Bring to the boil and simmer for 10 minutes. Add the vinegar, salt,
pepper and beaten eggs. Mix the water and cornflour together until smooth, add
the sesame oil, and stir into the soup. Bring to the boil and cook, stirring, until
the soup thickens. Serves 6.

Lentil and Lemon Soup

Tip

Brown lentils are better
soaked, as this reduces
the cooking time by
half, but even with
soaking and long
cooking they still keep
their shape, so I prefer
to use brown lentils for
salads or serve them as
a separate vegetable.

Red, yellow, green or brown lentils can be used for this simple soup. I usually
choose red ones, as they don't require soaking and disintegrate completely when
cooked. You can vary this recipe by lightly frying the diced bacon with a finely
chopped onion and adding it to the soup just before serving. Six to eight leaves of
washed and drained silver beet (Swiss chard) cut into ribbons and cooked with

the bacon and onion makes a pleasant change, or stir in 2 tablespoons of tomato paste (concentrate).

In the Middle East, where lentil soup is popular, a teaspoon of ground cumin or a little ground coriander is added and the soup is garnished with fresh parsley or chopped dill. For an extra rich soup, enjoyed in Turkey, sauté the onion with butter, add the silver beet and just before serving beat 2 egg yolks with the juice of a lemon, add a ladleful of the hot soup and beat well. Pour this mixture back into the soup gradually, stirring constantly, and bring the soup back to just below boiling point.

Lentil and Lemon Soup is very versatile. You can use brown, red, yellow or green lentils. Try adding a few leaves of shredded spinach just before serving, and for a spicy Middle-East flavour add a teaspoon of ground cumin or coriander.

> *1 cup (6 oz) lentils, picked over and rinsed*
> *6 cups (2³/₄ pints) water*
> *Salt and pepper*
> *3 rashers (slices) streaky bacon, diced*
> *3 potatoes, peeled and diced*
> *1 tablespoon lemon juice*

*W*ash the lentils and, if needed, soak them overnight in the water. Put them into a pan with their soaking water (or the 6 cups), adding a large pinch each of salt and pepper, and the diced bacon. Bring to the boil, reduce heat and simmer for 1¹/₂ hours or until the lentils are soft. Add the potatoes, simmer for a further 20 minutes or until the potatoes are soft. Mix well so that the potatoes thicken the soup; add the lemon juice. Serve very hot. Serves 6.

Gazpacho Andaluz

750 g (1¹/₂ lb) ripe tomatoes, skinned (see page 130)
1 cup (9 fl oz) white wine or stock
2 garlic cloves, crushed with salt and mixed with freshly
*   ground pepper and ¹/₂ teaspoon cumin*
³/₄ cup (3 oz) dry breadcrumbs
4 tablespoons olive oil
3 tablespoons wine vinegar
1 large red (Spanish) onion, finely diced
1 green capsicum (sweet pepper), seeded and finely diced
2 Lebanese (Continental) cucumbers, peeled and finely diced
12–16 ice cubes

Cook half the tomatoes with the wine for 5 minutes (this evaporates the alcohol) and push through a sieve or purée in an electric blender or food processor. Set aside. Cut the remaining tomatoes into small dice.

Mix the crushed garlic with the breadcrumbs, then very gradually stir in the oil. Add the vinegar, a little at a time, then the tomato purée. Combine with the diced tomatoes, onion, capsicum and cucumbers, mix well and chill for 2–3 hours before serving. Place 2–3 ice cubes in each bowl of gazpacho. Serves 6.

Zuppa di Stracciatella

A bunch of spinach or half a bunch of tender silver beet leaves
2 tablespoons grated Parmesan cheese
4–6 cups (1³/₄–2³/₄ imperial pints) homemade chicken stock
2 large eggs
A pinch of nutmeg

Wash the spinach leaves thoroughly and remove all the stalks. Roll up about 4 leaves of spinach at a time into a fat cigar and cut across into very thin shreds. Place a handful in each soup bowl and top with the grated Parmesan cheese.

Bring the chicken stock to a gentle simmer. Whip the eggs to a froth; add the nutmeg. Add the egg mixture to the simmering broth, whip for a second or two with a fork, then remove from heat. Ladle the stock mixture into the bowls over the spinach and cheese and serve as quickly as possible. Serves 4–6.

Zuppa di Stracciatella, a hot soup with little ragged flakes of beaten eggs, is ladled over bowls of very finely shredded spinach and Parmesan cheese. The soup just softens and partially cooks the greens.

Tip
In this soup the egg mixture breaks into flakes; it is not meant to be smooth. The hot soup just softens and partially cooks the spinach. It is delicious. For a tangy lemon soup, add 2 tablespoons of lemon juice when whipping the eggs.

Vegetables and Salads

Good vegetable dishes range from the tenderest green beans tossed in butter and lemon juice to a wonderful mixed vegetable combination tossed in garlicky mayonnaise, which the French call aigroissade.

Vegetables can be appreciated not just as accompaniments to meat, but as dishes to be served on their own. For many of us it is an easy matter to produce beautiful vegetable dishes, as there seems to be no end to the variety of vegetables in tip-top condition available at most greengrocers.

I do believe that vegetables are all too often not accorded the treatment they deserve. By learning to care for the vegetables you bring into the home, and by cooking them skilfully, you will be making a valuable contribution not only to your own and your family's health, but to your enjoyment as well. In this chapter you will find recipes that follow the new approach to cooking, eating and enjoyment—recipes for vegetables to be used as an accompaniment and others for complete vegetable meals.

Eggplant Parmigiana, a lovely Italian dish that's easy to make. You can vary the cheese; look for fontina, a rich, firm cheese with superb melting qualities.

ARTICHOKES (GLOBE)

To microwave. Wash and trim 4 artichokes, place in bowl with ½ cup (4½ fl oz) of water, cover and cook on maximum power 10–20 minutes, until bases are tender when pierced with a fork. Turn each artichoke round halfway through cooking. Let them stand for 2–4 minutes. Other recipes may be adapted to microwave cooking, using this recipe as a guide to time, etc.

*A*rtichokes may be served as a separate course as an entrée, or as a dressed vegetable with the main course. The most prized part of the artichoke is the 'fond', or bottom, which is used as a garnish for many classic French dishes. The regal globe artichoke should not be confused with the small cream tuberous Jerusalem artichoke, which is a winter vegetable, most often puréed and used to make an excellent soup.

To prepare globe artichokes for cooking. Remove the tough outside leaves and then cut one-third off the top of the artichoke with a sharp knife and trim the stalk and outer leaves with scissors. As each one is prepared, place it in a bowl of cold water to cover, into which is squeezed plenty of lemon juice to prevent them discolouring. This method of preparing them gives a most attractive shape. Alternatively, the sharp points of the leaves may simply be trimmed with scissors and the stalk cut off level with the base. Place in water with lemon juice as you prepare them.

To cook. Place them in boiling salted water with a slice of lemon and boil gently. The exact time will depend on the age and size. A baby, very fresh young artichoke will be tender in 15–20 minutes, while larger ones will require up to 45 minutes. Artichokes must not be overdone. A good way to test them is to pull off an outer leaf and test for tenderness with the point of a knife; also, the leaves should pull off easily. Artichokes should not be cooked in an aluminium pan.

Artichokes Clamart

Artichokes Clamart, being fragile and delicate, can be cooked in a sauté pan or earthenware cocotte and served in the same dish (to avoid disturbing the arrangement).

This is one of my most successful dishes. Guests enjoy the unexpected combination of two popular vegetables. When artichokes are tiny they are trimmed but left whole; larger artichokes are quartered.

> *8 small young artichokes or 4 large ones*
> *30 g (1 oz) butter*
> *1 lettuce, washed and shredded*
> *2 cups (12 oz) shelled peas*
> *½ teaspoon salt*
> *1 teaspoon sugar*
> *½ cup (4½ fl oz) stock*

Trim small artichokes down to tender hearts; if they are large, trim them down to the heart and then quarter them; cut out the choke if it is there. Melt the butter in a heavy saucepan, add the shredded lettuce and place the artichokes and peas on top. Season with the salt and sugar and moisten with the stock. Simmer gently with lid on for about 30 minutes. This vegetable, being delicate and fragile, may be prepared in a heavy enamelled cast-iron pot, a flameproof casserole or a copper sauté pan and served in the same dish to avoid damaging the appearance. Serves 6–8.

Artichokes Crécy

Prepare as for Artichokes Clamart, replacing the peas with very small young carrots.

Tip
To eat a whole, cooked artichoke, pull off a leaf at a time and, holding the tip in your fingers, scrape off the tender base of the leaf between your teeth. When you come to the heart, remove the hairy choke with a spoon and eat the bottom with a knife and fork.

Braised Artichokes

I know many cooks boil artichokes and serve them with vinaigrette or hollandaise sauce. I prefer them braised in stock or white wine or prepared à la Grecque with chopped tomatoes added.

Braised Artichokes, cooked in a good white wine and olive oil, are ready when a leaf pulls out easily. Remove the hairy choke with a spoon, then enjoy the base.

> *6 artichokes*
> *1 onion, chopped*
> *2 garlic cloves*
> *1 tablespoon chopped parsley*
> *1 bay leaf*
> *A sprig of oregano (or a good pinch if dried)*
> *3 tablespoons olive oil*
> *1 cup (9 fl oz) white wine*
> *Salt and freshly ground pepper*

Prepare the artichokes as described in the introductory remarks. Put them in a large, heavy saucepan or enamel-coated iron casserole, with the onion, garlic, parsley, bay leaf, oregano, oil and wine. Season with salt and pepper, cover and simmer slowly for 40 minutes. Artichokes are cooked when a leaf pulls out easily. Serve warm. Serves 6.

Artichokes à la Grecque

Prepare as for braised artichokes, adding 2 peeled, seeded and chopped tomatoes (see page 130). Serve warm with some of the pan sauce spooned over, or cold, cut into quarters and again with some of the delicious sauce in which they were cooked. Top with chopped parsley.

ASPARAGUS

To microwave: Wash and trim 500 g (1 lb) of asparagus. Place it on a plate with 2 tablespoons of water, cover and cook on maximum power for 4–6 minutes. Let stand for 2–4 minutes. Use as a guide to adapt other recipes.

Asparagus with Lemon is one of the simplest ways of enjoying this lovely vegetable, an edible member of the lily family.

Asparagus is considered a luxury vegetable throughout the world. Indeed, it is such a special vegetable that devotees serve it as a course on its own with just a simple dressing of a little butter and freshly ground pepper and salt and maybe a squeeze of lemon juice.

The classic hollandaise sauce makes it even more special, and this rich butter and egg sauce still has a place in today's healthy lifestyle. Simply make sure that the egg and butter are considered as part of the daily ration.

To cook: Asparagus is at its best prepared simply, but most carefully. Wash the spears and refresh them by standing them cut end down in water. Any tough ends should be trimmed off and used to flavour stocks. If the asparagus seems stringy, pare off the outside stringy skin near the base of the stem. Tie in serving-sized bundles.

Lower the bundles into simmering salted water and cook gently for 12–20 minutes, depending on the age and natural tenderness of the asparagus. When the asparagus is very young and tender, a small but deep saucepan is ideal—the bundles stand in the simmering water and an upturned cake tin or heatproof bowl can be used as a cover. In this way the delicate tips are steamed while the firmer base cooks in the water. A double boiler is ideal, using the base to cook the asparagus and the top upturned to contain the steam.

It is important not to overcook asparagus. The stalks should be tender but not limp, and the flower firm. Asparagus should be very well drained before being served and sauced. Lift the spears out of the saucepan as soon as they are tender, and drain on kitchen paper towels.

Asparagus with Lemon

One of the best ways of enjoying asparagus, with a simple dressing.

> *3 large bunches asparagus, about 1 kg (2 lb)*
> *¹/₃ cup (3 fl oz) olive oil*
> *2 tablespoons lemon juice*
> *2 tablespoons chopped parsley*
> *¹/₂ teaspoon salt*
> *¹/₄ teaspoon freshly ground pepper*

Cook and drain the asparagus as described in the introductory remarks. Beat the oil, lemon juice, parsley, salt and pepper thoroughly—the mixture should thicken a little. Arrange the asparagus on a hot serving platter or individual plates, and spoon the sauce over. Serves 6.

Asparagus Prosciutto au Gratin

A good recipe using those lovely green asparagus spears with their own special flavour. The crunchy buttered crumbs and a very good dry-cured ham give an exceptional result.

> *3 bunches asparagus, about 1 kg (2 lb)*
> *6 thin slices prosciutto*
> *30 g (1 oz) butter, melted*
> *6 slices bread*
> *¹/₂ cup (2 oz) grated Parmesan cheese*
> *Freshly ground pepper*

Prepare and cook the asparagus as described in the introductory remarks and cook until barely tender. While the asparagus is cooking, prepare the topping. Stack the slices of prosciutto and cut them into thin match-size strips. Trim the crusts off the bread, cut into fine cubes or blend to make crumbs, and toss them in the melted butter. Combine the Parmesan and the buttered crumbs.

Arrange the drained asparagus in a lightly buttered ovenproof dish or 6 individual ones, and season with pepper. Strew strips of prosciutto over the asparagus, and dust with cheesed crumbs.

Place the dish in a hot oven (230°C/450°F) until the top is golden, or heat gently under a hot grill (broiler). The crumbs should be crisp and golden and a little crunchy. Serve in the baking dish or the individual dishes. Serves 6.

BEANS

reen beans, which are very easy to prepare, are a delicacy when young and fresh and cooked with care. There is a variety of string or green beans on the market, and many of these are stringless—which means that, if at all, only their ends have to be broken off before cooking.

To cook: Beans should first be dropped into a little boiling salted water, brought to the boil, then simmered without a lid for 6–15 minutes, depending on their age and size, or until they are barely tender. Begin testing for doneness by tasting a bean after 6 minutes. It is important that they should not be overcooked, as they will then lose both flavour and texture. With a little practice you will soon gauge the heat required to cook vegetables by this light method—just take care not to let the vegetables cook dry.

Drain them in a colander. Return them to the saucepan and shake to remove excess moisture. Serve with a squeeze of lemon juice and freshly ground pepper. If they have to be kept, plunge them very briefly in cold water to halt the cooking process; they may then wait for an hour or more before finishing off. Just before dressing them and completing their cooking, place them in a large frying pan (skillet) and shake the pan over moderate heat for about 2 minutes to heat them and rid them of excess moisture.

To microwave: Place 250 g (8 oz) of prepared green beans on a dish or plate with 4 tablespoons of water, cover and cook on maximum power for 4 minutes. Let stand for 2–4 minutes. Use as a guide to adapt other recipes.

Beans Provençale

750 g (1 ¹/₂ lb) green beans, trimmed

1 tablespoon olive oil

2 garlic cloves, crushed

1 onion, chopped

4 ripe tomatoes, peeled, seeded and chopped (see page 130)

6 sage leaves, or winter savory

Salt and freshly ground pepper

ook, drain and dry the beans as described in the introduction to this section. Heat the oil in a large saucepan over medium heat, add the garlic and onion, and cook until the onion begins to colour. Add the tomatoes and sage, season with salt and pepper, and simmer for about 5 minutes. Add the beans, toss them lightly with the tomatoes, correct the seasoning. Simmer for 2–3 minutes, and then turn them out into a hot vegetable dish. Serves 4.

BEETROOT (BEETS)

eetroots are mostly cooked whole, whether they are the tiny beets of spring or the larger ones of winter. They are not peeled or cut.

To cook: When cooking whole beets, leave on 2.5 cm (1 in) of the stem and the root ends. Wash well and cook, covered, in unsalted water to cover until tender when tested with a fork. Small young beets take ½–1 hour; older beets 1–2 hours. When tender, drain and slip off the skins. Allow 1 kg (2 lb) of beets, with tops removed, for four servings.

To microwave: Wash and trim 500 g (1 lb) beetroot, cut in halves. Place cut side down on a dish or plate, cover loosely and cook on maximum power for 7–8 minutes. Let stand for 7–8 minutes, then peel.

Beetroot with Orange

¼ cup (2 oz) sugar
2 teaspoons cornflour (cornstarch)
½ teaspoon salt
1 tablespoon cider vinegar
4 tablespoons water
Grated rind and juice of 1 orange
4–6 cooked or canned beetroot (beets), quartered
1 tablespoon butter (optional)

ombine the sugar, cornflour, salt, vinegar and water in a saucepan, and gradually bring to the boil. Stir until clear. Stir in the orange rind and juice and the beetroot. Heat gently and, before serving, stir in the butter if using. Serves 4–6.

BROCCOLI

To microwave:
Prepare 250 g (8 oz)
broccoli and separate
into florets. Place on
a dish or plate with
3 tablespoons of water
and cook covered on
maximum power
4–5 minutes. Leave
stand 4 minutes. Use
as a guide to adapt
other recipes.

*F*resh broccoli with its rich green flower heads has a very delicate flavour. Never buy a bunch in which the flowers have started to yellow.

To cook: Trim off any thick base stalks. Separate the heads into florets and stand them upright in a saucepan in which they will fit snugly, in sufficient boiling salted water to come halfway up the stalks. Bring to the boil, reduce heat, and simmer for about 10–15 minutes. When the base of the thicker stalks is easily pierced with a fork, the broccoli is fully cooked. Drain well. A squeeze of lemon juice and a grinding of pepper is a simple and delicious way of serving it. A light dusting of Parmesan cheese is good; and like many lightly cooked vegetables, broccoli is enhanced by a dab of butter.

This beautiful vegetable is sometimes called Roman broccoli. A member of the family of brassicas, it is treated like broccoli or cauliflower.

BRUSSELS SPROUTS

To microwave: Place
250 g (8 oz) of
prepared Brussels
sprouts in a
microwave-safe dish or
plate with 3–4
tablespoons of water,
cover and cook on
maximum power for
7–8 minutes. Leave
stand 3–4 minutes.
Use as a guide to adapt
other recipes.

*B*russels sprouts look like tiny cabbages, and like so many vegetables lend themselves to a variety of different treatments. To prepare sprouts, trim the stems, discard any outside leaves that are yellow, and cut a small cross in the bottom of each little core. Wash and drain them before cooking. Brussels sprouts, when simply steam-cooked, may be treated in many of the ways suggested for asparagus and broccoli.

To cook: Drop 750 g (1 1/2 lb) of prepared sprouts into a saucepan containing 1 cup (9 fl oz) of boiling salted water, and simmer uncovered for 5 minutes. Cover and continue cooking 6–10 minutes longer, or until just tender. Drain, return to heat to dry off, add 2 teaspoons of butter, a squeeze of lemon and a fresh grinding of pepper. (Butter may be omitted.)

Purée of Brussels Sprouts

750 g (1 1/2 lb) cooked Brussels sprouts
Stock, milk or cream (single, light)
Butter
Nutmeg (optional)

Cook the Brussels sprouts as described in the introduction. Put them in an electric blender or food processor (using the sharp blades); moisten with a little stock, milk or cream and process until the mixture is fairly smooth. Season with a little butter and, if liked, a touch of freshly grated nutmeg. Serves 4–6.

CABBAGE

There are many varieties of cabbage, including the elegant, elongated sugarloaf, the loose-leafed savoy, and tightly packed white cabbage and red cabbage. As a general rule, choose a head that is firm.

Steamed cabbage. The old way of cooking cabbage is to cut it into wedges and boil it in a lot of water for hours. The new way is to shred it finely, or cut it into wedges, and steam it: barely cook it in very little water or stock—about 5 minutes if shredded, 10 minutes if quartered.

To shred cabbage, cut the head in two, or if large in four; then, with the curved side down, press the point end firmly on a board and with a sharp knife cut long thin shreds off the side. Discard the cores.

To microwave: Trim and shred 500 g (1 lb) of cabbage. Place on a dish or plate with 3 tablespoons of water. Cover and cook on maximum power 7–8 minutes. Leave to stand 3–4 minutes. Use as a guide to adapt other recipes.

Cabbage Alsacienne

The cabbage should be slightly crisp. Serve with smoked Continental sausage or grilled (broiled) pork chops.

2 tablespoons olive oil
1 onion, sliced
6 celery sticks, sliced
1 small white cabbage, shredded finely (see above)
1/2 cup (4 1/2 fl oz) white wine or stock
A squeeze of lemon juice
1 tablespoon chopped parsley

*H*eat the oil in a deep pan and add the onion and celery. Cook gently for a few minutes, add the cabbage and liquid. Season well, cover and cook slowly for 15–20 minutes or until barely tender. Add the chopped parsley just before serving. Serves 4–6.

Steamed Cabbage Chinese Style

Cabbage cooked this way should become limp, a lovely bright green colour and just a little crisp to the bite. It is delicious and seldom needs salt and pepper, but these can be added just before serving.

2 tablespoons peanut (groundnut) oil or other vegetable oil
1 garlic clove, smashed
2 spring onions (scallions), cut into short lengths
4 slices green (fresh) ginger
1/2 white or green cabbage, shredded (see page 107)

Tip
To smash garlic, place the clove on a board, lay the flat of a broad knife on top, and smash it with your fist. This loosens the peel, which you can then remove. The garlic clove can then be chopped or crushed or used as is.

*H*eat the oil gently with the garlic, spring onions and green ginger. For a more delicate taste remove garlic and ginger. Add the shredded cabbage, cover the pan and allow to steam for about 5 minutes, tossing every now and then as the cabbage begins to soften. Serves 4.

CAPSICUMS (SWEET PEPPERS)

*C*apsicums belong to the nightshade family, but they are not at all deadly. Indeed, the opposite—they have such outstanding nutritional value that it is regrettable that they are not used as much as they deserve to be. Ripe and red, yellow, orange or green, they are like precious jewels when used properly.

Since the C vitamins double on ripening, use the red ones when available. Actually they are much sweeter and milder than the green ones. When the lovely elongated yellow and bright orange ones appear in the market, make use of them, for their season is all too short.

A simple way to cook capsicums is to halve them, flick out the seeds, remove the ribs and cut the flesh into strips, fry in a little oil, perhaps flavoured with garlic. Season with salt and pepper and serve with grills. Halved and drizzled with oil, they may be grilled (broiled) along with meat.

Skinning. Capsicums are the better for being skinned. The simplest method of doing this is to hold them by a long fork over an open flame until they are

To microwave: One capsicum, halved, takes 3 minutes to cook on maximum. One sliced capsicum and 1 chopped tomato make a delicious sauce; cook, covered, for 3–4 minutes on maximum.

charred and blackened, or halve them and char under a hot grill (broiler). Place them in a brown paper bag or wrap in a clean tea towel and allow them to steam for a few minutes. Rinse them under cold water, and scrape the charred skin off with a knife. The core end should then be cut out and the pith and seeds removed. This is a bit tedious, but it is well worth the time spent, for the result more than justifies the effort. (Red capsicums skin more easily than green.)

Italian Capsicums with Capers

In this antipasto the sweet roasted capsicum holds a zippy light stuffing of capers, anchovy, pine nuts and parsley—a very good mix.

> *1 cup (2 oz) fresh breadcrumbs*
> *6 anchovy fillets, chopped*
> *2 tablespoons capers, chopped*
> *3 tablespoons pine nuts or walnuts, chopped*
> *3 tablespoons chopped parsley*
> *Salt and freshly ground pepper*
> *Olive oil*
> *3 red or yellow capsicums, quartered and seeded*

Combine the breadcrumbs with the anchovies, capers, pine nuts and parsley. Season with salt and pepper. Fork in enough oil to just combine, about 2 tablespoons. Stuff each capsicum quarter with this mixture and arrange in a shallow baking dish. Drizzle lightly with oil. Bake in a moderately hot oven (190°C/375°F) for 30 minutes. Serve as part of an antipasto tray or first course appetiser, either warm or at room temperature. Serves 6.

Capsicums (sweet peppers) are green and turn a bright red and become sweeter as they ripen. Yellow ones are closer in flavour to red. Some varieties are such a dark purple they are called black capsicums.

109

CARROTS

*Y*oung spring carrots need only be lightly scraped or, if they are tiny, cooked whole. They are delicious cooked in a very little water or chicken stock and a little butter in a tightly closed saucepan that permits them to steam until they are just tender. A little sugar or honey enhances the natural sweetness of the carrots.

Vichy Carrots

A favourite carrot dish—French, of course.

> *500 g (1 lb) young carrots*
> *1/2 cup (41/2 fl oz) water*
> *15 g (1/2 oz) butter*
> *2 teaspoons sugar*
> *Parsley, chopped*

*S*crape the carrots and cut them into thin slices. (If very young, leave whole.) Place them in a heavy saucepan with the water, butter and sugar. Cover the pan and cook for about 5 minutes until the carrots are tender. Remove the lid, add a pinch of salt and continue cooking until the liquid has evaporated, leaving a syrupy glaze on the carrots. Serve sprinkled generously with chopped parsley. Serves 4.

CAULIFLOWER

*T*he best cauliflower has very white, closely packed florets, and the
surrounding leaves should be still fresh and green. Before cooking, all
the dark outside leaves should be broken off. Cauliflower will cook more evenly
if it is then broken up into florets with no more than 3 cm (1 ½ in) of stem.

Some recipes require cauliflower to be cooked whole, and it makes a very
attractive presentation. Before cooking it whole, cut off all of the thick central
stem and make deep incisions with a sharp knife into all the remaining smaller
stems, so that the heat will penetrate them more easily. Sometimes the tender
young leaves are left on; when lightly cooked they enhance the look of any whole
cauliflower dish.

Cauliflower lightly cooked so that it still has a crunch is delicious in salads.

To microwave: Trim
500 g (1 lb) of
cauliflower and cut it
into florets. Place on a
dish or plate with 4
tablespoons of water,
cook covered on
maximum power
9–10 minutes. Let
stand for 4 minutes.

Mexican-Style Cauliflower

I make this dish when I want a substantial vegetable to serve with grilled or
barbecued meat.

> *1 medium head of cauliflower, trimmed into florets*
> *3 tomatoes, peeled, seeded and chopped (see page 130)*
> *2 tablespoons chopped parsley*
> *⅛ teaspoon cloves*
> *¼ teaspoon cinnamon*
> *1 tablespoon capers*
> *2 tablespoons stuffed olives, chopped*
> *3 tablespoons grated Cheddar cheese*
> *2 tablespoons fine breadcrumbs*
> *1 tablespoon olive or salad oil*

*P*reheat the oven to moderately hot (220°C/425°F). In a covered saucepan
cook the cauliflower in a small amount of boiling salted water until barely
tender. Drain.

Mix the tomatoes, parsley, spices, capers and olives in a small saucepan, and
heat gently to make a sauce. Pour a little of the sauce into a heatproof baking
dish, add the cauliflower and cover with the remaining sauce. Sprinkle with the
cheese and breadcrumbs, drizzle with the oil, and bake until brown. Serves 6.

111

Cauliflower Parmigiana

1 large cauliflower, separated into florets
2 tablespoons vegetable on olive oil·
2 cups (4 oz) fresh breadcrumbs
¹/₂ cup (2 oz) grated Parmesan cheese
2 tablespoons chopped parsley

Boil the cauliflower in 2 cups (18 fl oz) of lightly salted boiling water for about 8 minutes or until the florets are tender, then drain them carefully in a colander. Heat the oil and fry the breadcrumbs. Oil a shallow baking dish, sprinkle it with a little of the Parmesan cheese, arrange the florets in the dish and sprinkle them with the breadcrumbs mixed with the remaining Parmesan cheese. Put the dish in a hot oven (230°C/450°F) for about 5 minutes, or until the top is golden. Remove from the oven and sprinkle with parsley. Serves 6.

SWEET CORN

To microwave: Trim 2 corn cobs, wrap each loosely in kitchen paper towels or plastic wrap (cling film), cook on maximum power for 4–6 minutes. Let stand for 2–4 minutes.

Corn (maize) was cultivated by the ancient South American Indians. Look for corn with fresh, dark green husks and plump yellow kernels. Fresh corn looks moist and has a sweet taste. Old corn looks hard and shrunken and tastes floury. Corn deteriorates quickly after picking, so it should be cooked as soon as possible. If storing corn before cooking, refrigerate with husks left on.

To cook corn on the cob: Remove husk and silk from the corn. Put it in a deep saucepan with enough boiling water to cover the cobs. Sugar can be added to the water. Return the water to the boil and boil for 8 minutes. Overcooking will toughen, not soften, the kernels. Serve with butter, salt and freshly ground pepper, or serve a butter sauce to which has been added fresh or dried tarragon. Never add salt to the cooking water—it toughens the corn.

Barbecued corn on the cob. Remove husk and silk, rub the cobs generously with butter, salt and freshly ground pepper and wrap each cob in aluminium foil, folding in ends to seal it well. Place on the grill of the barbecue over hot coals. Cook about 15 minutes, depending on the size of the cob, turning frequently. A dash of soy sauce may be added to each cob with the butter before wrapping in foil. Alternatively, cobs can be boiled for 5 minutes, removed from the water, brushed generously with melted butter, then barbecued over hot coals for 10 minutes. Brush occasionally with melted butter.

To cook fresh corn cut from the cob: Cut the kernels off the cob with a corn scraper or a sharp knife, then simmer them in their own juice and a little butter in a covered saucepan for several minutes until tender. Season with salt and pepper; moisten with milk or cream. Devil by adding 1 tablespoon of Worcestershire sauce and finely chopped garlic.

Creole Sweet Corn is at its best when made with young, fresh sweet corn.

Creole Sweet Corn

In the Deep South, Americans enjoy corn cooked in a variety of ways. It seems a necessary adjunct to most meals.

> *1 onion, chopped*
> *$1/_2$ green capsicum (sweet pepper), chopped*
> *45–60 g (1 $1/_2$–2 oz) butter*
> *2 tomatoes, peeled and chopped (see page 130)*
> *1 teaspoon sugar*
> *1 teaspoon salt and $1/_4$ teaspoon pepper*
> *2 cups (12 oz) fresh or canned whole-kernel sweet corn*

Cook the onion and capsicum in butter until lightly browned. Add the tomatoes, sugar, salt, pepper and sweet corn. Simmer 10 minutes. Serves 6.

EGGPLANT (AUBERGINE)

*T*he dark purple skin of the eggplant (aubergine), smooth, firm and shiny, makes this one of the most decorative vegetables. Never buy one that is spongy to the touch, and use it as soon as possible, for it does not store well. The flavour of eggplant goes well with onions, tomatoes, garlic and oil—it has a satisfying quality that makes it a good choice for a light main dish. Sliced and lightly sautéed, it is a good accompaniment to grills and other meals. Although there are several varieties and sizes of eggplant, the best known and most generally used are the reddish purple, oval variety and the long slim ones—about 12 × 2 cm (5 × 1 in).

To prepare: The flesh of eggplant is extremely watery, and to eliminate as much water as possible before cooking it should always be sprinkled with a liberal amount of salt and allowed to drain on kitchen paper towels or a rack. If it is being cooked sliced, salt on both sides of the slices, lay the slices on the paper towel, and weight with a pastry board or any convenient similar weight for 1 hour; then thoroughly wash the salt off and dry the slices on paper towels. If the eggplant is to be cooked cut in half, make deep incisions in the flesh of each half, going to within 6 mm ($^1/_4$ in) of the skin, sprinkle a little salt in the incisions and place the halves, cut side down, on a rack for 1 hour. Wash off the salt. Squeeze the halves gently but firmly between the hands to press out as much of the remaining water as possible.

To microwave: Prepare 500 g (1 lb) of eggplant as at right and cut in circles or dice and place on a dish or plate with 2 tablespoons of water. Cook covered on maximum power for 5–6 minutes; let stand for 2–4 minutes. Use as a guide to adapt other recipes.

Grilled Eggplant

1 medium eggplant (aubergine), cut into thick slices
2 garlic cloves, chopped
$^1/_4$ cup (2$^1/_4$ fl oz) olive oil seasoned with 1 teaspoon grated onion and $^1/_2$ teaspoon salt
Grilled (broiled) bacon for garnish (optional)

Tip
A ribbed grill may also be used for grilling eggplant.

*P*lace the eggplant slices on a greased baking tray (sheet) and brush with the seasoned oil. Grill (broil) under a preheated griller about 10 cm (4 in) from the source of heat for 5 minutes, basting once with the seasoned oil. Turn the slices, using a pancake turner or egg slice, and brush with the remaining seasoned oil. Cook until tender, about 2 minutes longer. Serve plain or with tomato sauce. Garnish with the bacon, if liked. Serves 4.

Eggplant Parmigiana. Grill (broil) the eggplant slices as directed. When tender, transfer them to a baking dish. Spread with Fresh Tomato Sauce (see page 184) and sprinkle generously with grated Parmesan cheese. Top each piece with a thin slice of mozzarella or mild Cheddar cheese and grill until lightly browned and bubbly. Serve as a luncheon or supper entrée.

LEEKS

*L*eeks are most often used to enhance the flavour of a good stock or soup, but they are also excellent as a cooked vegetable. Before cooking, the roots and the green tops must be trimmed off; only the white part and a little of the green of leeks is edible. Leeks usually have a great deal of dirt and grit between their leaves at the base of the stalks, and they must be washed very thoroughly. They may be cut in half lengthwise almost half the way to the base and washed under running water while gently spreading their leaves apart.

To microwave: Trim and slice 500 g (1 lb) of leeks. Place them on a dish or plate with 3 tablespoons of water. Cook, covered, on maximum power for 7–9 minutes. Let stand for 3–4 minutes. Use as a guide to adapt the following recipes.

Braised Leeks

Serve hot with toast, or chill and serve with French dressing.

> *4–6 leeks*
> *1 tablespoon vegetable or olive oil*
> *1 small white onion, peeled and chopped*
> *1 cup (9 fl oz) chicken stock*
> *Salt and freshly ground black pepper*

*T*rim and wash the leeks as described in the introductory remarks. In a frying pan (skillet) heat the oil, add the onion and sauté slowly until softened. Add the leeks, stock, salt and pepper. Cover and simmer until the leeks are tender.

Leeks Niçoise

A fabulous way of cooking leeks. They can be left whole or cut in 5 cm (2 in) lengths. Serve as a first course or a light luncheon with crusty French bread.

Leeks Niçoise, as the name implies, calls for the flavours of tomato, garlic, parsley, olive oil and tiny black olives. Serve at room temperature or cold as a first course.

> *8–10 medium leeks*
> *$^1/_2$ cup (4$^1/_2$ fl oz) olive oil*
> *1$^1/_4$ cups (11 fl oz) water*
> *1 tablespoon tomato paste (concentrate)*
> *1 teaspoon sugar*
> *Salt and pepper to taste*
> *Lemon juice*
> *$^3/_4$ cup (4 oz) small black olives*
> *Parsley, chopped*

Trim and wash the leeks as described in the introductory remarks. Place them in a heavy frying pan (skillet) or saucepan in which the whole leeks will fit or a deeper pan if the leeks are cut up. Add the oil, water, tomato paste and sugar. Season with salt and pepper and cook, covered, for about 15 minutes, until the leeks are very tender. Add lemon juice to taste. Lift onto a platter and serve sprinkled with the olives and parsley. Serves 4–8, depending on whether the leeks are served as an entrée or a light meal.

MUSHROOMS

To microwave: Wipe and leave whole 125 g (4 oz) of button mushrooms. Place on a dish or plate with 1 tablespoon of water. Cook, covered, on maximum power for 2$^1/_2$–3 minutes. Let stand for 2–3 minutes. Use as a guide to adapt other recipes.

Who would expect a little vegetable that grows under the ground or in dark cellars to emerge so pearly white, sheltering such delicate pink gills? Mushrooms are essential to good French cooking. Dieters love them because they are low in calories, and all cooks prize them for their versatility and the wonderful flavour they can add to rich savoury meats or light, delicate chicken, fish or egg dishes. Mushrooms lend themselves to a huge variety of dishes, but they are delicious cooked simply and served as a dish on their own.

Preparing mushrooms. Cultivated mushrooms are picked and delivered to us in such a short time that preparation has become quite quick and simple. Peeling is not generally necessary, even with the large flat mushrooms. If, however, the skin seems to be tough, peel and save the peelings for flavouring stocks or a casserole. Wipe mushrooms with a soft cloth dipped in a bowl of water acidulated with a squeeze of lemon juice. Avoid washing mushrooms—they become soggy and lose

116

much of their flavour. If the stalk ends are tough and dry, a slight trim cut on the slant is all that is needed; again, keep the trimmings for flavouring other dishes.

To sauté: Use enough butter or good quality oil to just cover the surface of the pan. For 500 g (1 lb) of mushrooms, allow 1 tablespoon of butter or 2 tablespoons of oil. A squeeze of lemon juice enhances the flavour. Cook over a moderately high heat for no longer than 5 minutes to preserve shape and flavour, shaking the pan frequently. If you are holding the mushrooms for another dish, do not cover, as this will draw out the juices. At first the mushrooms will seem dry, but they will absorb the fat. Do not crowd the pan or they will stew—it is better if cooking a lot of mushrooms to do them in several batches.

Storing mushrooms: Mushrooms keep well either in a paper bag, a small box if you have a lot, or just uncovered and put in the refrigerator. Plastic wrap (cling film) or polythene bags tend to make the mushrooms turn soggy and disintegrate more quickly.

Mushrooms Lyonnaise

Mushrooms make a delightful first course. Serve them in their own little bowls or dishes with crusty bread to mop up the juices.

> *3 tablespoons olive oil*
> *1 garlic clove, peeled*
> *1 bay leaf*
> *2 whole cloves*
> *750 g (1¹/₂ lb) fresh mushrooms, quartered if large*
> *3 tomatoes, peeled, seeded and chopped (see page 130), or 12*
> *   tiny toms (cherry tomatoes), whole*
> *Salt and freshly ground pepper*
> *A pinch of nutmeg*
> *1 tablespoon chopped fresh parsley or chervil*
> *6 spring onions (scallions), chopped*

*H*eat 2 tablespoons of oil in a flameproof casserole with the garlic, bay leaf and cloves. When hot, discard the seasonings and add the mushrooms. Cook over a high heat for 5 minutes, stirring constantly. Add the tomatoes, and season to taste with salt and pepper and the nutmeg. Bring to the simmer; cook, covered, for a further 10 minutes. Heat the remaining oil, add the parsley or chervil and spring onions, toss lightly and add to the mushrooms. Serve with toast or with crusty bread. Serves 4.

Freezing mushrooms: Wipe whole mushrooms carefully with acidulated water and place on a baking tray to fit in freezer. Freeze one tray at a time, and only the quantity that will fit on the tray without mushrooms touching. When frozen, pack into plastic (polythene) bags, seal well and return to freezer until wanted. They should last about 3 months.

Mushrooms Lyonnaise, a well-flavoured vegetable dish that may be served as a first course. Good warm or cold.

119

Grilled Mushroom Caps

A simple first course or snack. Serve on freshly made toast.

> *3 tablespoons soft breadcrumbs*
> *1 tablespoon chopped parsley*
> *$\frac{1}{2}$ garlic clove, peeled and finely chopped*
> *12 large mushrooms, stems removed*
> *2 tablespoons olive oil*
> *Salt and freshly ground pepper*

Grilled Mushroom Caps, a simple first course or snack. The mushrooms are rolled in breadcrumbs, oil, garlic and parsley, then grilled (broiled) —delicious.

*M*ix the breadcrumbs, parsley and garlic together. Brush the mushrooms with oil and roll in the breadcrumb mixture. Sprinkle with salt and pepper. Put on a griller rack lined with aluminium foil and place under a preheated moderately hot grill (broiler). Cook for about 6 minutes. Drizzle on a little more oil if necessary. Serves 4.

ONIONS

The indispensable onion! What would any good cook do without it? Fortunately, onions are always available and keep well in a string bag hanging in a cool place, so they should always be readily on hand.

As well as the well-known white and brown onion, it's worth buying some of the more seasonal ones such as the small pickling onion and the red (Spanish) onion that is perfect for salads. The sweet white Vidalia is a favourite of mine.

There is some confusion about how to refer to the onion in its early stages of growth. The immature green onion, picked before the bulb has formed, is referred to in Australia as a shallot, in the United States as a green onion or scallion, and in Britain as a spring onion. However, a spring onion is properly one at a slightly more mature stage, where a white bulb has formed. A shallot is a different member of the onion family and looks something like reddish-brown garlic—the bulb separates into cloves in the way a head of garlic does. In this book it is referred to as a golden shallot to avoid confusion. The terms *green shallots*, *scallions* and *spring onions* are used interchangeably to refer to the green stages.

For cooking, onions should be cut in even slices or chopped in even bits so that all the onion is cooked uniformly.

To microwave: Peel 2 onions and slice or chop them. Place them in a dish with 2 teaspoons of oil or butter. Cook, covered, on maximum power for 3–4 minutes. Whole onions will take 4 minutes. Let stand for 3 minutes. This is a convenient way of sautéeing or frying onions for all kinds of dishes.

PEAS

Peas are a delicious vegetable, and when flavoured with mint and fresh butter they make a superlative dish. Fresh, tender peas should have bright green pods that are smooth and plump. When buying peas, remember that after shelling, the peas weigh about half the original weight. If shelling peas some time before cooking, keep them well covered to avoid any loss of moisture. When peas are kept at room temperature, enzymes quickly convert the sugar into starch, which causes a loss of flavour as well as sweetness. It is a good idea to cover shelled peas with some pods, wrap them in a tea towel or put them in a covered bowl in the refrigerator.

You will need about 1 kg (2 lb) for 4 healthy servings. When cooking peas, a few young pea pods are often added for flavour. Any water remaining in the saucepan after the peas have been cooked can be added to stock or used instead of water to make a gravy.

Be careful not to overcook them.

Fresh Peas French Style

This dish should be made with the youngest, freshest peas you can get. It does make frozen peas acceptable.

> *2 cups shelled peas (about 1 kg/2 lb in the shell)*
> *6 tiny white onions, peeled*
> *5–6 lettuce leaves, shredded*
> *3 sprigs of parsley, tied together*
> *$1/_2$ teaspoon salt*
> *A pinch of sugar*
> *1 tablespoon butter*
> *$1/_4$ cup (2$1/_4$ fl oz) stock or water*
> *1 teaspoon plain (all-purpose) flour*

*I*n a saucepan combine the peas, onion, lettuce, parsley, salt, sugar and half the butter. Mix together and add the stock. Cover closely and cook over medium heat until all but a little of the moisture evaporates, about 20 minutes. Cream together the remaining butter and the flour. Add to the liquid in the pan and shake the pan in a circular movement to mix it in (stirring with a utensil breaks the peas). When the liquid has thickened and returned to the boil, remove the pan from the heat. Remove the parsley and serve. Serves 4.

POTATOES

*P*otatoes are a most valuable vegetable, nutritionally speaking. Rich in vitamins B and C, plus many minerals, they should be included regularly in the diet. Not that most people have to be coaxed to eat potatoes, for they are a much loved vegetable. In recent years they have been maligned as being fattening; a potato is in fact equal in kilojoules (calories) to the same-sized apple.
Cooking potatoes. Whenever possible, cook potatoes with their skins on. Scrub them first, of course. Boiled new potatoes are delicious with their skins—and who can resist the crisp skin of a jacket-baked potato? Peeling the potato removes much of its goodness, as the minerals and vitamins are concentrated just under the skin.

Select the right potato for your cooking method. Old floury potatoes are wonderful for mashed potatoes or potatoes baked in their jackets—their texture allows them to absorb the buttery or creamy sauces. New potatoes have a firmer

and finer texture—the small ones are best served boiled or steamed and whole, and the larger ones are good for potato salads and gratins. Growers are now supplying us with a wide variety of potatoes. Look for them and try them out.
New potatoes. Smooth, white new potatoes that hardly need washing are delicious just plainly boiled, with a hint of butter. They also respond well to chives, mint or parsley chopped finely and added to the cooked potatoes at the last minute with butter. They are the best potatoes for salads because of their firm, waxy texture. The skin can be lightly scraped away before cooking, or peeled away after boiling. They are dropped into boiling water and cooked gently for about 12–15 minutes until just tender.

New Potatoes with Sun-Dried Tomato

Serve in a large bowl at an alfresco meal as an accompaniment to grilled, barbecued or cold meat. These are always a hit. Both sun-dried tomatoes and the paste are available at most good delicatessens and gourmet shops.

> *1 kg (2 lb) new potatoes*
> *Salt*
> *1 tablespoon butter, melted, or good olive oil*
> *1–2 tablespoons sun-dried tomato paste*
> *6 sun-dried tomatoes, chopped (optional)*

New potatoes, smooth, pearly white, steamed or boiled, respond to a final toss in fresh herbs—dill, chives, mint, basil—or sun-dried tomatoes. A spoonful of sun-dried tomato paste or spread does wonders.

Boil the potatoes in lightly salted water for about 20 minutes or until they are just tender. Drain, toss in butter or oil together with the sun-dried tomato paste and the sun-dried tomatoes if they are being used. Heat gently through, tossing every now and then. Put them into a serving dish for presentation. Serves 6.

Creamy Mashed Potatoes

This is one of the world's favourite ways of cooking potatoes.

> *4–6 medium-sized potatoes, peeled and halved*
> *Salt to taste*
> *1/2–1 cup (41/2–9 fl oz) milk, scalded*
> *30 g (1 oz) butter*
> *Freshly ground pepper*

Tip
Never add cold milk to hot mashed potatoes—it changes the light, fluffy character of the dish completely.

Tip
To keep mashed potato
hot without spoiling,
cook potatoes as
described above, then
mash and press down
well in the saucepan
with the potato
masher. Pack tightly,
levelling the top. Add
butter, spoon about 4
tablespoons of hot milk
over, cover with a well-
fitting lid and leave in
a warm place. Before
serving, beat well,
adding more hot milk
if necessary. The
potatoes will keep up
to 20 minutes.

Put the potatoes into a saucepan of cold, lightly salted water to cover. Cook with the lid on until the potatoes are easily pierced with a fork, about 20 minutes. Drain thoroughly, then shake the pan over heat a few minutes until all surplus moisture has evaporated and the potatoes are quite dry. Mash with a potato masher or potato ricer. Beat the potatoes with a wooden spoon until very smooth. Add the butter, then gradually beat in the hot milk until the potatoes are light and fluffy. Season to taste. Serves 4–6.

New Potatoes with Dill

1 kg (2 lb) new potatoes
Salt
1 tablespoon butter, melted, or good olive oil
3 tablespoons coarsely chopped fresh dill

Boil the potatoes in lightly salted water for about 20 minutes, or until they are just tender. Drain, toss in butter and half the basil over a medium heat. Put them into a serving dish and sprinkle with the remaining dill. (You can substitute mint, basil or chives for the dill.) Serves 6.

Fish Potatoes

1 kg (2 lb) old potatoes
Salt
Parsley, chopped

Peel the potatoes and cut them into halves lengthwise. Using a potato peeler, pare the sharp edges to shape into ovals. Put the potatoes in a colander over a saucepan of boiling water, or in a steamer, sprinkle with salt, cover with a lid and steam for about 15 minutes or until they are tender. Transfer them to a hot serving dish, sprinkle with parsley and serve.

Baked Stuffed Potatoes

The traditional dollop of sour cream or butter topped with chives or parsley is always popular with jacket potatoes. While a little butter is often used to finish off many vegetables, the danger with jacket potatoes is that the potatoes absorb so much of the butter or cream that these enriching fats are used to excess.

Scrub and dry medium even-sized old potatoes and bake on the rack in a hot oven (200°C/400°F) for 1 hour or until soft when pricked with a skewer.

Remove them from the oven, cut a cross in the top, press lightly to open the cut and scoop out the soft centre, placing it in a bowl. Mash lightly with a little butter, season with salt and freshly ground pepper. Pile mixture back into potato skins and return to the oven for a further 10 minutes to heat through.

Sauté Potatoes

1.5 kg (3 lb) Pontiac or good boiling potatoes
2 tablespoons olive oil
30 g (1 oz) butter
Rind of 1 lemon, grated
2 garlic cloves, chopped
A good grating of nutmeg
Salt and freshly ground pepper

Tip
Serve crusty sauté potatoes with grills, roasts, sausages, pork chops, steak or fish.

*P*eel the potatoes and cut them into thick slices; halve if large, or, if you prefer, cut them into cubes or chunky pieces. Boil them in salted water for about 4 minutes. Drain. Melt the oil and butter in a large frying pan (skillet), preferably non-stick, over a moderately high heat. When very hot, add the potatoes, toss and turn them frequently for several minutes, shaking the pan until they begin to brown. When they are brown, add the lemon rind, garlic, nutmeg, and salt and pepper. Continue sautéeing and tossing until the potatoes are as brown and cooked as you wish.

Sauté potatoes will keep well for 15 minutes over a low heat, partially covered. Just before serving uncover and reheat the potatoes to piping hot. Serves 6.

Other flavours. One of the following may be added along with garlic: tiny sprigs of rosemary, 1 tablespoon of sliced basil leaves, 2 tablespoons of chopped parsley or 3 tablespoons of chopped golden shallots.

A bouquet of herbs is lovely in the kitchen. Here we have lavender, sage (some of it gone to seed), rosemary and borage.

SPINACH AND SILVER BEET (SWISS CHARD)

To microwave: Wash, trim and shred about 250 g (8 oz) of spinach leaves. Pile into a bowl, cover and cook on maximum power for 6–8 minutes. Let stand for 2–4 minutes. Use as a guide to adapt other recipes.

Spinach or any leafy green vegetable, like cabbage, should be lightly cooked. The flavour of these vegetables is at its best when they are steamed in the water that clings to the leaves, just long enough to soften them.

Wash and chop the leaves only just before cooking. As much as half a cup ($4^1/_2$ fl oz) of water will cling to the leaves of a bunch. If carelessly allowed to remain in the leaves, this water not only dissolves out the valuable minerals and vitamins, but makes the leaves turn an unpleasant olive-grey.

Immediately after washing, shake the excess water off the leaves, drop them into a pot and allow to cook over a low heat, covered. They should be stirred frequently until steam is formed.

Creamed Spinach Tiffany

1 kg (2 lb) bunch spinach or silver beet (Swiss chard)
1 tablespoon butter
$1/_2$ teaspoon dried tarragon
Salt and freshly ground pepper to taste
2 tablespoons (dairy) sour cream
$1^1/_2$ tablespoons horseradish relish

Prepare and cook the spinach as described in the introductory remarks. Drain the spinach well, put it into a sieve and press with a spoon to remove all the moisture.

Heat the butter in a saucepan, add the spinach, tarragon, salt and pepper. Gently heat through. Just before serving, stir in the sour cream and horseradish relish. Serves 4–6.

Tomatoes Hassler, as served at the hotel of that name which stands at the top of the Spanish Steps in Rome. A lovely antipasto or first course.

TOMATOES

Nothing can quite equal the tangy flavour of a fresh tomato that has been fully ripened on the plant. Whenever these are available, usually at the height of summer, take advantage of them and adapt your menu to include them. Whether fresh, canned or concentrated, tomatoes are always a must in any

kitchen. They can be made into tasty, warming soup with finely chopped onions and garlic, a little chicken stock and a handful of freshly chopped herbs. Pasta with a rich garlic-flavoured tomato sauce is always a favourite, or the tomato sauce can be served in many other ways, such as with eggs, grilled (broiled) meats or fried fish. Vegetables such as zucchini (courgettes), green capsicums (sweet peppers) and green beans go further mixed with a few tomatoes quickly tossed in a little butter. Tomato paste (concentrate) is indispensable when making casseroles, sauces, soups and curries.

To skin (peel) and seed a tomato: Often tomatoes should be skinned, seeded and drained of excess juice before cooking. To peel a tomato, plunge it into boiling water for a few seconds (counting to ten is a good way of guarding against overheating) and then into iced water. Cut out the top of the tomato at the stem end (this top section may be reserved for the stockpot) and peel the skin down from there. To extract the seeds and juice, cut the tomato in half crosswise and squeeze gently in the palm of the hand, shaking out as many of the seeds and as much of the juice as possible.

Tomatoes Hassler

Italian cooks are adept at making remarkable dishes using vegetables and just a little meat or fish. This dish I enjoyed from the buffet table at the lovely Hassler Hotel in Rome. It is good served warm or at room temperature.

> *6–8 small ripe tomatoes*
> *Salt*
> *1 1/2 cups cooked long-grain rice (2/3 cup [4 oz] uncooked)*
> *4 tablespoons chopped fresh parsley or basil*
> *1/4 cup (2 1/4 fl oz) olive oil*
> *6 canned anchovy fillets, drained and chopped*
> *4 garlic cloves, peeled and crushed*
> *Freshly ground black pepper*
> *Sugar*

Cut a slice from the top of each tomato and set these slices aside. Scoop out the pulp, leaving a shell about 1 cm (1/2 in) thick; set the pulp aside. Sprinkle inside the shells with salt and stand upside down to drain. Chop the pulp finely, discarding the seeds.

Place the rice, parsley or basil, oil, anchovies, garlic and 1/2 cup (4 1/2 fl oz) of the tomato pulp in a bowl and mix lightly together. Season to taste with salt and

130

pepper and a dash of sugar. Arrange the tomatoes in an oiled shallow ovenproof dish just large enough to hold them in one layer and fill them with the rice mixture. Cover the tops with the reserved slices. Bake in a moderately hot oven (190°C/375°F) for 10–15 minutes, basting with the cooking juices every now and then. Serve hot or at room temperature. Makes 6–8.

TURNIPS

Steamed White Turnips

Peel 4 young white turnips and cut them into large cubes or quarters. Cook, covered, in 1 cup (9 fl oz) of boiling salted water until soft, about 5 minutes. Drain and toss in a little butter, shaking the pan often. Serve sprinkled with chopped parsley. Baby turnips are trimmed, left whole and cooked this way.

To microwave: Peel and dice 250 g (8 oz) of turnips. Place them on a dish or plate with 2 tablespoons of water and cook, covered, at maximum power for 6–7 minutes. Let stand for 2–4 minutes.

ZUCCHINI (COURGETTES) AND BABY SQUASH

Zucchini and baby squash possess a very delicate but pleasing flavour and are popular with the French and Italians. They are frequently cooked in just a little lightly salted water, and great care should be taken not to overcook. Zucchini are deceptive in that they will soften considerably after being drained, and 3 or 4 minutes is usually sufficient to tenderise them.

Zucchini are versatile as well as delicate. They can be quickly pan fried in oil or stewed with onions and/or tomatoes. Cut them into long strips or on the bias

Zucchini (courgette) flowers ready for the pan. The male flower is used; the shorter-stemmed female is left attached to the ripening fruit. Dipped in a batter and deep fried, it is a delicacy. The flowers may also be stuffed with a light forcemeat, then battered and fried.

into thick or thin oval shapes and lightly sauté or steam. The Italians like to cut them into miniature chips and deep-fry them. They can be stuffed, served raw, thinly sliced in salads, cooked then mashed, or coarsely grated and steamed in stock and butter for a minute.

To prepare: Before cooking, wash the zucchini and cut the ends off, then slice them about 1 cm ($1/2$ in) thick or halve them, depending on the recipe. Baby squash are trimmed and halved or cooked whole. Sprinkle the cut surfaces with salt and place the pieces on a plate or in a colander and allow them to stand for 10–15 minutes; then rinse off the salt and proceed with the recipe. Very young zucchini do not need this treatment with salt.

MIXED VEGETABLE DISHES

There are many interesting combinations of vegetables, and there are vegetables that enjoy a short season and are all too often neglected.

Stuffed vegetables, vegetable soufflés, vegetable tarts and pies and mixed vegetable dishes like the famous vegetable stew of France, ratatouille, are appearing more and more on restaurant menus and are served for family meals and when entertaining. Vegetables have the appeal that merits them taking centre stage. Serve a plate of vegetables on their own, lovingly cooked, with a dab of butter, a squeeze of lemon, a little sea salt and plenty of freshly ground pepper, a sprinkling of freshly chopped herbs or a creamy herb sauce.

Herb sauce. Mix together 2 tablespoons of thick natural (plain) yoghurt, 2 tablespoons of thick (double, heavy) cream, 2 finely chopped garlic cloves (optional), 6 tablespoons of freshly chopped herbs, choosing one or two among parsley, basil, chives, watercress and chervil, and a little salt and freshly ground pepper to taste. Use two spoons to serve a dollop on each vegetable plate.

Steamed Vegetables

A collapsible steamer is a most worthwhile investment. It allows the cooking of a wider variety of vegetables at one time, and as steamed vegetables cook so quickly and don't lose their goodness in the water, their flavour is more intense.

Simply prepare the vegetables as usual, place them in a steamer over boiling water in the base of a saucepan or wok, and cover with the lid. It is important that the vegetables are not sitting in water; there should be sufficient room between water and food for the steam to develop and rise up through the

*Gourmet vegetables—
a mixture of the
freshest young
vegetables both
steamed and grilled
(broiled) and served
with a light herbed
sauce.*

vegetables. Start with the firmest vegetables, and add the softer ones
progressively according to the length of cooking time each requires.

As a guide, sliced carrot, pumpkin (winter squash) or small new potatoes take
about 15 minutes, beans take 8 minutes, and zucchini (courgettes), snow peas,
spinach or cabbage take about 5 minutes.

Best of all is a selection of baby vegetables, carefully chosen and prepared.

Grilled Eggplant and Baby Squash

A few young eggplants (aubergines) and tiny baby squash, halved
Salt and freshly ground pepper
Olive oil
1 lemon

Arrange the prepared vegetables in a colander, sprinkling layers liberally
with salt. Leave to drain for about 30 minutes, then rinse and pat dry.
Preheat a grill (broiler) and arrange the vegetable halves on an oiled grilling
(broiling) rack or use a heated and oiled well-seasoned ribbed-grill pan. Brush
the vegetables with oil. Grill, turning once and brushing with oil as they cook,
until coloured and tender. Keep them on a plate in a warm place until all are
cooked. Drizzle with a little extra oil, season with pepper and lemon juice.

Sauté of Ratatouille Vegetables

A light vegetable dish to accompany fish, lamb or indeed any grill or roast. If baby zucchini (courgettes) and eggplants (aubergines) are unavailable, choose small ones cut into cubes or thick slices, depending on size. For a softer result, prepare as described, double the quantity of olive oil and, after the tomatoes have been added, simmer covered for an additional 15 minutes.

6 spring onions (tiny white onions), peeled
A sprig of fresh thyme or lemon thyme
1 small bay leaf
2 tablespoons olive oil
3 garlic cloves, peeled and halved
6 tiny zucchini (courgettes), halved lengthwise or left whole
6 baby eggplants (aubergines), halved or, if tiny, left whole
A handful of cherry tomatoes or 1 tomato cut into eighths
1 tablespoon chopped fresh mixed herbs
Salt and freshly ground pepper

134

*P*ut the onions in a large sauté pan with 1 cup (9 fl oz) of water, thyme and bay leaf. Cover and simmer for 5 minutes; drain off the water. Add the olive oil and garlic and allow to sauté gently while cooking the other vegetables.

In a large saucepan of boiling salted water cook the zucchini for 3 minutes. Scoop them up with a slotted spoon and add to the sauté pan with the onions. Keep the water at simmering point, add the eggplant and cook for 4 minutes, then add it to the sauté pan with the other vegetables. Toss the vegetables together and continue to sauté, covered, for 5 minutes, adding more olive oil if necessary. By this time the vegetables should be tender. Uncover the pan and add the tomatoes, herbs, salt and pepper to taste. Cook for a further minute and serve. Serves 6.

Caponata Siciliana

This Sicilian dish has a sweet-sour flavour—a legacy of Ancient Roman days, when sweet dates were used instead of tomatoes and sugar. This recipe is ideal for accompanying cold meats and makes an excellent part of an antipasto.

> *1 medium eggplant (aubergine), cut into small cubes*
> *4 tablespoons olive oil*
> *2 celery stalks, thinly sliced*
> *1 onion, thinly sliced*
> *2 tomatoes, peeled and chopped (see page 130)*
> *1 tablespoon capers, drained*
> *2 teaspoons pine nuts*
> *5 black olives, halved and pitted*
> *1 tablespoon sugar*
> *2 tablespoons wine vinegar*
> *Salt and freshly ground pepper*

*S*prinkle the eggplant cubes with salt and leave to drain for 30 minutes. Wash and pat dry. Heat half the oil in a deep frying pan and fry the cubes a few at a time until browned and soft, adding a little more oil as necessary.

Return all the cooked eggplant to the pan with the celery, onion and tomatoes. Simmer for 15–20 minutes and then add the capers, pine nuts and olives. Stir the sugar in the vinegar until dissolved and add to the pan. Season with salt and pepper and simmer very gently for a further 15 minutes. Taste and add a little more vinegar if necessary. Cool and leave for several hours for the flavours to develop fully. Serve the caponata cold with Italian bread. Serves 6.

Grilled Vegetable Platter

6–8 tablespoons olive oil

3 garlic cloves, chopped

3 tablespoons chopped fresh parsley

A few sprigs of thyme

Freshly ground black pepper

3 large capsicums (sweet peppers), any colour, quartered and seeded

6 zucchini (courgettes), trimmed and halved lengthwise

6 baby eggplants (aubergines), halved lengthwise, or 1 medium
*   eggplant, sliced*

3 tomatoes, halved crosswise

Grilled Vegetable Platter. An assortment of vegetables can be roasted on a ribbed grill or over a charcoal grill. Serve with bruschetta or toasted country bread.

Combine the oil, garlic, parsley, thyme and pepper. Brush the surfaces of the prepared vegetables with the seasoned oil. Reserve the remaining oil.

Heat a ribbed grill (or if you are using a barbecue for other purposes, grill over the hot coals; they give a marvellous smoky taste to the vegetables). Grill the vegetables for about 3 minutes on each side; start with the capsicums, then the zucchini, the eggplant and lastly the tomatoes. Arrange the vegetables on a large platter and sprinkle them with the remaining seasoned oil. Allow them to marinate for about 15 minutes before serving. Serves 6.

SALADS

Today's salads are looking prettier, more colourful, more varied and certainly most inviting with the vast variety of foods, salad greens, fruit and vegetables that go into them. A salad must look appetising and be made with fresh ingredients. It must smell and taste good—easy with today's superb oils, vinegars, mustards, seasonings and herbs, the vast variety of seafoods, cured and fresh meats, pasta, grains, cheese, baby-tender vegetables, all offering such scope.

Salad Greens

*N*ever before has there been such an abundance of delightful green leaves of every shape, size, colour and taste to mix and match, and to add enormous interest to our meals.

Lettuce comes first to mind. We can choose from crisp round iceberg, elongated cos (romaine), soft butterheads and mignonette. In the same family there are endives and chicory—curly endive (chicorée frisée), and broad-leafed escarole, the long, smooth, fat, cigar-shaped witloof, sometimes called Belgian endive or chicory, all with a slightly bitter taste that you soon learn to enjoy.

Chinese cabbage, savoy, sugarloaf, the large, green, white and red cabbages, although winter vegetables, are around for the early summer months and are popular for coleslaws and other salads.

Among the cresses and tiny leaves we can now get watercress, green and peppery corn salad (lamb's lettuce), shaped like a lamb tongue and called *mache* in France; it has a delicious nutty taste. New for many of us are the peppery arugula (rocket), the slightly bitter red radicchio, the green and brown very curly frisée lettuce, and the lovely mescluns. Mesclun is a very convenient way of buying salad greens. It is a mixture of baby greens, such as oak-leaf lettuce, tiny cos, butterhead and coral lettuce leaves along with arugula, snow pea shoots and marigold flower petals, depending on what is available.

Mesclun and Radicchio Salad is so pretty you could eat it! It should be dressed with the very best virgin olive oil.

Mesclun and Radicchio Salad

1 tablespoon wine vinegar or 1 teaspoon balsamic vinegar
Salt and freshly ground pepper
3 tablespoons olive oil
1 tablespoon extra virgin olive oil
8 radicchio leaves, rinsed and dried
250 g (8 oz) mesclun (see above)

*I*n a large bowl whisk together the vinegar, salt and pepper to taste, and the oils added in a stream, whisking until the dressing is lightly emulsified. Toss the radicchio with the dressing and divide it among 4–6 plates, first allowing the excess dressing to drip off the leaves into the bowl. Toss the mesclun with the remaining dressing in the bowl and divide it among the plates. Serves 6.

Caesar Salad

This salad was created by a Mexican, Alexander Cardini, for his brother Caesar, who had gone to London to seek fame and fortune as a chef. I consider this one of the most elegant salads when made properly.

1 cos (romaine) lettuce
4 canned anchovies
1 garlic clove, crushed
8 slices French bread
1 egg
Salt to taste
Freshly ground black pepper
Juice of ¹/₂ lemon
3 tablespoons olive oil
1 teaspoon Worcestershire sauce
3 tablespoons freshly grated Parmesan cheese

Caesar Salad, made according to the recipe given to me by the creator of this famous salad.

Wash the lettuce, separate the leaves and dry thoroughly. Crisp in the refrigerator. Mash the anchovies with the garlic and spread on the slices of French bread. Bake in a slow oven (150°C/300°F) until crisp and dry. Allow to cool. Place the egg gently into boiling water and cook for 50 seconds only. Arrange the lettuce in a salad bowl, season with salt and pepper. Combine the lemon juice, olive oil and Worcestershire sauce in a small bowl and beat well with a fork. Pour it over the salad, sprinkle the cheese over and add the bread. Break the coddled egg into the salad. Roll the leaves in dressing until each leaf is glistening with the dressing. Be gentle, and do not bruise the leaves. Serve at once. Serves 4.

Crudités

A favourite hors d'oeuvre of provincial France, the simple arrangement of crisp, young, fresh, raw or blanched vegetables is popular with everyone. Serve the arranged vegetables with Aïoli (garlic-flavoured mayonnaise, page 191) and Vinaigrette (French dressing, page 188) for dipping, or with Coriander Chutney (page 187). Prepare the vegetables as follows:

Carrots. Wash, peel and trim small young carrots, leave whole or cut each into quarters or strips. Drop into iced water to crisp.

Radishes. Use only firm, round, bright red radishes. Trim top leaves, leaving small leaf intact. (This makes it easier for guests to eat radishes with their fingers.) Wash radishes well. Place in iced water.

Spring onions (scallions, green shallots). Wash, remove outside leaf and trim off root and green tops about 5 cm (2 in) above the fork of the leaves. Fray ends and keep in iced water until ends curl.

Tomatoes. Use very firm, small tomatoes, preferably the cherry tomato variety. Wash and chill. If using larger tomatoes, halve or quarter them.

Celery. Wash and cut stalks in 12 cm (5 in) lengths. Fray ends by making 2.5 cm (1 in) cuts 5 mm ($^1/_4$ in) apart, lengthwise at each end of stalk. Drop into a large bowl of iced water and leave for 45 minutes to 1 hour to allow stalks to curl and become crisp.

Cauliflower. Separate into florets, trim and wash. Place in iced water.

Asparagus. Trim or break tough ends. Steam in a pan of lightly salted water about 5 minutes. Drain and refresh under cold water. Drain.

Snow peas (mangetout). Tip and tail, drop into lightly boiling salted water for 30 seconds. Drain and refresh under cold water. Drain.

Green beans. Cut off stem ends. Steam in a pan of lightly salted water about 5 minutes. Drain and refresh under cold water. Drain.

Beetroot and Endive Salad. The baby beetroot help to make a new version of this classic combination.

Beetroot and Endive Salad

Belgian endive, with its elongated white leaves and pleasant sharp tang, combines well with distinctive flavours such as pickled walnuts, orange or beetroot (beets). To be at its best the beetroot should be freshly cooked and just allowed to cool, not be chilled.

> *4 heads of Belgian endive (witloof, chicory)*
> *Lemon juice*
> *Extra virgin olive or walnut oil*
> *Salt and pepper*
> *2 large beetroots (beets), or 12 baby beetroots, cooked and skinned*

Tip
Now that you can buy baby beetroot, use them on special occasions. They take 10–15 minutes to cook (in boiling salted water). Trim the stalks before cooking; slip skins off when cooked and leave whole.

*D*iscard the outer leaves of the endive. Break off the crisp leaves or cut through into 2.5 cm (1 in) lengths or have a mixture of both whole leaves and sliced. Squeeze just a little lemon juice over to prevent discoloration. Season with good olive or walnut oil, salt and pepper, and roll gently until all leaves are glistening. Cut the beetroot into julienne strips (leave baby beetroot whole) and just before serving strew them over the endive. Serves 4.

Tip
Fennel can be sliced
and added to give a
crunchy, crisp texture
to this salad.
Alternatively, for
something a little out
of the ordinary, add
snow peas (mangetout)
tipped and tailed and
lightly blanched in
boiling water for
30 seconds.

*Fresh Pear and
Watercress Salad is a
course on its own. The
peppery watercress
complements the
ambrosial perfume of
ripe fresh pears.*

Fresh Pear and Watercress Salad

2 tablespoons wine vinegar or sherry vinegar
1 tablespoon French (Dijon) mustard
1 teaspoon finely grated green (fresh) ginger
Salt and freshly ground black pepper
Crushed garlic to taste
1/2 cup (4 1/2 fl oz) olive oil
A bunch of watercress
4 ripe pears

Place the vinegar and seasonings in a small bowl. Using a fork, gradually beat in the oil until a thick dressing is formed; use more oil if needed.
Wash the watercress well and break into sprigs, removing the tough stalks. Spin dry. Peel the pears, halve them, remove the cores and cut into slices. Put watercress and pears into a salad bowl and toss with dressing. Serves 4–6.

Potato Salad

5 or 6 medium potatoes
Salted water
1 teaspoon salt
Freshly ground pepper
2–3 tablespoons vinegar
6–7 tablespoons olive oil
4 tablespoons stock or hot water
Parsley, chives, chervil and tarragon, chopped
Spring onions (scallions), chopped (optional)
1/2–3/4 cup (4 1/2–6 3/4 fl oz) mayonnaise (optional)

Boil the unpeeled potatoes in just enough salted water to cover until tender. Drain, peel, and cut them into thick slices. While the potatoes are still hot, season them with the salt and a little pepper, and sprinkle with the vinegar and oil, well beaten together with a fork. Add the stock and chopped herbs to taste. Chopped spring onions may also be added. Let the salad stand at room temperature until most of the liquid is absorbed. Turn the potato slices carefully to ensure even seasoning. Serve the salad without chilling. For a creamy salad, spoon the mayonnaise over the potatoes. Top with chopped parsley. Serves 4–6.

Escalivada

This Spanish roasted vegetable salad is delicious warm or at room temperature with a generous hunk of bread. Look for the baby eggplants (aubergines) and spring onions (scallions).

500 g (1 lb) medium or baby eggplants (aubergines)
1 bunch spring onions, peeled and trimmed
2 yellow or red capsicums (sweet peppers)
3 large garlic cloves, peeled
$^1/_2$ cup ($4^1/_2$ fl oz) olive oil
Salt
Chopped parsley and pitted, halved black olives to garnish

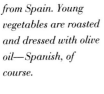

Escalivada, a dish from Spain. Young vegetables are roasted and dressed with olive oil—Spanish, of course.

*I*n a heavy baking dish roast the vegetables in a moderate oven (180°C/ 350°F) until very soft. Cover tightly with a lid or aluminium foil and leave for 10 minutes or so. Uncover and peel the capsicums and eggplants if liked and cut into long, thin strips. If the eggplants are baby ones you may prefer to leave them unpeeled and whole. Leave the spring onions whole.

While still warm, dress with the olive oil and season with salt. Turn into a serving dish and scatter with parsley and olives. Serves 6.

Spanish Orange Salad

For an exotic variation to this salad, add 2 tablespoons of Pernod or anisette to the dressing. These liqueurs are available in miniature bottles, so there is no need to go to the expense of buying a large bottle of liqueur.

4 medium-size oranges
1 small red or salad onion
3 tablespoons dry sherry
Juice of 1/2 lime or lemon
1 tablespoon olive oil
Freshly ground white pepper
Watercress to garnish

*P*eel the oranges and remove any pith. Cut the oranges into 1 cm (1/2 in) slices. Set aside. Peel and thinly slice the onion and separate into rings. Place in a bowl, sprinkle over the sherry and leave to marinate for 1 hour. In a small bowl, blend the citrus juice, oil, pepper and sherry marinade. Whisk well. Arrange the watercress in a glass bowl. Place orange slices on top and then onion. Pour on the dressing and toss carefully. Serves 4.

Tomato Salad

Tomatoes dressed in olive oil and just a touch of lemon juice, topped with blanched spring onions (scallions), must be one of the simplest yet most delicious salads. To blanch the spring onions, drop them into a saucepan of boiling water for 30 seconds, then refresh them under cold water.

4 firm, ripe tomatoes
Salt and freshly ground pepper
2 tablespoons olive oil, preferably virgin
1 teaspoon lemon juice or vinegar (wine or balsamic)
6–8 spring onions (scallions) chopped and blanched
Fresh parsley or chives, chopped

*W*ithout peeling, cut the tomatoes crosswise into thin slices (use a serrated-edge knife) and arrange them overlapping on a flat dish. Season well. Mix the oil and lemon juice or vinegar and sprinkle over the tomatoes. Sprinkle with spring onions and some chopped parsley or chives. Serves 4–6.

Carpaccio with Arugula and Artichoke Dressing

375 g (12 oz) trimmed piece of beef fillet (tenderloin)
1 cup sliced arugula (rocket) leaves, washed well and dried
A small wedge of Parmesan cheese
Freshly ground black pepper
DRESSING
3–4 drained marinated artichoke hearts in olive oil
1 tablespoon sherry vinegar or red wine vinegar
1 tablespoon fresh lemon juice
Salt and pepper
4 tablespoons olive oil, preferably virgin
2 tablespoons warm water

Carpaccio with Arugula and Artichoke Dressing—the thinnest slices of raw beef, arugula (rocket) leaves and shavings of Parmesan cheese.

Wrap the beef well in plastic wrap (cling film) and semi-freeze it for 1 hour or until it is firm but not frozen solid. Using a very sharp knife cut the fillet across the grain into very thin slices. To make the slices even thinner, arrange them on sheets of plastic wrap, cover with additional sheets of wrap and gently roll them with a rolling pin, testing a slice as you roll to make sure they do not become too thin to transfer to serving plates. Roll up the sheets loosely and chill the beef for at least an hour.

Tip
Make Parmesan curls by shaving the wedge of cheese with a vegetable peeler or cheese plane.

Divide the beef among 4 chilled plates, lining the plates with a single layer of the slices. Mound the arugula in the centre with about 5 Parmesan curls. Give each serving a good grinding of pepper, and drizzle a little of the dressing over each. Serve the remaining dressing separately. Serves 4.

Dressing. In an electric blender or food processor, purée the artichoke hearts with the vinegar, lemon juice, and salt and pepper to taste. With the motor running, add the oil in a stream and the warm water, blending the mixture well.

Warm Seafood Salad

1 kg (2 lb) baby octopus, cleaned

Salt and freshly ground pepper

2 bay leaves

6 peppercorns

30 g (1 oz) butter

500 g (1 lb) squid (calamari), cleaned and cut into strips

250 g (8 oz) raw (green) prawns (shrimp), shelled (optional)

250 g (8 oz) scallops (optional)

1 small onion, finely chopped

1¼ cups (11 fl oz) olive oil

2 large ripe tomatoes, peeled, seeded and chopped (see page 130)

4 tablespoons wine vinegar

3 tablespoons chopped parsley

3 tablespoons snipped chives

2 garlic cloves, peeled and halved

Mixed green salad leaves

4 tablespoons Hot Vinaigrette (page 189)

Snow pea (mangetout) shoots and chopped parsley for garnish

Warm Seafood Salad is served on a bed of mixed salad greens. The hot vinaigrette brings out the flavour of the seafood and is a contrast to the cool, crisp greens.

Place the octopus in a saucepan with cold water to cover. Add a little salt and pepper, the bay leaves and peppercorns. Bring slowly to the boil, then turn the heat down very low so that the liquid just trembles. Cover and continue cooking until the octopus is tender. (This will depend on the octopus and may take 1–2 hours. Test at intervals with the point of a knife.) Remove the pan from the heat and leave the octopus to cool in the cooking liquid. When cool, drain and cut into bite-size pieces.

Melt the butter in a heavy saucepan and add the strips of squid. Stir briskly over low heat until the squid turns opaque. This will take only a short time. Remove the squid, add the prawns and scallops, if using, turning over a low heat until opaque. Remove from heat.

Cook the onion slowly in ¼ cup (2¼ fl oz) of the olive oil until soft. Add the tomatoes, cover and simmer until the mixture is thick. Season lightly with salt and pepper and set aside to cool.

In a bowl mix the vinegar with a little salt and pepper and beat in the remaining cup of olive oil a little at a time. Add the tomato mixture, parsley, chives and garlic. Season to taste, add the seafood and mix thoroughly. Place in a covered container and refrigerate for 1–3 days—the longer the time, the better

151

the flavour of the salad. Wash and dry the salad greens. Toss in Hot Vinaigrette and heap on six individual plates. Warm the seafood, pile on top, garnish with snow pea shoots and sprinkle over some of the remaining marinade. Sprinkle each salad with a little chopped parsley. Serves 6.

Korean Beef Salad

Korean Beef Salad is perfect for picnics or an alfresco brunch. The dressing is a fascinating blend of sweet and exotic.

750 g (1¹/₂ lb) boneless sirloin steak, trimmed

4 onions, chopped

6 tablespoons sake or dry sherry

6 tablespoons light soy sauce

3 tablespoons sesame oil

1¹/₂ teaspoons coarsely ground pepper

2 tablespoons vegetable oil

250 g (8 oz) small mushrooms

125 g (4 oz) snow peas (mangetout), blanched in boiling salted water for 10 seconds, drained, patted dry and strings discarded

Pitta pockets or flat mountain bread for serving

2 cups pea shoots as accompaniment

DRESSING

1 garlic clove, chopped

1 tablespoon Dijon mustard

2 teaspoons honey

3 tablespoons rice wine vinegar

3 tablespoons light soy sauce

3 tablespoons sesame oil

6 tablespoons vegetable oil

*I*n a baking dish large enough to hold the beef and the onions in one layer, whisk together the sake, soy sauce, sesame oil and pepper. Add the beef and onions and let the mixture marinate, covered and chilled, stirring the onions and turning the beef several times, for at least 3 hours or overnight.

Remove the beef and the onions from the marinade, pat the beef dry and reserve half the marinade. In a large frying pan (skillet) heat the oil over moderately high heat until it is hot and in it sauté the beef, turning it once, for 8 to 10 minutes for medium-rare meat. Transfer the beef to a cutting board and let it stand for 10 minutes.

In the frying pan cook the onions, stirring for 5 minutes, or until they are tender but still slightly crisp, and transfer them with a slotted spoon to a bowl of dressing (see below). Add the mushrooms with the reserved marinade to the frying pan, cook until almost all liquid is evaporated, and transfer to the bowl. Slice the beef thin across the grain. Add to the vegetable mixture along with the snow peas and toss well. Transfer to a serving dish or portable container (if taking to a picnic) and serve it in the pitta pockets with the pea shoots, or eat as a light meal with steamed rice and the pea shoots. Serves 8.

Dressing. In a large bowl combine the garlic, mustard, honey, vinegar, and soy sauce, add the sesame oil and the vegetable oil in a stream, whisking, and whisk the dressing until it is emulsified. The dressing may be made a day in advance and kept covered and chilled.

Mixed Lettuce and Nasturtium Salad

Tip
Flowers are turning up in salads these days. They look pretty and have a flavour that adds interest. Pansy, violet or nasturtium flowers from the garden can all be used. Mesclun, the salad-green mix (page 138), may replace the varied lettuce in this salad.

1 bunch arugula (rocket), washed gently and dried

2 heads of lettuce (butterhead, mignonette or frisée), the leaves separated, rinsed, dried, and torn into bite-size pieces

2 teaspoons fresh lemon juice

1 teaspoon snipped fresh tarragon or chervil leaves

1/4 teaspoon sugar

1/4 teaspoon freshly grated nutmeg

1/4 teaspoon salt

1 garlic clove, peeled and crushed

1/3 cup (3 fl oz) virgin olive oil

8 nasturtium flowers

Trim the rough stem ends of the arugula; cut in two if long.

In a salad bowl toss together the arugula and the lettuce. In a small bowl whisk together the lemon juice, snipped herb, sugar, nutmeg, salt and garlic. Add the oil in a slow stream, whisking constantly. Drizzle this dressing over the greens, and toss well. Divide the salad among 4 salad plates; scatter over the flowers. Serves 4.

Fattoush

Toasted pieces of pitta bread form the basis of this Syrian vegetable salad.

2 whole-wheat pitta breads
Juice of 2 lemons
2 garlic cloves, peeled and crushed
¹/₂ cup (4¹/₂ fl oz) olive oil
Salt and freshly ground pepper
2 Lebanese (Continental) cucumbers, peeled thinly and diced
1 bunch spring onions (scallions), chopped
4 firm ripe tomatoes, diced
1 green capsicum (sweet pepper), diced
1 cup Italian (flat-leaved) parsley sprigs, chopped
3 tablespoons chopped fresh mint

Tip
Thinly peel Lebanese cucumbers so as to retain much of the green directly under the skin. When chopping spring onions, include half the length of the green parts.

Open out the pitta breads and toast in a moderate oven (180°C/350°F) for 10 to 15 minutes until crisp and browned. Break them into small pieces and put them in a shallow salad bowl. In a small bowl whisk together the lemon juice, garlic and olive oil, adding salt and pepper to taste. Toss with the bread pieces.

Add the cucumber and spring onions to the bread with the tomato and capsicum. Add the parsley and mint and toss together. Check for seasonings and serve. Serves 6.

Thai Pork Salad

500 g (1 lb) pork, lean and finely chopped or minced (ground)
3 tablespoons water
2 tablespoons lemon juice
2 tablespoons Thai fish sauce (nam pla)
¹/₂ teaspoon finely sliced fresh chilli (chili pepper)
2 tablespoons roasted peanuts (groundnuts), skinned
1 red or salad onion, finely sliced
6–8 green shallots (spring onions), cut in short lengths
2 tablespoons finely shredded fresh ginger
6–8 mint leaves
¹/₂ cup torn coriander (Chinese parsley) stems and leaves
8 or more crisp lettuce cups

Tip
The wok is an all-purpose utensil and quickly cooks pork for this light salad. Try using minced or finely chopped chicken in place of pork. This is a warm salad, so much in tune with today's eating.

*P*lace the pork and water in a wok, cook over medium heat, stirring to prevent lumps forming, until the pork is tender. Turn the pork into a bowl to cool. Add the lemon juice and all the other ingredients except the lettuce leaves; toss lightly.

Serve with the lettuce cups. The guests wrap the lettuce cups around the pork and eat it in the hand. Serves 4–6.

Avocado and Chicken Salad

Avocado and Chicken Salad—a new-wave salad of freshly cooked food in a great dressing served on a bed of crisp greens.

1 tablespoon lemon juice
¼ teaspoon Tabasco sauce
2 teaspoons chopped fresh oregano
5 tablespoons extra-virgin olive oil
1 small red or salad onion, finely chopped
4 half breasts of chicken with the skin
1 tablespoon olive oil
Salt and pepper to taste
¼ cup black olives, pitted and halved (optional)
3–4 tablespoons chopped fresh mint leaves
3 tablespoons chopped fresh parsley
6–8 sun-dried tomatoes, quartered
2 firm ripe avocados, halved lengthwise, pitted and sliced
About 16 leaves of butterhead or other soft-leafed lettuce or a
*   bag of mesclun (see page 138)*

*I*n a large bowl mix together the lemon juice, Tabasco and 1 teaspoon of the oregano: add the oil in a stream, whisking the dressing until it is emulsified. Stir in the onion. Heat a well-seasoned ribbed grill pan over moderately high heat, or use a preheated grill (broiler). Pat the chicken dry, rub with the olive oil, and sprinkle it with the remaining oregano and salt and pepper to taste. Grill the chicken, skin side down (up, if using a broiler), pressing the thickest part occasionally with a metal spatula, for 7 minutes; turn it, and grill it in the same manner for 7 minutes more, or until it is cooked through. Transfer the chicken with tongs to a plate, and let it cool to room temperature.

Cut the chicken into thick slices, add it to the dressing, and let it marinate at room temperature, stirring occasionally, for 15 minutes. Add the olives, mint, parsley and tomato and toss the salad well. Add the avocados. Toss the salad gently and season it with salt and pepper. Put the lettuce leaves on a platter and top them with the salad. Serves 6.

Vegetarian Dishes

It's a sign of the times: you ask a group of friends for a meal and inevitably find that there's one or two who will announce, 'Love to, but I'm vegetarian.' They like to add, 'Don't go to any extra trouble,' but you inevitably feel you must. Once over the initial surprise, you soon realise that much of the best food in the world is vegetarian.

I never find it a challenge to prepare such meals. Indeed, some of my most successful luncheon and dinner parties have catered for vegetarians and non-vegetarians at the same time. It's been a revelation to everyone. I may start the meal with Artichokes Clamart (page 98) followed by soufflé gnocchi—choux pastry with good cheese, poached in water. These light and tender dumplings are topped with cheese and baked. I would follow this with a sparkling mixed green salad combining some of the wonderful salad varieties available to us now (see chapter 5), which I simply dress at the table using balsamic vinegar and olive oil. When the main course is fairly simple, you can afford to go all out for the dessert course, a lovely Gâteau Pithiviers (page 338) or a dish of caramel oranges or a prune tart.

With recipe ideas from this chapter plus the others throughout these pages, you'll find it fascinating putting together simply wonderful vegetarian meals.

Vegetable Chilli Bowl is a wonderful mélange of dried beans, fresh vegetables, herbs and spices. It is served here with Spoon Bread, that aristocrat of corn breads, light as a soufflé.

Vegetable Chilli Bowl

Have a bowl of this vegetable variation of a chilli con carne ready for any informal meal. It has the lively spicy taste of any good chilli. The finishing touch is to serve it with Spoon Bread, and I include the recipe.

1/2 cup (4 1/2 fl oz) olive oil
2 onions, roughly chopped
3 garlic cloves, finely chopped
2 red capsicums (sweet peppers), cored, seeded and cut into
  squares
2 zucchini (courgettes), cut into cubes or chunks
1 tablespoon chilli powder
1 tablespoon ground cumin
2 400 g (14 oz) cans peeled tomatoes
Salt and plenty of freshly ground pepper
440 g (15 oz) can red kidney beans
440 g (15 oz) can chickpeas (garbanzos), drained
1/2 cup chopped parsley
1/2 cup chopped coriander (Chinese parsley)
2 tablespoons fresh lemon juice

*H*eat the oil in a deep flameproof casserole over a moderate heat and add the onion, garlic and capsicum. Sauté for about 5 minutes. Add the zucchini and continue to sauté for about 3 minutes. Stir in the chilli powder and cumin and stir for a minute. Add the tomatoes, roughly chopped, with their juice. Season with salt and pepper and stir in the drained kidney beans and chickpeas.

Cover and simmer for 15 minutes, until all the vegetables are tender. Lastly, stir in the parsley, coriander and lemon juice to give the dish a fresh taste.

Serve the vegetable chilli with bowls of grated Cheddar cheese, green shallots and sour cream or yoghurt alongside for everyone to help themselves. Spoon Bread makes this dish even more special. Serves 6.

Spoon Bread

3 cups (27 fl oz) milk, scalded
125 g (4 oz) butter
1 cup (5 oz) corn (maize) meal
1 teaspoon salt
1 teaspoon sugar
3 eggs, separated

*P*reheat the oven to moderate (180°C/350°F). Combine the milk and butter in a small pan and bring to the boil. Add the corn meal, salt and sugar and cook for 5 minutes. Cool slightly, then beat in the egg yolks. Whisk the egg whites until stiff, and fold into the mixture. Bake in a buttered baking dish for about 45 minutes, until risen, golden and crusty. Serve as soon as it comes out of the oven. Serves 6.

Mediterranean-Style Stuffed Vegetables

This basic stuffing can be used to fill a variety of vegetables. While the instructions given here use a set quantity of stuffing for each vegetable, you can use a few different vegetables and divide the stuffing accordingly. Cook each vegetable type separately or pack in a large roasting pan and bake, covered with aluminium foil, in a moderately hot oven (190°C/375°F). Arrange the stuffed vegetables on a large platter with lemon wedges for sprinkling juice, and serve as a first course. The stuffing ingredients are:

1 cup (5 oz) long-grain rice, well washed
4 onions, chopped
$^1/_2$ cup (4$^1/_2$ fl oz) olive oil
3 tablespoons pine nuts or slivered almonds
2 teaspoons salt
400 g (14 oz) can tomatoes, chopped
1 cup (4$^1/_2$ fl oz) boiling water
3 tablespoons currants or chopped raisins
$^1/_2$ teaspoon each ground pepper and allspice
2 teaspoons sugar
2 tablespoons chopped mint
2 teaspoons dried dill

*I*n a large bowl cover the rice with boiling water and let it stand until the water cools to room temperature. Drain and rinse with cold water; drain again thoroughly. Meanwhile, cook the onions in the olive oil with the pine nuts and salt until the onions are pale golden. Add the drained rice and stir until rice is coated with oil, for about 5 minutes. Add the tomatoes with juice, and the remaining ingredients. Reduce the heat and cook a further 15 minutes until the liquid is completely absorbed. Allow to cool completely.

Stuffed capsicums (sweet peppers). Cut the tops off 10–12 small capsicums, or halve 6 large capsicums, and remove the seeds. Fill with 1 quantity of stuffing, without packing tightly. Arrange them close together in a heavy pan and sprinkle with 2 tablespoons of olive oil. Pour over $^{1}/_{2}$ cup ($4^{1}/_{2}$ fl oz) boiling water, cover and simmer 25–30 minutes or until the rice and vegetables are tender. Add more water if necessary to avoid burning. Cool in the pan. To cook in the oven, pack the capsicums into a roasting pan, add $^{1}/_{2}$ cup ($4^{1}/_{2}$ fl oz) water and cook, covered, in a moderately hot oven (190°C/375°F) for 30 minutes.

Stuffed tomatoes. Cut the tops off 15 medium tomatoes, and remove the pulp with a small spoon (the pulp can be used in place of the tomatoes in the stuffing recipe). Fill the tomatoes with the stuffing. Arrange the tomatoes in a large pan on a rack, if possible, so that they don't sit in water while cooking. Sprinkle with 2 tablespoons of olive oil, and pour over $^{1}/_{2}$ cup ($4^{1}/_{2}$ fl oz) boiling water. Cover and simmer until the rice and tomatoes are tender, about 15–20 minutes, adding a little more water if necessary. Cool in the pan. To roast the tomatoes in the oven, pack them into a roasting pan (do not add the water, as for peppers) and roast uncovered in a moderately hot oven (190°C/375°F) for 15 minutes.

Stuffed vine leaves. Use 250 g (8 oz) preserved, washed and blanched vine leaves. One at a time, lay the leaves, shiny side down, on a board and top with a spoonful of stuffing. Roll each leaf a little, then tuck the edges in to seal. Continue rolling, squeeze gently, and arrange them flap down in a heavy pan. Sprinkle with 3 tablespoons of olive oil, then cover with an upturned heatproof plate. Pour the juice of half a lemon and $^{1}/_{2}$ cup ($4^{1}/_{2}$ fl oz) of boiling water over the plate, to prevent the leaves from unfolding. Cover and simmer until rice and leaves are tender, about 30 minutes. Cool in the pan.

Stuffed eggplant (aubergine). Halve 3 medium eggplants and scoop out the flesh, leaving a shell to hold the stuffing. Chop the eggplant flesh, add to the stuffing along with the onions in the frying pan (skillet) and fry until soft, then proceed with the cooking as above. Fill the eggplant shells with the stuffing. Arrange them in a roasting pan, drizzle with 3 tablespoons of olive oil and roast in a moderately hot oven (190°C/375°F) for 30 minutes. Cover with aluminium foil if the surface of the stuffing seems to dry out.

Mediterranean Stuffed Vegetables, a dish that has travelled to the Western world from Turkey, Armenia, Greece, Egypt, Iran, Lebanon and North Africa among other places. Vegetables, rice, spices, herbs, nuts and fruits and good olive oil combine to make a filling for various kinds of vegetables.

Pumpkin-Stuffed Cabbage Leaves

This lovely dish of stuffed cabbage leaves with a wonderful fragrance of herbs makes a great family meal. It is economical (for most of us) but very good, and shows what interesting things can be done with the humble cabbage.

12 large cabbage leaves
1 medium onion, peeled and chopped
1 garlic clove, crushed
1 tablespoon olive oil
375 g (12 oz) cubed pumpkin or butternut squash, boiled or
*   steamed and puréed*
4 tablespoons cooked rice or fresh breadcrumbs
1 egg, lightly beaten
2 tablespoons chopped parsley
1 teaspoon chopped lemon thyme
1 teaspoon chopped oregano
1 tablespoon chopped celery tops
1 teaspoon ground cinnamon
Salt and freshly ground pepper
400 g (14 oz) can of peeled tomatoes, chopped and the
*   juice saved*
1/2 cup (4 1/2 fl oz) each white wine and water
4 tablespoons olive oil

Pumpkin-Stuffed Cabbage Leaves is a complete dish in itself. The pumpkin can be any of the golden squash family.

Scald (blanch) the cabbage leaves in a large pan of boiling water until they are limp and tender. Drain, cool and remove the tough parts, then lay the leaves out flat ready for stuffing. Sauté the onion and garlic in the tablespoon of olive oil until softened. Place in a bowl with the pumpkin, rice or breadcrumbs, egg, herbs, cinnamon and salt and pepper and mix thoroughly.

Put a large tablespoon of filling on each cabbage leaf, roll a little, tuck in the sides, and roll up completely into a small, fat sausage, securing it with a toothpick. Continue with the remaining cabbage leaves, arranging them in a lightly oiled gratin dish. Top with the chopped tomatoes and juice and pour in enough wine and water to come two-thirds of the way up the cabbage. Trickle over the 4 tablespoons of oil.

Cover tightly with aluminium foil and bake in a preheated hot oven (220°C/425°F) for 10–15 minutes. Reduce the temperature to slow (150°C/300°F) and continue to cook for 1 hour. Serves 4–6.

Capsicum Salad

This simple version of capsicum (sweet pepper) salad, made in a trice, omits the fiddly peeling of the thin skin but with very good results.

4 red and yellow capsicums (sweet peppers)
3 tablespoons olive oil
Juice of 1/2 lemon
1 garlic clove, chopped
Fresh herbs (parsley, oregano, chives, basil)

Cut the capsicums into quarters, remove the seeds and ribs. Lay the quarters out, skin side up, on a grilling tray and roast under a red-hot grill (broiler) till the skin is blistered. Remove the skins if you wish. Cut each quarter into three or four strips and place them in a serving dish. Dress with olive oil, lemon juice, garlic and herbs, tossing lightly. Allow to cool to room temperature.

Basic Thick Polenta

Polenta is made from finely ground yellow corn meal and in the north of Italy sometimes takes the place of pasta and even bread. After it is boiled, it may be fried in oil, toasted on a grill or baked in the oven with or without a sauce. Polenta blends well with meat, game and fish dishes and is often served as a course on its own, baked with a tomato or meat sauce.

6 cups (2 3/4 imperial pints) water
2 teaspoons salt
1 1/2 cups (8 oz) fine polenta

In a thick, heavy saucepan bring the water to the boil with the salt and gradually add the polenta, stirring constantly with a wooden spoon to keep it smooth. Cook over a moderate heat, stirring frequently for about 20 minutes or until the polenta comes away cleanly from the sides of the pan. This produces a thick polenta, suitable for baked, grilled or fried dishes. Use as required. At this stage, the polenta may be turned into a greased baking tray (sheet), left to cool, then cut into squares to be pan-fried in oil. Or it can be turned into a greased cake tin, then turned out to be served with meats, poultry or chicken livers and mushrooms or cut into squares and served warm with freshly grated Parmesan cheese.

Polenta Baked in Tomato Sauce

1 quantity Basic Thick Polenta (opposite page)
1 cup (9 fl oz) Fresh Tomato Sauce (page 184)
Parmesan cheese, freshly grated

Turn the cooked polenta into a greased baking tin approximately 20 cm (8 in) square. When cool, cut into 5 cm (2 in) squares. Place them in a lightly greased shallow ovenproof dish, spoon over the tomato sauce and sprinkle generously with Parmesan cheese. Bake in a moderately hot oven (190°C/375°F) for 30–40 minutes or until golden brown. Serves 6–8.

Risotto with Tomatoes and Basil

About 5 cups (2 imperial pints) chicken stock
75 g (2$^1/_2$ oz) butter
1 tablespoon vegetable or olive oil
1 medium onion, finely chopped
750 g (1$^1/_2$ lb) ripe but firm tomatoes, peeled, seeded
  (see page 130) and chopped
Salt and freshly ground pepper
1$^1/_2$ cups (10 oz) Arborio or short-grain rice
$^3/_4$ cup (3 oz) freshly grated Parmesan
12 fresh basil leaves, shredded

Tip
In northern Italy risotto is one of the specialty dishes and is much loved, but it is a dish that has to be cooked with care. The results justify the attention to detail. Do buy the short-grain Arborio rice; long-grain rice is kept for pilafs, the Eastern rice dish.

Bring the stock to a gentle simmer in a pan. In another large heavy-based pan, melt half the butter with the oil and onion and sauté gently until pale golden. Add the tomatoes, salt and pepper. Cook, stirring every now and then, for 5 minutes. Add the rice and stir a few times to coat thoroughly. Add a ladle of stock and stir constantly to keep the rice from sticking to the pan.

Continue this process, adding a ladle of stock at a time and stirring until the rice has absorbed the liquid and is tender. Add the remaining butter, cheese and basil, stir and taste for salt and pepper. Serve as soon as it is made. Serves 6.

Summer Pasta Salad

Summer Pasta Salad is something between a hot pasta dish and a warm salad, a combination that is increasingly popular. The vegetables should be cooked tender-crisp and retain their fresh, bright colour.

Pasta salads are one of the most interesting offerings as a light summer meal. Almost any pasta shape or variety—tomato, spinach—can be used and almost any young summer vegetable. To round it off, serve with crusty garlic bread or Bruschetta (page 49).

1 bunch of asparagus

125 g (4 oz) snow peas (mangetout) or sugar peas

125 g (4 oz) tender green beans

1 carrot

4 small zucchini (courgettes) or button squash

250 g (8 oz) pasta shapes (fusilli, conchiglie, farfalle, bucatini, gemelli, ruote, etc.)

¹/₂ cup (2 oz) freshly grated Parmesan cheese

DRESSING

1 tablespoon tarragon vinegar

1 garlic clove, crushed

2 teaspoons tarragon or Dijon-style mustard

3 tablespoons good olive oil

*C*ut the asparagus into short finger lengths, discarding any tough bottoms. Remove the strings from the peas. Cut the beans in two or three. Slice the carrot and zucchini obliquely.

In a saucepan of boiling salted water, cook each variety of vegetable separately for 1–2 minutes. When each vegetable is tender crisp, lift it out with a slotted spoon and cool under running tap water. Snow and sugar peas will take only 1 minute, green beans 2 minutes.

Prepare the dressing in a small bowl. Beat together the vinegar, garlic and mustard with a fork or small whisk, then gradually beat in the olive oil, drop by drop, to create a thick emulsion. Give the mixture a quick beating before adding it to the salad.

Bring a large pan of salted water to the boil, drop in the pasta and cook according to the packet instructions or until it is *al dente*—firm to the bite. Drain, and while it is still hot add it to the vegetable mixture along with the dressing, tossing the mixture until it is well combined. Serve the pasta warm or at room temperature with the Parmesan cheese. Serves 4.

Esau's Soup

An old biblical dish, very simple but good and nourishing too. Use either full cream milk or one of the light, low-fat milks.

> *1 cup (6 oz) brown lentils*
> *1 onion, stuck with 4 whole cloves*
> *1 bay leaf*
> *600 ml (2 1/4 cups, 1 imperial pint) milk, scalded*
> *Salt and freshly ground pepper*
> *30 g (1 oz) butter*
> *Croutons, fried in butter*

*S*oak the lentils in water for several hours. Change the water to cover and cook with the onion and bay leaf until the lentils are tender. Remove the onion and bay leaf. Force the lentils though a food mill or purée them in a food processor, using a little of the liquid if necessary.

Combine the purée and the hot milk. Cook the soup, stirring frequently, without letting it get too thick. Season with salt and freshly ground pepper.

Just before serving, add the butter; as soon as it melts, serve. Garnish with croutons. Serves 4.

Roman-Style Semolina Gnocchi

Roman-style Semolina Gnocchi. The finest ground semolina is cooked and spread on a dish and allowed to cool, then cut into squares or rounds. They can be fried in butter and served with cheese or mixed with honey, nuts and raisins, or they can be cooked au gratin, as in this recipe.

1 small onion, peeled and halved
¹/₂ bay leaf
3³/₄ cups (1³/₄ imperial pints) milk
³/₄ cup (4 oz) semolina
1¹/₂ teaspoons salt
Freshly ground pepper to taste
³/₄ cup (3 oz) freshly grated Parmesan cheese
60 g (2 oz) butter
A little dry mustard

Put the onion in a heavy pan with the bay leaf and milk. Bring very slowly to the boil to allow the milk to take on the flavour of the seasonings. Remove the seasonings and stir in the semolina, gradually. Add the salt and pepper and, stirring frequently, cook over a gentle heat until the mixture is very thick, about 15 minutes.

170

Remove from the heat, stir in half the Parmesan cheese, a little of the butter and the dry mustard. Spread out on an oiled baking tray (sheet) to a thickness slightly less than 10 mm ($^3/_8$ in) and allow to cool. When cold, cut into circles with a 5 cm (2 in) pastry (cookie) cutter or in squares with a knife.

Preheat the oven to hot (200°C/400°F).

Have ready a well-buttered shallow gratin dish, and in it arrange the circles or squares of gnocchi, slightly overlapping. Sprinkle with the remaining cheese. Melt the remaining butter and drizzle it over the top. Bake for 20–30 minutes until the top is brown and crisp. Serve immediately, while still bubbling, either as it is or accompanied with Fresh Tomato Sauce (page 184). Serves 4.

Herbed Spinach Roulade

This light soufflé-type mixture is baked in a Swiss roll tin (jelly roll pan) or paper case, filled with a savoury mixture, then lightly rolled. Roulades are delicious and deceptively simple to make.

> *500 g (1 lb) spinach or silver beet (Swiss chard)*
> *4 eggs, separated*
> *3 tablespoons chopped parsley*
> *1 teaspoon each oregano, thyme and chives, chopped*
> *Salt and pepper*
> *Grated nutmeg*
> MUSHROOM SAUCE
> *2 tablespoons butter*
> *4 green shallots (spring onions, scallions), chopped*
> *185 g (6 oz) mushrooms, sliced*
> *1 tablespoon plain (all-purpose) flour*
> *$^3/_4$ cup (6 $^1/_2$ fl oz) milk*
> *Salt and pepper to taste*
> *1 tablespoon grated Parmesan cheese*

*B*utter and line a 30 × 25 cm (12 × 10 in) Swiss roll tin (jelly roll pan) with baking paper smeared with butter. Preheat the oven to moderately hot (190°C/375°F).

Wash the spinach well and trim off the stalks; if using silver beet, remove all white stalks. With just the water clinging to the leaves after washing, cook the spinach in a large covered saucepan for 5 minutes. Drain thoroughly and squeeze dry, then chop finely.

Place the chopped spinach in a bowl with the egg yolks, herbs, salt, pepper and nutmeg to taste. Mix well. Whisk the egg whites until stiff, and fold them into the mixture. Spread the mixture into the prepared tin. Bake for 10–15 minutes or until risen and firm.

Mushroom sauce. Heat the butter in a saucepan, add the shallots and fry until they are soft. Add the mushrooms and fry for 2–3 minutes. Stir in the flour, then gradually stir in the milk. Add salt and pepper, and simmer for 2–3 minutes.

Sprinkle the grated cheese over a sheet of greaseproof (waxed) paper. Turn the roulade out onto the paper and peel off the lining paper. Spread with the filling and, with the long side facing you, roll up like a Swiss roll. Serve immediately, cut in slices, a little on the diagonal. Serves 4 as a main course.

Mung Bean Dhal

One of India's best known foods, rich in protein, dhal is made with either mung beans, the dark green beans used for bean sprouts, or green split peas. Serve as part of a vegetarian meal with a rice dish.

> *1 cup (6 oz) mung beans or split peas, picked over and rinsed*
> *1 tablespoon curry powder*
> *1 teaspoon salt*
> *1 whole hot chilli*
> *¹/₄ cup (4¹/₂ fl oz) vegetable oil*
> *2 medium onions, sliced thinly*

Soak the beans in water to cover for several hours. Bring to the boil and add the curry powder, salt and chilli. Cover and cook for 1¹/₂ hours or until the beans are tender. Remove the chilli and discard. Purée the beans in an electric blender or push them through a coarse sieve. A little more liquid may be added if necessary.

Heat half the oil in a frying pan (skillet) and fry the onion until golden brown. Spoon the dhal into a serving dish, garnish with the fried onion and drizzle with the remaining oil. Serves 4.

Mixed Vegetable Curry

An introduction to the pleasures of Indian cooking usually includes delectable mixed vegetable dishes.

2 tablespoons ghee or clarified butter or peanut oil
2 onions, chopped
6 garlic cloves, chopped
A 5 cm (2 in) piece of fresh ginger, peeled and chopped
4 cardamom pods, split
A 2 cm (1 in) piece of cinnamon
4 cloves
1 teaspoon turmeric powder
3 teaspoons poppy seeds
Chilli powder
3 green or red chillies (chili peppers), chopped
1/2 cup diced carrots
1 cup (6 oz) peas
1 cup cauliflower florets
3 potatoes, boiled and peeled, and cut in cubes
2 large tomatoes, peeled (see page 130) and quartered
Coriander (Chinese parsley) and mint leaves
Salt

Heat the ghee in a heavy saucepan and fry the onions until crisp and golden. This should be done slowly; it takes a long time and onions must not burn. Add the garlic and ginger with the cardamom pods, cinnamon, cloves, turmeric, poppy seeds, chilli powder to taste and chillies. Fry for 5 minutes, stirring all the time. Add the carrots and peas and cook slowly for 5 minutes. Add the cauliflower and potatoes, cook until the cauliflower in tender, about 5 minutes. Add the tomatoes and cook a further 3 minutes. Add a few chopped coriander and mint leaves. Season to taste with salt. Serves 4.

Garnish. Slice an onion finely and fry in ghee or peanut oil until golden brown; remove. Split 10 almonds into halves and fry until golden, then remove. Fry 2 tablespoons raisins until plump, about 1 minute. Sprinkle over vegetables.

Baked Ricotta

1.5 kg (3 lb) fresh ricotta
Salt and freshly ground pepper
1 egg, beaten
Virgin olive oil

Baked Ricotta served at room temperature with a well-flavoured capsicum (sweet pepper) salad makes a lovely dish for a casual lunch. Offer toasted bruschetta or focaccia; the crisp texture goes well with the soft cheese and salad.

Turn the ricotta into a colander set over a shallow bowl. Cover with plastic wrap (cling film) or aluminum foil and leave to drain overnight in the refrigerator. Turn into a bowl and season the ricotta with salt to taste (about 1 teaspoon) and a good grinding of pepper. Mix well.

Pack the cheese into a buttered loaf pan. Bake in a preheated moderate over (180°C/350°F) for approximately 1 hour. Remove from the oven and allow to cool for about 15 minutes. Turn out onto a small ovenproof dish. Brush with the beaten egg, return to the oven and cook until the egg cooks to a rich golden crust. Invert the loaf pan over the ricotta (if cheese is very fresh it may crack) and allow to cool to room temperature.

Serve cut into slices drizzled with a little virgin olive oil, accompanied with a well-flavoured salad or a salad of skinned red and yellow capsicums (see recipe on page 166). Offer crusty bread or a good sliced rye bread. Serves 6–8.

Khichri

¹/₂ cup (3 oz) yellow split peas, picked over and rinsed
2 cups (10 oz) long-grain rice
60 g (2 oz) ghee or clarified butter or vegetable oil
2 small onions, sliced thinly
6 small onions, peeled and left whole
1 teaspoon salt
1 teaspoon ground cumin
1 teaspoon garam masala (Indian spice mix)
1 garlic clove, crushed
A 1 cm (¹/₂ in) slice of fresh ginger, peeled and chopped finely

Soak the split peas in 1¹/₂ cups (13¹/₂ fl oz) of water overnight. Drain well. Soak the rice in a bowl containing 5 cups (2¹/₄ imperial pints) of water for 30 minutes. Drain well.

Melt the ghee in a heavy-based saucepan and add half the sliced onions. Cook over a moderately high heat for 10–15 minutes or until crisp and golden.

Lift out the onion and drain on kitchen paper towels and set aside. Add the 6 whole onions to the fat with the remaining sliced onion. Sauté gently until they are golden. Add the rice, split peas, salt, cumin, garam masala, garlic and ginger. Reduce the heat to moderately low and cook the mixture for 7–10 minutes, stirring constantly, until the rice and peas are coated with ghee. Add 3^1/$_2$ cups (1^1/$_2$ imperial pints) of water, bring to the boil and cook over a moderate heat, stirring, for 4 minutes. Cover the pan with aluminium foil and a tight-fitting lid, and simmer for 25 minutes. Serve on a heated dish garnished with the reserved onion. Serves 4–6.

Saffron Pilaf

An Indian pilaf is one of the most satisfying dishes. It is often the main attraction on the table, for not only does it look appetising but its fragrant smell stimulates the appetite. It goes well with spiced foods or grilled meats or poultry.

Tip
Saffron—the stamens of the crocus—is a marvellous flavouring. It is expensive but to my mind, well worth the cost. Turmeric may be substituted; use twice as much turmeric as you would saffron and you'll get a good yellow rice.

60 g (2 oz) butter or ghee
1 onion, finely chopped
2 cups (10 oz) long-grain rice
Salt
8 peppercorns
2 whole cloves
4 cardamom pods, bruised
4 cups (1^3/$_4$ imperial pints) chicken stock (page 68)
^{1}/$_2$ teaspoon saffron
125 g (4 oz) unsalted cashews
60 g (2 oz) ghee
^{2}/$_3$ cup (2–3 oz) raisins

Melt the butter in a heavy saucepan and add the onion. Allow it to cook gently until soft and golden. Stir in the rice, add the salt, peppercorns, cloves and cardamom. Heat the stock with the saffron and pour it onto the rice. Stir the rice and allow the liquid to come to the boil. Cover the saucepan tightly and lower the heat.

Cook the rice gently for about 18–20 minutes or until all liquid is absorbed and the rice is tender. Remove the lid and allow the rice to cook for a further few minutes to release the steam. Fry the cashews in ghee for a few minutes until golden. Add the raisins and cook for a further 2 minutes.

Spoon the pilaf onto a hot serving dish. Remove the spices if you wish. Fork the rice up and scatter the cashews and raisins over it. Serves 6.

Lemon Rice

I like to use the fragrant long-grain basmati rice for this dish. It has a lovely fresh taste and goes well with many spiced foods as well as grilled poultry, meat or fish.

1 cup (5 oz) long-grain rice, well washed
1/2 teaspoon ground turmeric
2 tablespoons ghee or unsalted (sweet) butter
2 tablespoons cashew nuts
1/2 teaspoon mustard seeds
4 curry leaves (optional)
2 green chillies (chili peppers), seeds removed and chopped
A pinch of salt
1/2 cup (4 1/2 fl oz) coconut milk
2 tablespoons lemon juice
Fresh coriander (Chinese parsley), chopped

Drain the rice and cook it in 1 cup (9 fl oz) of water, which should be boiling and tinted with the turmeric. When three-quarters cooked, remove from the heat, drain and set aside.

Heat the ghee and fry the cashews, mustard seeds, curry leaves and green chillies for 3 minutes. Add the rice and salt, and stir for 2 minutes. Add the coconut milk and lemon juice. Cover and cook on low heat for a further 5–10 minutes. Toss lightly with a fork, then lightly toss in the coriander.

Couscous with Vegetables

500 g (1 lb) packaged couscous grains
75 g (2¹/₂ oz) butter
2 garlic cloves, crushed
1 teaspoon salt
1 teaspoon cumin
Freshly ground black pepper
¹/₂ teaspoon ground ginger
1 bay leaf
2 tablespoons tomato paste (concentrate)
2 fresh red chillies
4 medium carrots, scraped, cut into quarters lengthwise then
  across into 5 cm (2 in) lengths
4 zucchini (courgettes), cut the same size as the carrots
3 large tomatoes, peeled (see page 130) and quartered
500 g (1 lb) potatoes, peeled and cut into 5 cm (2 in) lengths
Water
Harissa sauce (see below)

Couscous is one of the great dishes of North Africa. The couscous grains are a type of fine semolina made from crushed wheat. This vegetarian version is sensationally good. The steamed couscous is served with tender vegetables, and the spiced buttery juices are spooned over. Harissa Sauce provides a touch of fire.

Cover the couscous with cold water, stir with the fingers and drain. Let the couscous stand for 15 minutes to allow it to swell. Repeat this process.

Meanwhile, melt 60 g (2 oz) of the butter in a large, heavy saucepan, add the garlic and sauté for 1–2 minutes until softened. Add the salt, cumin, pepper, ginger, bay leaf and tomato paste and stir well. Add the whole chillies, carrots, zucchini and tomatoes and just enough water to cover, then bring to the boil.

Place the swollen couscous in a colander or steamer lined with a fine tea towel which will fit snugly into the top of the pan. Place this over the vegetables, cover well and simmer gently for about 40 minutes—the couscous grains should not touch the liquid. After 20 minutes, add the remaining butter to the couscous and add the potatoes to the vegetables. Fluff up the couscous occasionally with a fork during cooking.

To serve, pile the couscous onto a large serving platter, make a well in the centre and pile the vegetables into the centre, or make a peak of the couscous and arrange vegetables around the base; spoon over the juices from the vegetables. Serve immediately with harissa sauce. Serves 6.

Harissa sauce. Combine 2 tablespoons each of ground chilli powder, ground cumin, olive oil and tomato paste and 1 teaspoon of salt, and mix well. Store in an airtight container or screw-top jar.

Sauces

A sauce is often the making of a dish, adding delicacy or piquancy to the food with which it is served. The right sauce can make an otherwise bland dish interesting, and often by contrast making two flavours blend into one whole.

For many of us, classic mayonnaise, béchamel and hollandaise have become part of life. A simple salad of eggs mayonnaise is almost the first dish to disappear at one of my picnics or buffet parties. Béchamel I use for many dishes; the rich buttery hollandaise, like béarnaise, is a treat served on rare occasions and used very lightly.

While I have included recipes for a few of the standard sauces, I have also included some of the newer ones. A recipe for yoghurt mayonnaise (eggless) is great news for dieters or those on low-cholesterol diets, for it really tastes good while not being so rich as traditional mayonnaise.

Sauces are one of the easiest ways to make food interesting. Remember it is the actual flavour of the ingredients used which is important to the sauce— nothing else can give the same taste and appearance. So make sure everything you use is of the best quality and in the best condition.

Mayonnaise is one of the best and most useful sauces. It adds lustre and interest to eggs, potatoes, fish and shellfish and countless other foods. Rémoulade is an another exquisite sauce. Like mayonnaise, it enhances eggs, potatoes, shellfish and, if you eat them, pig's trotters.

Béchamel Sauce

Béchamel is the classic white sauce and has many uses. It is the basis of many deliciously flavoured sauces for a great variety of dishes. While egg yolks and cream may be added to enrich the basic recipe, they do add unwanted fats and cholesterol. Instead, whip in 2 tablespoons of dry powdered milk.

1¹/₂ cups (13¹/₂ fl oz) milk
1 bay leaf
1 whole onion or 2 spring onions (scallions), chopped
5 whole peppercorns
30 g (1 oz) butter
2 tablespoons plain (all-purpose) flour
Salt and white pepper

$\mathcal{H}$eat the milk slowly in a saucepan on low heat to scalding point with the bay leaf, onion and peppercorns. Remove from heat, cover and let it infuse for 7–8 minutes. Melt the butter in a small heavy saucepan, draw away from heat, stir in the flour, cook for about 1 minute, then add the strained and slightly cooled milk. Stir continuously over medium heat until boiling. Simmer 2–3 minutes. Add salt and pepper to taste. Makes about 1¹/₂ cups (13¹/₂ fl oz).

Mornay Sauce. Beat 2 tablespoons of grated sharp (mature) cheese into 1 quantity of béchamel sauce and add 2–3 teaspoons of French mustard, such as Grey Poupon from Dijon, and extra salt and pepper to taste. If the sauce has to be heated, do not boil. Serve with pasta, cooked poultry or fish. Use to coat food that is to be reheated in the oven or under a grill (broiler). If the food is to be served *au gratin*, top with a little grated cheese and/or breadcrumbs and brown under the grill or in the oven.

White Butter Sauce (Sauce Beurre Blanc)

This creamy, butter-coloured sauce is actually nothing but warm butter flavoured with shallots, wine or vinegar, salt and pepper. It is much in evidence in top restaurants. Use it with baked or steamed fish, shellfish, asparagus, chicken, cauliflower, poached eggs and warm vegetable mousses and terrines. Make half the quantity if this amount is too much.

3 shallots (spring onions, scallions), finely chopped
30 g (1 oz) butter
1 tablespoon water
¹/₂ cup (4¹/₂ fl oz) dry white wine
Freshly ground pepper
250 g (8 oz) unsalted butter, chilled and cut into small cubes
¹/₂ teaspoon balsamic vinegar

Cook the shallots gently in the 30 g of butter until soft. Add the water, wine and a grinding of pepper. Boil until reduced to about 2 tablespoons of liquid. Remove from the heat and beat in 2 pieces of butter with a wire whisk. Return to low heat and beat in the remaining butter, one piece at a time; the sauce will thicken to the consistency of cream. Season to taste with salt and balsamic vinegar. Strain through a fine sieve. Use warm. Do not reheat this sauce, as it may become thin and oily. Serves 6–8.

Hollandaise Sauce

2 egg yolks
¹/₂ cup (4 oz) butter, melted
1 tablespoon boiling water
2 teaspoons lemon juice
¹/₄ teaspoon salt
A dash of cayenne pepper

Put the egg yolks in the top of a double boiler and beat slightly. Slowly stir in the butter. Add the boiling water gradually, beating constantly. Cook; stirring, over hot water until thickened; water in the double boiler should not touch the top pan. Remove from heat, stir in the lemon juice, salt and cayenne pepper. Cover and stand over warm water until ready to serve. Serve with cooked vegetables or fish. Makes about ³/₄ cup (6¹/₂ fl oz).

Fresh Tomato Sauce

This light, fresh-tasting sauce is very versatile. Serve it with vegetables, sautéed veal, roast beef, pasta, gnocchi and chicken liver mousse.

1 tablespoon olive oil
1 garlic clove, peeled and crushed
1 spring onion (scallion), chopped
4 medium tomatoes, peeled, seeded and juiced (see page 130)
    and chopped
1 teaspoon tomato paste (concentrate)
A bouquet garni (page 31)
²/₃ cup (6 fl oz) chicken stock (page 68)

From the top: luscious Mayonnaise, rich with eggs and olive oil; Yoghurt Mayonnaise, eggless with little oil, the one to use when on a low-cholesterol regime; light, fresh-tasting Tomato Sauce; and Green Sauce, used with pasta, boiled meats, chilled seafood and some salads.

Heat the olive oil in a saucepan, add the garlic and spring onion and cook for 2–3 minutes. Add the tomatoes, tomato paste, bouquet garni and stock; cook over gentle heat for 15 minutes. Remove the bouquet garni and purée the sauce in an electric blender or food processor, or push through a sieve, or leave chunky. Check the seasoning. If the sauce is too thin, reduce by boiling. Makes about 2 cups (18 fl oz).

Chunky Tomato and Basil Sauce

This is a very fresh-tasting sauce; the tomatoes are just heated through. Serve this sauce with pasta or gnocchi or as an accompaniment to grilled poultry or meats.

3 tablespoons olive oil
4 firm ripe tomatoes, peeled and seeded (see page 130) and cut
    into chunks
1 teaspoon Dijon mustard
1 garlic clove, peeled and crushed
Salt and pepper
1 tablespoon chopped spring onions (scallions)
2 tablespoons chopped parsley
8 fresh basil leaves, shredded

Heat the oil in a saucepan, add all the other ingredients and cook, covered, over gentle heat, about 15–20 minutes. More fresh basil leaves may be scissored into the sauce just before serving. Makes about 2 cups (18 fl oz).

Green Sauce

Tip

Green Sauce is
excellent over boiled
potatoes, over boiled
rice to make a salad, or
with pasta. This
quantity of sauce is
sufficient for 125 g
(4 oz) of pasta or 2
cups of cooked rice. It
is also served with
chilled seafood, hot
boiled beef and some
salads.

1 tablespoon chopped capers
1 tablespoon chopped parsley
1 tablespoon chopped watercress or basil
1 garlic clove, chopped
1/4 teaspoon salt and freshly ground pepper to taste
6 tablespoons olive oil
3 tablespoons lemon juice

*I*n a small bowl mash with a fork or beat the capers; add the parsley, watercress, garlic, salt and pepper and continue beating until it forms a smooth paste. Add the oil, a tablespoon at a time, beating well after each addition until the oil is absorbed. Add the lemon juice slowly, beating well all the time. Makes about 1 cup (9 fl oz).

Mustard and Dill Sauce

Tip

Mustard sauces add
great interest to
poached fish and
chicken. This sauce is
particularly good with
Gravlax (page 205).

4 tablespoons highly seasoned prepared Dijon mustard
1 teaspoon dry mustard
3 tablespoons sugar
2 tablespoons white vinegar
4 tablespoons vegetable oil
3 tablespoons chopped fresh dill

*M*ix mustards, sugar and vinegar to a paste. Using a whisk, gradually beat in the oil until it forms a thick emulsion. Stir in the dill. Keep refrigerated in a tightly covered container and whisk before using. The sauce will keep for 3 or 4 days in the refrigerator. Makes about $^{3}/_{4}$ cup ($6^{1}/_{2}$ fl oz).

Coriander Chutney

This bright, herby green chutney is a good accompaniment to little meatballs or fried fish, and it makes a good dip for crudités.

2 bunches fresh coriander (Chinese parsley) leaves
1 small bunch mint leaves
6 spring onions (scallions), cut into short lengths
1 tablespoon grated fresh ginger
1 garlic clove, peeled and crushed
1 teaspoon salt
1 teaspoon sugar
1 tablespoon lemon juice
$^1/_2$ cup ($4^1/_2$ fl oz) natural (plain) yoghurt

Put all the ingredients except the yoghurt into an electric blender or food processor fitted with a steel blade. Blend until finely chopped. If you don't have a blender, then everything will have to be finely chopped. Add the yoghurt and whirl in the blender only long enough to mix through. Serve in a small bowl. Makes about 1 cup (9 fl oz).

Pesto (Genoese Basil Sauce)

2 cups fresh basil leaves
2 tablespoons chopped pine nuts or walnuts
2 garlic cloves, mashed
A pinch of coarse salt
$^1/_4$ cup (1 oz) grated Parmesan cheese, preferably combined
*   with 2 tablespoons romano or pecorino cheese*
$^1/_2$ cup ($4^1/_2$ fl oz) oil, preferably olive

This sauce is easily made in a food processor fitted with a steel blade or in an electric blender (done in several batches). Combine the basil, nuts, garlic and salt, and grind in a food processor or with a pestle, crushing the ingredients to form a paste. Add the grated cheese and grind again until the mixture is blended. Add the oil and blend it into the mixture. The mixture should have the consistency of a smooth paste, similar to mayonnaise. Makes about 1 cup (9 fl oz).

Tip
Generally, 2–3 tablespoons of pesto are sufficient for four servings of pasta, and only 1 tablespoon in soups or on potatoes. When serving pesto with the grated cheese already incorporated into it, do not serve additional cheese or you will be disturbing the balance of flavours.

Vinaigrette (French Dressing)

Vinaigrette varies with its use. For a light, delicate salad, mix the dressing just enough to create a liaison; for a more robust dressing, add the oil drop by drop and the mixture will thicken. Garlic and fresh herbs also may be added.

> 2 tablespoons good vinegar
> 1/4 teaspoon salt
> 1 teaspoon French (Dijon) mustard
> Freshly ground black pepper
> 8 tablespoons olive oil

Tip
When adding herbs to vinaigrette it is best to sprinkle half of the freshly chopped herbs over the salad, adding the remaining herbs to the dressing. Tarragon, basil, chives and parsley add their own distinctive flavour. They may be used separately or in combination. One or two spoonfuls of chopped herbs are sufficient.

*P*ut the vinegar into a small bowl with the salt, pepper and mustard. Mix well with a fork or whisk and slowly add the oil, beating until the mixture thickens slightly. If the dressing tastes sharp, add more oil or a pinch of caster (superfine) sugar. If the dressing is too oily for your taste, add more salt. An alternative way is to combine all the ingredients in a glass jar, cover and shake well until the mixture thickens. Makes about $^3/_4$ cup ($6^1/_2$ fl oz).

Garlic. There are several ways to add garlic to your dressing. If you like a pungent dressing, crush 1 or 2 cloves of garlic to a paste with salt, add the vinegar and other seasonings and then the oil. You can chop garlic and add it to the finished dressing for a more rustic salad. For a more delicate flavour, bruise the peeled garlic and steep it in the vinegar for 1–2 hours. The vinegar brings out a more delicate flavour of the garlic, while oil brings out the stronger flavour.

The importance of good oil cannot be overstressed. From the deep green first pressing of hand-picked olives, the extra virgin olive oil, used to drizzle over bread or a special dish, to the excellent lighter oils, there is an oil for every culinary need. Make Vinaigrette just as you need it; a light whisk in a small bowl is all it takes.

Hot Vinaigrette

> 4 tablespoons olive oil
> 4 tablespoons white wine vinegar or $^1/_2$ wine and $^1/_2$ balsamic
>   or sherry vinegar
> 1 tablespoon finely chopped green shallots (spring onions)
> Ground black pepper
> 1 teaspoon Dijon mustard
> 1 tablespoon chopped parsley

*H*eat the oil, vinegar, shallots and a fresh grinding of pepper. Whisk in the mustard, add the parsley and serve. Spoon over warm salad and toss lightly. Makes about $^1/_2$ cup ($4^1/_2$ fl oz).

Mayonnaise

Homemade mayonnaise with its sumptuous texture and fresh, subtle flavour is one of the great sauces. It takes only about 10 minutes to make by hand once you have mastered the technique and is faster still with a food processor.

2 egg yolks
1/2 teaspoon salt
A pinch of white pepper
1/2 teaspoon dry mustard
2 teaspoons vinegar or lemon juice
1 cup (9 fl oz) olive oil, salad oil or a mixture of both

*H*ave all the ingredients at room temperature. Warm the eggs and oil in hot water if they are cold. Rinse out a mixing bowl with hot water and wrap a damp cloth round the base to keep it steady.

Place the egg yolks, seasonings and 1 teaspoon of the vinegar or lemon juice in the bowl and beat with a wire whisk to combine. When they are thick, begin to add the oil, drop by drop, whisking constantly and incorporating each addition thoroughly before adding the next. As the mixture thickens, the oil flow can be increased to a steady thin stream, but you must keep beating constantly. Stop pouring every now and then to check that the oil is well blended. If the mayonnaise should show signs of breaking or curdling, beat in a teaspoon or two of boiling water before adding more oil. When all the oil is incorporated, beat in the remaining vinegar or lemon juice. Makes about 1 cup (9 fl oz).

Mayonnaise made in a food processor or blender. Place one egg yolk and one whole egg, seasonings and 1 teaspoon of the vinegar or lemon juice in the bowl and blend for a few seconds. With the motor running, add the oil gradually, ensuring that each addition has been absorbed before adding more. When all the oil has been incorporated, add the remaining vinegar or lemon juice.

Garlic Mayonnaise or Aïoli. Crush 2 or 3 cloves of garlic to a paste with salt in a bowl. Add the egg yolks and seasonings and mix until thick, then add the oil as for the basic recipe. Do not add too much vinegar. Serve with boiled meats, fish and cold cooked or raw vegetables.

Rémoulade Sauce. To 1/2 cup (4 1/2 fl oz) of mayonnaise add 1 good teaspoon of French (Dijon) mustard and 1 tablespoon each of chopped gherkins, capers and parsley, and a teaspoon of tarragon all mixed together. When thoroughly combined, stir in a few drops of anchovy essence (extract). Serve with egg salads, fish, prawns (shrimp) and pig's trotters. Makes about 1/2 cup (4 1/2 fl oz).

Tip
If either hand-made or machine-made mayonnaise refuses to thicken or if it curdles, take a clean, warmed bowl and beat an egg yolk with 1/2 teaspoon of vinegar, then gradually beat in the curdled mayonnaise very slowly at first and then more quickly.

Crudités, an arrangement of crisp, young fresh vegetables, raw or blanched, is served with the garlicky mayonnaise Aïoli.

191

Yoghurt Mayonnaise

This is sometimes referred to as eggless mayonnaise. It is the one to use when dieting, or if you are on a low-cholesterol diet. I use it because I like it as a change from true mayonnaise.

> *3 teaspoons Dijon mustard*
> *1¹/₂ tablespoons olive oil*
> *³/₄ cup (6¹/₂ fl oz) natural (plain) low-fat yoghurt*
> *1 tablespoon lemon juice*
> *Salt and freshly ground pepper*

*P*lace the mustard in a mixing bowl, add the oil gradually, beating vigorously with a fork or whisk. Blend in the yoghurt. Add the remaining ingredients until the mixture is smooth. Refrigerate until required. Makes about 1 cup (9 fl oz).

Guacamole

This famous dish of mashed and seasoned avocado has many uses. It may be piled in a bowl, surrounded by fresh crisp vegetables and used as a dip. Little triangles of fried tortillas or corn chips are often served with guacamole—just scoop up the spread with the crunchy bits. Guacamole may be served as a sauce with fish, or over poached chicken breast, grilled (broiled) steak or with tacos. The little green chillies (chili peppers) are available canned in specialty sections of large grocery departments and supermarkets, some health food shops and delicatessens.

> *1 large avocado, halved and pitted, then mashed*
> *1 small onion, finely chopped*
> *1 tablespoon canned green chillies (chili peppers), seeded and*
> *   chopped, or Tabasco sauce to taste*
> *3 fresh tomatoes, peeled (see page 130) and chopped*
> *1 tablespoon fresh coriander (Chinese parsley), chopped*
> *Salt and freshly ground black pepper*

*C*ombine all ingredients well—guacamole can be made mild or very hot with chilli peppers or Tabasco. Cover with plastic wrap (cling film) and chill until ready to use. Makes about 1 cup (9 fl oz).

Ingredients for making Guacamole, the Mexican avocado sauce that is good with fish and chicken. It is often served as a dip with corn chips or fried tortillas, and of course it goes with tacos.

Tip
Burying the avocado seed (pit) in the guacamole will prevent the sauce from discolouring.

193

Fish

Those who love fish envy people who have a fisherman in the family, someone who can be relied on to return home with a successful catch. Nothing equals the flavour of fish that is caught and cooked the same day.

Fortunately, fast fishing boats with fishermen skilled at looking after their catch, refrigerated trucks, air cargo and modern processing and freezing have improved to the point where the fish we buy is almost as good as freshly caught fish. We can enjoy fish even when we are hundreds of kilometres inland.

Whether your choose a rich, oily fish, a finer fleshed white fish, a fresh mountain trout or an expensive shellfish, there are dozens of ways to cook it. The main warning: it is a crime to overcook fish. Fish is easy to cook, but it's also easy to spoil.

Barbecued Red Mullet. Each little fish is brushed with oil, wrapped in grape vine leaves, fresh if available, and barbecued over glowing coals. Sardines and other small fish may be treated this way.

Grilled Fish

Potato cakes: Arrange 2 peeled and finely sliced potatoes in overlapping layers to make a small circle, building up to about 3 layers. Make 4 separate 'cakes'. Heat a tablespoon each of olive oil and butter in a frying pan (skillet) and lift the cakes into the sizzling pan. Fry gently until golden; turn carefully to cook the other side. A lovely garnish for grilled fish, steak or poultry.

*T*he secret of success with cutlets or steaks (slices) or thick fillets of fish is to grill (broil) them on one side only, in the grill pan itself or on a metal tray—never use the grilling (broiling) rack. The point is that the heat striking down on the metal makes it very hot, so the fish is also cooked from underneath.

Fish cooks much quicker than many of us realise. An average steak about 2 cm (1 in) thick cooks in 8 minutes. A thinner fillet will be cooked in 4–5 minutes, depending on its thickness. Thick fillets may be slashed, for even cooking.

Heat the grill pan—or use the grilling rack topped with aluminium foil (turn the edges up to catch the juices). Melt 15 g ($^1/_2$ oz) of butter (or use 1 tablespoon of oil, preferably olive oil) per steak in the grill pan. Season with salt and pepper and turn in the melted butter or oil to coat. During grilling, baste once or twice with the buttery juices in the pan. For a herby taste, sprinkle with a few fresh snipped chives or parsley halfway through cooking. Reduce heat if necessary. Transfer to a heated serving dish.

Small whole flat fish can be grilled the same way. Other whole fish are grilled on both sides. If the fish is thick, make a few slashes through the thicker part, so that it cooks as quickly as the thinner part.

Poached Fish

Grilled Fish Steaks. The fish steaks or fillets are grilled (broiled) on one side only; if thick, the fillets are slashed for even cooking. Pictured is a fillet of an exotic reef fish, red emperor, served here with steamed mixed vegetables and a thin, crisp potato cake.

*G*entle simmering in a well-flavoured liquid is good for all fish, giving moistness to dry fish and flavour to bland fish. Sauces to accompany poached fish can be made from the liquor in which it cooks.

Lower the fish into the liquor (see court-bouillon recipe below) in a saucepan or ovenproof dish. Place a large fish on a strip of aluminium foil; this will help you remove the fish when cooked. Simmer very gently over direct heat, or in a moderately slow oven (160°C/325°F), until the fish flakes easily. Fish must never boil. Atlantic salmon (whole or in cuts) is cooked this way. Allow 15 minutes for every 500 g (1 lb) for whole fish.

Court-bouillon. Court-bouillon is a slightly acid liquor for poaching fish. It is made by simmering together, for 15 minutes, $2^1/_2$ cups (22 fl oz) of white wine and $1^1/_4$ cups (11 fl oz) of water (or $2^1/_2$ cups [22 fl oz] of water and 1 tablespoon of white vinegar) with 1 bay leaf, 2 parsley stalks, a sprig of dill, 4 peppercorns, 1 onion, 2 slices of carrot, 1 celery stick and 1 teaspoon of salt. Strain and cool. Store in the refrigerator or freeze for future use.

Sautéed Fish Meunière

*T*his is the simplest and one of the truly classic ways of preparing fish
fillets. Dip the fillets in milk and dust them lightly with seasoned flour.
Melt a little olive oil and butter in a pan—just enough to cover the base; let it
heat through. Add the fish and cook over brisk heat until it is nicely browned on
one side. Turn and brown it on the other—this should only take about 5 minutes.

Remove the fish to a hot plate. Season and garnish with thin slices of lemon,
add a little more butter to the pan and, when it has melted and turned a golden
nut brown, pour it over the fish. Top with an ample quantity of chopped parsley.

Variations

Amandine. Add thinly sliced (slivered), chopped or whole almonds to the sauté.
Almonds may be sautéed with the fish or separately with extra butter and added
to the hot fish platter. Chopped hazelnuts may be used in the same manner.

Fines herbes. Combine equal quantities of chopped parsley, chives and tarragon
and add to the pan just before pouring the sauce over the fish.

Lemon butter. Remove the fish from the pan, add 45 g (1^1/$_2$ oz) butter and
season. Add 1 tablespoon of lemon juice and 6 paper-thin slices of peeled lemon.
Cook for 2 minutes and use to garnish the fish.

Fish Steaks with Orange

The flavouring of citrus fruits goes well with most white fish.

> *4 fish steaks, weighing about 185 g (6 oz) each*
> *1 tablespoon butter*
> *Salt and freshly ground black pepper*
> *1 orange, ^{1}/$_2$ sliced, ^{1}/$_2$ juiced*
> *1 lemon, ^{1}/$_2$ sliced, ^{1}/$_2$ juiced*

*L*ay the fish in a lightly greased flameproof dish and dot with small pieces
of butter. Season the fish with salt and pepper. Combine the orange and
lemon juices and pour half over the fish. Set the grill (broiler) on high, place the
fish under it and cook for 4–5 minutes.

Remove, pour the remaining juice over the fish and top with the sliced fruit,
then return the fish to the grill and cook for a further 4 minutes or until it is
cooked through and golden. Serve with fresh green vegetables in season or a
tomato salad. Serves 4.

*Fish Steaks with
Orange reminds us
that it is a crime to
overcook fish. It also
reaffirms the old
adage that simplest
things are often best.
Just a few ingredients,
the right few, do
wonders for fresh fish.*

Fish Florentine

This is another classic way of cooking fish fillets. Have the fish, seasoned flour, beaten egg all at the ready and the vegetables and salad that you plan to serve prepared. Cook the fish at the very last moment.

> *750 g (1¹/₂ lb) fish fillets*
> *Plain (all-purpose) flour seasoned with salt and pepper*
> *1 egg, beaten*
> *Light olive oil for frying*

*W*ash the fillets and dry with a clean kitchen paper towel. Dip them into the seasoned flour, for a light coating, then in the beaten egg and again in the flour. Heat 6 mm (¹/₄ in) of oil in a heavy-based frying pan (skillet) and cook the fish gently for about 3–4 minutes on each side until golden brown. Drain on a kitchen paper towel. Serve with tartare sauce or lemon wedges. Serves 4–6.

Barbecued Red Mullet

Tip
This method of cooking is ideal for sardines, which are often seen at the fish market.

These delicious little fish, called *rougets* in France, where they are much prized, mustn't be confused with the similar in appearance yet inferior gurnard. Red mullet are usually about 10 cm (4 in) long and are prepared by slitting the stomach to remove the entrails, except for the liver, which is considered a delicacy by some. Rinse in lightly salted water and dry carefully (as the flesh is delicate) with kitchen paper towels. When I go to the fish market for red mullet, I look for the small ones but will buy larger mullet if that is all there is; they are both good.

> *24 fresh tiny red mullet, or several larger ones, cleaned*
> *Salt and freshly ground pepper*
> *3 tablespoons vegetable or olive oil*
> *24 fresh or preserved vine leaves*
> *3 lemons, quartered*
> *Parsley, chopped*

*P*lace the prepared fish in a bowl, season them lightly with salt and pepper and brush liberally with oil, inside and out. Wrap each fish in a vine leaf and arrange on a rack over glowing coals or under a hot grill (broiler) and cook for 2–3 minutes on each side; 5 minutes each side for larger fish. Arrange on a hot serving platter and garnish with the lemon quarters and a generous sprinkling of parsley. Serves 6.

Grilled Fish Steaks with Balsamic Vinegar

Grilled (broiled) fish responds well to the flavours of good olive oil and one of the specialty vinegars—sherry, tarragon or balsamic—which, though expensive, are well worth it for their wonderful aromatic fragrance.

> *4 snapper, jewfish or other fish steaks cut about 2.5 cm*
>   *(1 in) thick*
> *1 tablespoon olive oil*
> *2 teaspoons balsamic vinegar*
> *Freshly ground pepper*
> *2 teaspoons chopped spring onions (scallions, green shallots)*
> *A dash of Tabasco sauce*

Cover the griller (broiler) pan with aluminium foil, brush with a little of the oil and lay the fish on the foil. Mix the remaining ingredients and use the mixture to brush on the fish steaks. Grill the fish about 5 cm (2 in) from heat, basting, until the fish flakes easily, about 8–10 minutes. Serve with a green vegetable and steamed rice or Fish Potatoes (page 127). Serves 4.

Scampi are not unlike Dublin Bay prawns. Some of the scallops shown here in their shells have orange corals, others do not.

Steamed Fish Coriander

The Chinese have a magical touch with fish. They often steam it almost to the point of being cooked, place the fish on a hot platter, season it in a distinctive way, add a little soy sauce and pour boiling oil over just before taking it to the table. The hot oil finishes the cooking.

1 whole fish (perch or bream)
6–8 green shallots (spring onions, scallions)
4 slices fresh ginger
Fresh coriander (Chinese parsley)
1 cup (9 fl oz) fish stock or water
GARNISH
4 green shallots, shredded
1/2 cup coriander sprigs
6 slices fresh ginger, shredded
4 teaspoons soy sauce
3 tablespoons peanut (groundnut) oil
2 teaspoons sesame oil

Clean, scale and remove the head from the fish (Chinese leave the head on). Slash the fish in its thickest part and lightly salt it inside and out. Slice the green parts of 2 shallots and shred 2 slices of the ginger; place these in the stomach cavity of the fish with some coriander. Lay the remaining shallots, ginger and more coriander on a rack on the bottom of a flameproof dish to form a bed for the fish. Put the fish on top. Add the stock. Cover with aluminium foil or a lid and cook gently over medium heat for about 10–15 minutes.

Remove the fish to a heated serving plate and garnish with the shredded shallots, coriander sprigs, shredded green ginger and soy sauce. Bring the peanut and sesame oils to the boil in a small saucepan, pour this over the fish and serve immediately. Serves 4.

Steamed Fish Fillets with Ginger and Sesame Oil

500 g (1 lb) firm white fish fillets
2 tablespoons vegetable oil
2.5 cm (1 in) piece fresh ginger, cut into thin strips
2 spring onions (green shallots, scallions), cut into matchsticks
1 teaspoon sesame oil
1–2 tablespoons light soy sauce

Arrange the fish fillets in one layer in a microwave cooking dish and cover with plastic or microwave wrap. Cook in the microwave on High for 3 minutes or until just cooked. Remove from the microwave and keep covered.

In a small dish heat the vegetable oil and, when very hot, add the ginger and spring onions. Remove from the microwave and add the sesame oil and soy sauce. Arrange the fish fillets on heated serving plates and spoon over the ginger sauce. Serves 2–4.

Grilled Salmon Steaks

4 salmon steaks, cut 2.5 cm (1 in) thick
$1/2$ teaspoon black pepper, freshly ground
Juice of $1/2$ lemon
60 g (2 oz) Herb Butter (see below)

Put the fish in a glass or earthen dish. Combine the pepper and lemon juice and pour it over the fish. Leave the steaks to marinate for about 15 minutes, turning them several times. Drain them and place them on an oiled grill pan. Cook under a preheated grill (broiler) for 5–6 minutes, or cook on a preheated oiled ribbed grill, allowing the same time but turning once. Remove skin and centre bone from the steaks, if you like, and arrange on 4 individual plates or a serving dish.

Place one or two discs of herb butter on top of each steak. Serve with salad greens and a few steamed potatoes. Serves 4.

Herb Butter. Cream 60 g (2 oz) of butter with 2 tablespoons of chopped parsley, 1 tablespoon of snipped dill and some freshly ground pepper. Gradually beat in 2 teaspoons of lemon juice and 4 drops of Tabasco. Shape into a roll in aluminium foil and chill until firm. Cut the roll into discs as needed.

Gravlax
(Scandinavian Marinated Salmon)

Gravlax is a dish synonymous with Scandinavia. Fresh fish, traditionally salmon, is cured for 3 days before serving.

Gravlax, that wonderful raw salmon dish of Scandinavia, is traditionally prepared with salt, sugar and a big bunch of dill, then cured by being buried in the snow. Modern refrigeration has simplified this procedure.

> *750 g (1¹/₂ lb) fresh salmon or salmon trout fillets*
> *¹/₄ cup (2 oz) sugar*
> *¹/₄ cup (2 oz) coarse salt*
> *1 teaspoon white peppercorns, cracked*
> *A large bunch of fresh dill*
> *1 tablespoon cognac or brandy*
> *1 tablespoon dry white wine*

Place a fillet skin side down on a plate, sprinkle thickly with sugar, salt and cracked pepper, cover with plenty of dill sprigs, and press the seasonings onto the fish. Top with a second fillet of fish, skin side uppermost. Select a ceramic or glass dish just large enough to hold the fish, pour in the cognac or brandy and white wine and place fillets in it. Cover with plastic wrap (cling film), place a 1 kg (2 lb) weight on top and let marinate in the refrigerator for 3 days.

205

Turn the fish every 12 hours, basting with marinade and separating the fillets a little to baste the fish inside.

After 3 days, remove the weight and the plastic wrap. Using a slotted spoon, transfer the fish to a cutting board. Separate the fillets, scrape off the dill and the seasonings and cut the fish on the slant into 6 mm (^{1}/$_4$ in) slices, detaching each slice from the skin. Serve on slices of black bread, topped with a swirl of (dairy) sour cream mixed with mustard and a sprig of dill, or with Mustard and Dill Sauce (page 188). Serves 6–8 as an appetiser.

Poached Salmon Fillets with Butter Sauce

Poached Salmon Fillets with Butter Sauce is one of the most delectable of dishes. The butter sauce is of exquisite finesse and lightness, discreetly flavoured with the reduced stock in which the fish was cooked.

4 salmon fillets or steaks weighing about 185 g (6 oz) each
2 cups (18 fl oz) dry white wine
1 green or golden shallot, finely chopped
90 g (3 oz) butter, cut into dice
Salt and white pepper to taste
3 tablespoons snipped chives, dill or chervil leaves
1 teaspoon sea salt

*P*lace the salmon in a shallow pan and pour over the wine. Heat the wine to the barest simmer and poach the fish, covered, until just cooked, about 6 minutes. Drain the cooking liquid into a pan, add the shallot and reduce to about $^1/_2$ cup ($4^1/_2$ fl oz); strain and reserve. Cover the fish and keep it warm.

To make the sauce, heat the reduced wine liquid over a low heat and whisk the butter a piece at a time into the liquid, using a light, quick action. Continue whisking until all the butter is added; it should remain yellow and creamy without becoming oily. Season with salt and pepper.

To serve, arrange the fish on 4 heated dinner plates, spoon a little sauce over each and garnish generously with chives, dill or chervil. Offer the sea salt separately. Serves 4.

Trout with Ginger

Fresh ginger has a pungent and strong flavour, especially when it is fresh. It is most used in Asian cooking, but it is becoming popular throughout the world as supplies of fresh ginger come onto the market.

4 trout, each weighing about 250–375 g (8–12 oz)
Salt
4 tablespoons milk
$^1/_2$ cup (4 oz) plain (all-purpose) flour seasoned with salt and
   pepper
75 g ($2^1/_2$ oz) butter
A walnut-sized piece of fresh ginger, cut into matchsticks
A bunch of spring onions (scallions), cut into matchsticks
Juice of 1 lemon
Freshly ground black pepper

*G*ut and clean the trout under running cold water, and dry each one carefully. Salt them inside and outside and then moisten them with milk. Roll them in the flour so that they are lightly coated.

Heat the butter in a large, heavy pan, add the trout and fry gently over a medium heat until golden on both sides—the fish should be cooked in 8–10 minutes. Remove them from the pan and keep warm in a serving dish. Fry the ginger in the butter in same pan, increasing the heat, and almost immediately add the spring onions and the lemon juice. Stir all ingredients just for a minute, season with salt and pepper, then pour this sauce over the trout. Serve immediately. Serves 4.

Mediterranean Fish Stew

Based on the famous French bouillabaisse. Any stew containing fresh local fish and shellfish, sweet tomatoes, garlic, fragrant saffron, and olive oil is sure to be a winner. Don't forget the pepper and garlic sauce, called Rouille.

> *2 tablespoons olive oil*
> *1 small onion, chopped*
> *2 celery sticks, sliced*
> *3 garlic cloves, crushed*
> *A large pinch of saffron*
> *4 ripe red tomatoes, peeled (see page 130) and chopped*
> *2 cups (18 fl oz) water*
> *³/₄ cup (6¹/₂ fl oz) dry white wine*
> *Salt and freshly ground pepper and a sprinkling of cayenne*
> *1.5 kg (3 lb) mixed seafood: fish cutlets and fillets, mussels,*
> *   raw prawns (shrimp) and scallops, prepared for cooking*
> *Lemon juice to taste*
> *Parsley, freshly chopped*
> ROUILLE
> *4 garlic cloves, crushed*
> *1 canned pimiento (red pepper)*
> *3 egg yolks*
> *A pinch of saffron*
> *1 cup (9 fl oz) olive oil*

Mediterranean Fish Stew is something fishermen make for themselves after a fishing trip, using the freshest and most varied fish of their catch. It is cooked with care, the flavour and texture of each fish remaining distinct, each being added to the broth at the right moment. I make a rouille to serve with it.

Heat the oil in a heavy pan and sauté the onion gently until soft, about 5 minutes. Add the celery, garlic and saffron, stir for a minute or so and add the tomatoes. Cook, stirring, until thick and pulpy. Add the water, wine and seasonings. Add the prepared seafood in order of thickness and size.

When the fish is tender and whitened, the prawns pink and the mussels open, the seafood is cooked. Taste and add more seasoning if necessary. A little lemon juice can be squeezed over at this point. Garnish with chopped parsley and ladle into bowls. Have a basket of crusty bread on the table and hand around the Rouille for guests to add a spoonful to their stew as desired. Serves 4.

Rouille. Place the garlic in an electric blender or food processor with the pimiento, egg yolks and saffron. Purée until smooth; then, with the machine running, add the olive oil, drop by drop at first and more quickly as the sauce thickens. Spoon into a bowl to serve with the soup.

Squid with Tomato and Peas

Squid (calamari) and cuttlefish are of the same family and are an important part of Mediterranean cooking. This Italian dish makes a super first course, with crusty bread to mop up the juices.

500 g (1 lb) small squid (calamari) or cuttlefish, cleaned,
  prepared and cut into thin strips or squares
1 small onion, sliced
1/2 cup (4 1/2 fl oz) wine vinegar
2 tablespoons olive oil
1 quantity Fresh Tomato Sauce (page 184)
2 cups (12 oz) shelled green peas

Put the pieces of squid or cuttlefish in an earthenware bowl with the onion, vinegar and oil and leave to marinate for 1–2 hours. Heat the tomato sauce in a medium saucepan, add the squid or cuttlefish, thoroughly drained, and the green peas. Cook gently for 20 minutes or until tender; cooking time will depend on size. Serves 4.

Squid (Calamari)

There are many kinds of squid. Some have a very white internal skeleton known as a cuttlebone, hence the name cuttlefish. These are not quite so tender as the squid with the transparent bone, but they are still delicious. Choose small squid for this quick method of cooking, and serve immediately—the flesh seems to toughen on standing. Cook the tentacles too.

> *500 g (1 lb) small squid (calamari), cleaned, prepared and cut*
> *into rings or strips*
> *3 tablespoons plain (all-purpose) flour seasoned with salt and pepper*
> *3 tablespoons olive oil*
> *Lemon wedges for serving*

Toss the rings or strips and tentacles of the squid in the seasoned flour. Heat the oil in a frying pan (skillet) and cook the squid, a few pieces at a time, for about 3 minutes, turning the pieces occasionally. Drain and serve with lemon wedges. Serves 4.

Grilled Sardines

Sardines are a saltwater fish of the pilchard family. They are especially popular in Italy, where Italian cooks prepare them in a wide variety of ways. They are a treat and worth including on the menu. Their heads may be removed before cooking, the stomachs slit and the tiny entrails removed.

> *24 fresh sardines, cleaned*
> *$1/_2$ cup (2 oz) plain (all-purpose) flour*
> *Salt and freshly ground pepper*
> *Juice of 1 lemon*
> *3 tablespoons vegetable or olive oil*
> *3 lemons, quartered*

Place the sardines in a bowl, dust them lightly with flour, season them lightly with salt and pepper, add the lemon juice and oil and mix lightly so that each sardine is well coated. Arrange them on the rack of the griller (broiler) lined with aluminium foil and grill under a high flame for 2–3 minutes on each side. Arrange them on a hot serving platter and garnish with the lemon quarters. Serves 6.

Tip
To clean and prepare squid (calamari), gently pull the tentacles from the body—the internal organs should come away with the head— then hold the body sac under cold running water to rinse away the black ink. Use a little salt to remove any stubborn pieces of ink. Pull out the hard material which forms the skeleton. Peel the skin off the body sac; the flesh can be siiced into rings or strips or squares or left whole. Cut the tentacles off the head just below the eyes and discard the rest of the head and viscera. Remove the hard 'beak' from the tentacles and discard that too. Dry the prepared squid on kitchen paper towels.

Baked Stuffed Squid

Baked Stuffed Squid. Stuffed with a simple mixture of breadcrumbs, parsley and lemon and cooked in a light tomato sauce, squid (calamari) are superb.

Serve as a first course, either warm or cold. The squid may be served whole with some sauce or sliced. I like to leave small squid whole and slice the larger ones.

1 garlic clove, crushed
2 tablespoons chopped parsley
1 cup (2 oz) fresh breadcrumbs
3 tablespoons vegetable or olive oil
1 teaspoon salt
Freshly ground pepper
Rind of 1 lemon, grated
1 kg (2 lb) small squid, cleaned and prepared (see page 211)
1/2 cup (41/2 fl oz) dry white wine
1 cup (9 fl oz) Fresh Tomato Sauce (page 184)
Chopped parsley and lemon wedges for garnish

*P*ut the garlic, parsley, breadcrumbs and oil in a bowl, season with salt, pepper and lemon rind, and mix thoroughly. Stuff the squid bodies with this mixture and sew the opening with string or secure it with toothpicks. Oil a baking dish large enough to accommodate all the squid, spread a thin layer of tomato sauce over the bottom, place the squid in the dish and pour the remaining sauce over them. Add the wine and bake for 45 minutes in a moderately hot oven (190°C/375°F). Remove and place the squid on a hot serving platter. Top with the parsley and lemon wedges. Serves 4–6.

Mussels with Sauce Poulette

Tip
If cream and egg yolk are not in your diet, serve the mussels with the liquor in which they were cooked. This liquor may be spiked with a tablespoon or two of either Pernod or whisky—the strong mussel flavour can really take the addition.

2 kg (4 lb) fresh mussels, cleaned
6 spring onions (scallions, green shallots), finely chopped
4 parsley sprigs
1 bay leaf
A sprig of thyme
Freshly ground black pepper
2 cups (18 fl oz) white wine
1/2 cup (41/2 fl oz) cream (single, light)
1 egg yolk
Parsley, chopped

*P*ut the mussels into a wide pan with the spring onions, herbs, pepper and wine. Cover and cook over high heat for 5 minutes, shaking the pan now and then. Remove the mussels as soon as they open, discarding half of each shell. Arrange the mussels in the remaining shells on warm soup plates. Strain the cooking liquor through a sieve and reserve.

In a small saucepan beat the cream and egg yolk, and add the mussel liquor. Whisk over moderate heat to thicken slightly. Pour this sauce over the mussels and sprinkle with chopped parsley. Serve at once with crusty bread and a bottle of chilled dry white wine. Serves 6.

Prawn and Pineapple Curry

1 lemon grass stalk or strip of lemon peel, roughly chopped
5 golden shallots, peeled
3 garlic cloves, peeled
3 fresh red chillies (chilli peppers), halved and seeded
1 teaspoon ground turmeric
3 tablespoons coriander (Chinese parsley), roughly chopped
6 tablespoons vegetable oil
1/2 teaspoon shrimp paste (trasi, blacan or mam tom)
1 cup (9 fl oz) coconut milk (canned, packaged or fresh)
500 g (1 lb) raw king prawns (shrimp), shelled and deveined
4 pineapple slices (canned or fresh), cut into triangles
Salt to taste

*U*sing an electric blender or food processor, grind the lemon grass with the shallots, garlic, chillies, turmeric and coriander.

Heat the oil in a wok or a pan and add the ground paste. Cook for a minute, then stir in the shrimp paste with the thin part of the coconut milk (if possible; alternatively just add half), added gradually. When the mixture is bubbling, stir in the prawns and the remaining coconut milk. Allow to heat for a few minutes, then stir in the pineapple. Continue to simmer until the prawns turn pink and are well flavoured, about 10 minutes. Serve with steamed rice. Serves 4.

Very young baby garlic, not often found in markets.

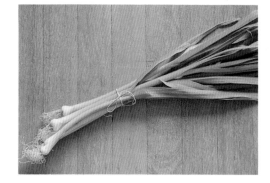

Raw Fish Salad

500 g (1 lb) firm white fish fillets, cut into very thin, almost
  transparent, slices
Juice and peel of 1 or 2 limes or lemons
1 tablespoon olive oil
Salt and pepper
4 tablespoons chopped spring onions (scallions, green shallots)
2 teaspoons green peppercorns, lightly crushed
2 canned pimientos (red peppers), cut into julienne strips
12 cherry tomatoes

*S*pread the fish on a chilled plate and dribble over the citrus juice. Combine the oil, salt, pepper, spring onions and peppercorns and sprinkle this over the fish; marinate for 15 minutes.

Cut the citrus peel into fine julienne strips, about the thickness of pine needles. Drop them into boiling water for 1 minute. Drain. Lift the fish out of the marinade and arrange the slices on 4 chilled plates with any leftover marinade. (If using the 3 different fish, keep them in separate small piles.) Scatter the citrus peel and pimiento strips over the fish and decorate with the tomatoes. Serves 4.

Tip
There are many ways of making this famous raw fish salad. Vary the fish used; sometimes use three different fish, a white fish, tuna and Atlantic salmon. Serve as a first course.

Scallops en Brochette

1 kg (2 lb) scallops
1 cup (9 fl oz) dry white wine
6 tablespoons chopped parsley
3 garlic cloves, chopped
9–12 thin slices prosciutto
125 g (4 oz) butter
1 large onion, finely chopped
3 tablespoons wine vinegar
Salt and pepper
Lemon juice

*W*ash and dry the scallops, retain the coral, trim off any brown bits.
Poach the scallops in the white wine for 2–3 minutes. Reserve the liquor. Mix the parsley and garlic on a plate, and roll the scallops in the mixture, then string them on 6 skewers, alternating with pieces of prosciutto. Melt a spoonful of

the butter and brush it over the scallops. Grill (broil) them gently for 10 minutes, turning them from time to time. Keep them warm while you make the sauce.

Put the onion and vinegar into a small pan with 3–4 tablespoons of the wine in which the scallops were poached. Reduce at a moderate heat so that the onion cooks and the liquid evaporates to 1½ tablespoons. Remove from heat, and when just tepid beat in the rest of the butter, bit by bit, to make a thick cream. Stir in any remaining parsley and garlic, plus chopped chervil if you have it. Correct the seasoning and sharpen with a little lemon juice.

Put the sauce into a bowl and serve with the brochettes. Serve with boiled rice and a crisp green salad. Serves 6.

Steamed Scallops with Ginger and Spring Onions

Steamed Scallops with Ginger and Spring Onions. The scallops are gently steamed in their shells (small ramekins can be used) and finished off with shredded fresh exotic aromatics, then sizzling soy and sesame oil. A truly wonderful inspiration from a Chinese chef.

In some fish markets you can get fresh scallops in their shells. What a treat! A true luxury, more so when cooked in this light, easy, quick and fragrant way. The Chinese have cooked according to the *jing* (steaming) method for centuries. It is a very healthy way to cook and brings out the full flavour. Fresh uncooked scampi or large king prawns (jumbo shrimp) may be cut in two and steamed in this way. They take only a few minutes to steam.

12 scallops, in shells
6–8 spring onions (scallions, green shallots), cut into matchstick strips
6 slices fresh ginger, shredded
3 tablespoons coriander (Chinese parsley) sprigs
4 teaspoons light soy sauce
2 tablespoons peanut (groundnut) oil
2 teaspoons sesame oil

Tip
If scallops in their shells are not available, arrange 4–5 scallops in 4 small buttered ramekins and cook in this way.

*A*rrange the scallops on a rack in a steamer (a large bamboo steamer is ideal, or use a cake rack in a wok with a lid which will fit). Scatter half the spring onions and ginger over the scallops, reserving the rest for garnish. Cover well with aluminium foil or lid and cook gently over a moderate heat until cooked (about 5 minutes). Remove the scallops to a heated serving dish and garnish with the reserved spring onions and ginger and the coriander. Sprinkle with soy sauce. Heat the peanut and sesame oils in a small saucepan, pour over the scallops and serve immediately (if the oil is hot enough there should be lots of sizzling as the garnish half-cooks). Serve immediately. Serves 4.

Meat

Meat has long been the star around which the rest of the meal revolves. It is the main ingredient in literally thousands of recipes.

In the Western world, grilled steak or lamb cutlets with young vegetables or a crisp green salad has been considered the most delightful of meat dishes. A leg of lamb roasted with vegetables has been the highlight of family meals and a weekly treat, with roast pork or a joint of beef introduced as a change. A casserole or ragout, most welcome in winter; cold meat to be enjoyed with salads for summer. This is how it has been for generations. And very good it has been too.

Not surprisingly, times have changed. The stir-fry technique of cooking is not only for the Chinese; we are all doing it. It is so quick and easy, and we love the fresh taste. Cooking on a hibachi or barbecue in the garden or on the veranda or balcony goes on in all climates, in both hemispheres. We are cooking meats with spices, herbs, vegetables and grains in ways unheard of (unless it was our own native way), a decade ago. We are learning techniques and flavour combinations from our neighbours near and afar—Korea, India, Malaysia, Greece, France, Italy. There's no stopping us now that we've got the idea.

Veal with Black Olives must be one of the best ways of treating the delicate but rather bland flesh of veal. Garlic, onion, black olives, rosemary and a dry white wine are used with a light touch, adding flavour that will intrigue.

Fillet of Beef Niçoise

This has long been a feature of my buffet table for both large and small parties—delicious, roasted fillet of beef (tenderloin) served at room temperature with herbed vegetables.

Tip
To trim a fillet of beef, remove the surface fat and membrane covering the meat with a sharp knife. (You can leave a little fat on to add extra flavour.) After trimming, tie the fillet neatly with string so that it will keep its shape during cooking.

1 kg (2 lb) fillet of beef (tenderloin), trimmed and tied (see tip)
Freshly ground black pepper
1 tablespoon olive oil
30 g (1 oz) butter
3 tablespoons brandy
250 g (8 oz) green beans, trimmed
250 g (8 oz) zucchini (courgettes), sliced into short lengths, or
*   patty pan squash*
500 g (1 lb) tomatoes, peeled and quartered, or whole cherry
*   tomatoes*
60 g (2 oz) black olives (optional)
¹/₂ cup (4¹/₂ fl oz) green herb vinaigrette (see below)
1 tablespoon finely chopped fresh herbs, such as parsley, basil,
*   oregano or tarragon*

Fillet of Beef Niçoise is a special-occasion dish. A well-trimmed fillet of beef is roasted 'pink' and served with the freshest of young vegetables and dressed with a herby vinaigrette.

Season the fillet with the pepper. Preheat the oven to 260°C (500°F). Heat the oil in a flameproof baking dish (roasting pan), then add the butter. When hot, add the beef and brown it well all over. Heat the brandy, set it alight and pour it over the beef. Shake the pan until the flames subside. Place the pan in the oven and turn the heat down to 220°C (425°F). Cook for 20 minutes.

Cook the beans and zucchini or squash for 4 minutes in boiling salted water; drain. Combine the tomatoes, beans, zucchini, and olives and toss them lightly in the green herb vinaigrette.

Remove the beef and allow it to cool, wrapped loosely in aluminium foil, until required. Remove the string and carve the meat into 1 cm (¹/₂ in) slices. Arrange on a serving dish and brush with a little of the green herb vinaigrette to keep the meat moist. Spoon the salad along the beef and sprinkle with chopped herbs. Serves 6–8; a large fillet will serve 8–10.

Green herb vinaigrette. In a screw-top jar combine ²/₃ cup (6 fl oz) good olive oil, 2 tablespoons white or red wine vinegar, 1 teaspoon French mustard, 1 clove of garlic (crushed), salt and freshly ground pepper, 3 tablespoons finely chopped mixed herbs—choose from chives, parsley, oregano, tarragon and basil. Shake well before using.

Fillet of Beef with Italian Green Sauce

One of the simplest dishes in the world to do well. Prime fillet of beef (tenderloin) is an expensive cut but makes a very special dish when entertaining. Serve the meat at room temperature. Serve with baby new potatoes boiled and tossed in a little butter or olive oil.

60 g (2 oz) butter
1.5 kg (3 lb) whole beef fillet (tenderloin), trimmed and
  seasoned (see tip)
3 tablespoons brandy
Salt and freshly ground black pepper
GREEN SAUCE
1 cup finely chopped parsley
8 small pickled gherkins
3 tablespoons capers
6–8 anchovy fillets
1–2 tablespoons green peppercorns
Grated rind of 1 lemon
²/₃ cup (6 fl oz) olive oil

Season the fillet well with freshly ground pepper. Preheat the oven to 260°C (500°F).

Heat the butter in a flameproof baking dish (roasting pan) and brown the fillet on all sides over moderate heat. Warm the brandy in a small saucepan, set it alight and pour it over the beef. Shake the pan until the flames subside, spooning the juice over the meat.

Place the baking dish in the oven and immediately turn the heat down to 220°C (425°F). Roast for 15 minutes for very rare beef, 20 minutes for medium rare. Lift the fillet out of the oven, season with salt and freshly ground pepper, cover with foil and leave to stand at least 15 minutes while making the sauce. (This standing time is important, as it allows the juices to settle and carving can be done without much loss of juices.)

The simplest way to make the green sauce is to place all the ingredients together in an electric blender or food processor and process until a smooth sauce is formed. Alternatively, pound the ingredients in a mortar with a pestle.

Remove the string from the beef fillet, and slice the meat fairly thickly. Spread the green sauce over the base of the platter and arrange the beef slices on top. Serve with new potatoes. Serves 10–12.

Medallions of Beef with Dill Sauce

1 kg (2 lb) fillet of beef, well-trimmed
Salt and freshly ground black pepper
2 tablespoons butter
125 g (4 oz) mushrooms, thinly sliced
1 tablespoon finely chopped golden shallots or green shallots
2 tablespoons red wine vinegar
2 tablespoons capers
1 cup (9 fl oz) light (dairy) sour cream
1 tablespoon finely chopped fresh dill (or parsley)

Cut the fillet into medallions of equal size—about 1 cm (¹/₂ in) thick. Sprinkle them with salt and pepper to taste. Melt half the butter in a frying pan (skillet) large enough to hold the medallions comfortably without crowding. Cook the medallions over moderately high heat for about 30 to 45 seconds on one side—they should be nicely browned—then turn and cook about 30 to 45 seconds on the other side. Immediately transfer the meat to a warm serving platter. Add the remaining butter and mushrooms and stir. Add the shallots and cook about 20 seconds. Add the vinegar and capers and stir, then add the sour

Tip
Have your butcher take the short fillet part off the rump and trim it well; it is a treat. I often cook it this way, the meat cut into medallions. The delicious sauce can also be served with hamburgers.

cream and stir. Let the sauce come to the simmer. Add any juices that have accumulated around the steak. Remove from the heat. Spoon the sauce over the meat and sprinkle the dill on top. Serve with steamed rice or creamy mashed potatoes. Serves 8.

Pan-Grilled Pepper Steak

Pan-grilled steaks are superb. You need a heavy frying pan or, better still, a ribbed grill. If your regular grill is a reliable one, you will also get good results. The same rules apply.

> *185–250 g (6–8 oz) rump steak (or boneless sirloin),*
>   *cut 2.5–4 cm (1–1^1/$_2$ in) thick, per person*
> *1 teaspoon black peppercorns, cracked, or green peppercorns*
> *Good olive oil*
> *Salt*

Pan-Grilled Pepper Steak requires a ribbed grill if you want that seared crossbar effect. Vegetables too can be cooked this way. A thick, heavy iron pan can also give meat that crusty outside and rosy pink inside that typifies the best grills.

Have the steak at room temperature. Cut it into portions or leave it in a large piece and cut it after grilling (this retains maximum juices). Slit the fat at intervals, cutting through just to the lean meat, to prevent the meat from buckling while it is cooking. Dry the meat well and press the peppercorns onto both sides. Brush lightly with oil and allow to stand 1–2 hours.

Heat a heavy frying pan or ribbed grill, brush it with the oil and, when it is just beginning to smoke, put the meat on. Keep the heat high and do not move the meat for 2 minutes after placing it on the pan, as it may stick at first but will release itself if you wait. (Turn it half-way around after 2 minutes when using a ribbed grill if you want the steak to have a grid-patterned surface.) Cook another 2 minutes, then turn it over and sear the other side in the same manner. Lower the heat and continue to cook until the steak is done to your liking, only 1–2 minutes.

When tiny beads of pink juice appear on the surface and the steak is pliant to the touch, it is rare. When it is more heavily 'dewed' with juice and springy to touch, it is medium-rare. If it is firm, it is well done.

Remove the meat to a hot dish and let it rest for 1 minute before slicing. Smear the surface with a little butter if you like.

Grilled vegetables. Quartered red capsicums (sweet peppers), sliced eggplant (aubergine), small tomatoes or sliced zucchini (courgettes) may accompany grilled steak. Brush with olive oil and a light sprinkling of herbs and place on the hot grill to sear and heat through.

225

Beef Salad with Cumin Vinaigrette

This salad can be made with leftover roast beef, but I usually pan-grill steaks especially, for this is such a lovely salad.

> *2 Pan-Grilled Pepper Steaks (preceding recipe)*
>
> *1 red or green capsicum (sweet pepper), cut into fine strips*
>
> *1 zucchini (courgette) or Lebanese (Continental) cucumber,
>   sliced*
>
> *$^1/_2$ red or salad onion or 6 shallots (spring onions, scallions),
>   sliced*
>
> *Mixed salad greens, washed and crisped (include some
>   arugula or watercress)*
>
> *3 tablespoons snipped fresh coriander (Chinese parsley) or
>   mixed herbs*
>
> CUMIN VINAIGRETTE
>
> *1 tablespoon white wine vinegar*
>
> *1 teaspoon Dijon-style mustard*
>
> *$1^1/_4$ teaspoons ground cumin*
>
> *3 tablespoons olive oil*

llow the steaks to stand for 5–10 minutes after cooking, then cut them into strips. Combine the meat with the capsicum, zucchini and onion. Toss with cumin vinaigrette. Cover and chill until required.

Arrange the salad greens on four dinner plates. Place the beef salad on the greens, lifting it up with a fork to give it a light appearance. Sprinkle the herbs on top. Serves 4.

Cumin vinaigrette. Combine the ingredients in a small screw-top jar and shake well just before using.

Thai Hot Beef Salad

Bupah, my daughter Suzanne's Thai friend, taught us to make this fabulous hot salad. Thais add two red chillies, which make it really hot; I prefer one. There are two schools of thought regarding preparation of the salad. One is that the meat should marinate in the seasonings and sauce for several hours before the meal is served. The other is that the meat should be tossed in the marinade while it is still warm and be served immediately on the crisp greens. I prefer the latter method of preparation.

> 750 g (1½ lb) rump or sirloin steak
> Freshly ground pepper
> ½ cup mint leaves (spearmint for preference)
> 1 large red onion or 2 large spring onions (scallions), thinly
>   sliced
> 1–2 red chillies, halved, seeded and very finely shredded
> Juice of 1 large lime or ½ lemon
> 2 tablespoons Thai fish sauce (nam pla)
> 1 teaspoon sugar
> Lettuce leaves, whole or halved cherry tomatoes and extra
>   mint leaves to garnish

eason the steak with pepper and cook it on a hot ribbed grill or under a preheated grill (broiler) for 5 minutes on each side or until done to taste. Remove, allow to stand 5–10 minutes. Cut the meat into very thin slices and place it in a bowl. Meanwhile, combine the mint leaves with the onion slices, shredded chilli, citrus juice, fish sauce and sugar. Stir well and add to the beef slices, tossing.

Arrange on a salad platter lined with lettuce, cherry tomatoes and extra mint leaves and serve. Serves 4–6.

Persian Meatballs in Spinach and Orange Sauce

This unusual dish of meat, vegetable and citrus juice shows imagination, for the combination is perfect.

MEATBALLS
750 g (1¹/₂ lb) minced (ground) beef
1 cup (2 oz) soft breadcrumbs
1 medium onion, grated
¹/₂ teaspoon salt
¹/₄ teaspoon freshly ground pepper
¹/₄ teaspoon cinnamon
3 tablespoons olive oil

VEGETABLE MIXTURE
500 g (1 lb) fresh spinach or silver beet (Swiss chard), finely
  chopped
1 cup parsley, chopped
³/₄ cup (6¹/₂ fl oz) water
³/₄ cup (6¹/₂ fl oz) orange juice
2 tablespoons lemon juice
1 tablespoon plain (all-purpose) flour
1 teaspoon salt
2 garlic cloves, finely chopped
1 tablespoon olive oil or butter

Tip
Wash thoroughly and dry spinach and parsley leaves before chopping them.

*P*ut the meat in a large bowl. Add the breadcrumbs, onion and seasoning and mix well. Form meatballs the size of small walnuts. Heat half the oil in a frying pan (skillet), and sauté the meatballs for 10 minutes, rolling the pan, until the meat is brown.

Heat the remaining oil in a frying pan and sauté the spinach and parsley for 10 minutes. Combine the meat and the vegetables, add the water, and let simmer on a low heat for about 10 minutes. Mix the orange juice, lemon juice and flour together. Add to the meat and vegetable mixture. Add salt if needed. Let simmer for another 20 minutes. Sauté the garlic in oil or butter and add it to the meat and vegetable mixture about 10 minutes before serving. Serve with steamed rice. Makes 4−5 servings.

Beef Patties Cordon Bleu

Beef Patties Cordon Bleu. Sandwiching a slice of Gruyère cheese and paper-thin prosciutto or other raw or boiled ham is one of the best things to do with chopped or ground beef.

The cheese used in this dish may be varied. Emmenthaler is good, or a little Gorgonzola or Roquefort. The ham may be smoked or a dry-cured ham like prosciutto or ham deluxe.

725 g (1¼ lb) chuck steak
4 thin slices of Gruyére cheese
4 thin slices of ham
Salt and pepper
1 tablespoon oil

Trim the steak and put it through a mincer or chop it in a food processor using the steel blade. Divide the minced beef into 8 patties. Put a slice of cheese and a slice of ham on each of half the patties, and top with the other half. Press the patty 'sandwich' back into shape. Season with salt and pepper. Heat the oil in a heavy pan, and when very hot cook the patties, allowing 3–4 minutes each side.

Serve in soft buttered buns with lettuce or serve on a plate with salad and crusty bread. Serves 4.

Potted Meat

This summertime meat loaf is one of the best cold meat dishes I know. A traditional accompaniment is a little dish of hot English mustard and another of vinegar. Ask your butcher to saw through the knuckles of veal.

2 large knuckles of veal
750 g (1¹/₂ lb) shin (shank) beef
1 onion, sliced
¹/₄ teaspoon mixed spice
2 cloves
8 whole peppercorns
Salt
1 tablespoon gelatine
3 anchovies, chopped and mashed

Potted Meat may be time consuming to make properly (the well-simmered meat is pulled apart with the tines of 2 forks); however, everyone agrees it is well worth the trouble. The sharp vinegar and hot mustard are the essential condiments.

*P*lace the meat in a large saucepan and cover with water. Bring slowly to the boil, skim, then reduce the heat. Add the onion, spice, cloves, peppercorns and salt to taste. Simmer gently for 3 hours or until the meat is coming away from the bones. Remove the meat from the bones and chop it finely or, better still, pull it apart using the tines of two forks. Strain the stock and reserve.

In a bowl, dissolve the gelatine in ¹/₂ cup (4¹/₂ fl oz) of the hot stock. Make up the liquid to 2¹/₂ cups (22 fl oz) with more stock and additional water if necessary. Add the anchovies and meat. Mix lightly. Adjust seasonings.

Spoon the mixture into a loaf tin or 5-cup bowl and refrigerate until firm. Unmould and serve with a pungent green such as arugula (rocket) or watercress, tomatoes and cucumbers, sliced or in quarters, and a dish of pickled gherkins or tiny cornichons.

Instead of the hot English mustard and vinegar accompaniment, you can make a sauce of 1 tablespoon of made mustard, 2 tablespoons of malt vinegar and 3 tablespoons of olive oil beaten in. This is one of the nicest sauces to serve with brawn and is the one taught at the Cordon Bleu in London. Serves 8.

Brawn. A variation of potted meat. Replace the knuckles of veal with 3 pig's trotters, either fresh or pickled, and cook as above. Alternatively, if your butcher can get half a pickled pig's head, use it; it makes an excellent brawn. It too cooks in about the same time. Pick the meat from the bone; try to remove any fragments of bone and gristle. Some of the skin may be retained. Mix the pork meat with the beef, and chop finely. The juice of 1 lemon will sharpen the flavour. Set as above.

Beef in Coconut

Rendang Daging is a dish you find on Malaysian and Indonesian menus; it is a great favourite. A lovely thick spicy sauce coats the meat. It needs very little oil for frying the meat, as the oil comes out of the coconut milk to help cook the meat and give the right sauce.

> *1 red onion, peeled and quartered, or 6 golden shallots*
> *2.5 cm (1 in) piece of fresh ginger, peeled and sliced*
> *4 dried red chillies*
> *2 lemon grass stalks or a strip of lemon peel*
> *2 garlic cloves, peeled*
> *1 tablespoon water*
> *2 tablespoons vegetable oil*
> *6 tablespoons freshly grated coconut or 4 tablespoons*
>   *desiccated (shredded) coconut*
> *750 g (1¹/₂ lb) beef topside or chuck steak, trimmed and cut*
>   *into cubes*
> *2 cups (18 fl oz) coconut milk*
> *1 teaspoon each sugar and salt*

*I*n an electric blender or food processor, grind the onion, ginger, chillies, lemon grass, garlic and water to a smooth paste. Heat the oil in a deep frying pan (skillet) or saucepan and gently fry the ground onion and chilli mixture for 3 to 4 minutes. Add the coconut, cook for a minute or two, then put in the beef and stir-fry until it changes colour. Add the coconut milk, sugar and

salt and bring to the boil. Reduce the heat and simmer, uncovered, until the meat is tender, about 45 minutes. If the sauce starts to dry out, add a little hot water.

Serve with steamed rice and an assortment of sambals, such as chopped tomato with mint, chopped cucumber with garlic, sliced banana, a pile of fried prawn crisps. Serves 6.

Escabeche of Tongue

When a friend from Uruguay has a party, this salad of ox tongue marinated in a vinaigrette is sure to be on the menu. Her parents are Spanish and Italian, but she tells me this recipe originally comes from Portugal. Start preparing the dish the day before you want to serve it.

1 fresh ox tongue
6 whole cloves
A bouquet garni (page 31)
1 onion, sliced
1 carrot, sliced
1 celery stalk, sliced
1¹/₂ teaspoons salt
3 garlic cloves, crushed
¹/₂ cup (4¹/₂ fl oz) wine vinegar
¹/₂ cup (4¹/₂ fl oz) olive oil
¹/₂ cup chopped parsley
2 hard-boiled eggs, roughly chopped
Freshly ground pepper

Place the tongue in a saucepan with water to cover and add the cloves, bouquet garni, onion, carrot, celery and salt. Bring slowly to the boil, skim the surface, and simmer, covered, for about 3 hours or until the meat is tender. Leave it in the liquid until cool enough to handle, then take the tongue out, remove any bone-like parts, and trim off any fat in the root end. Slit the underside of the skin and remove; it should peel off easily if you first push your thumbs underneath to ease the edges.

Cut the tongue lengthwise into thick slices, and cut these across into thick strips. Now whisk the garlic with the vinegar to mix and gradually whisk in the oil until emulsified. Add the parsley with the eggs and a good grinding of pepper. Leave to marinate, covered, in the refrigerator for several hours before serving. Serves 6.

Leg of Lamb Stuffed with Fennel, Mushrooms and Bacon

Leg of Lamb Stuffed with Fennel, Mushrooms and Bacon calls for both dried and fresh mushrooms, the lovely fennel of Florence, and fresh herbs for the unusual but successful stuffing. Served here with Sauté Potatoes.

Have the butcher tunnel-bone a leg of lamb so as to leave it fairly close to its original shape. The stuffing is most unusual for lamb; a variety of mushrooms, the lovely Florence fennel, garlic and fresh herbs. Serve with sautéed potatoes or a dish of steamed baby new potatoes.

60 g (2 oz) dried mushrooms, such as ceps or porcini
60 g (2 oz) pancetta or coppa ham or bacon, finely chopped
15 g (¹/₂ oz) butter
1 small heart of fennel, chopped
250 g (8 oz) fresh mushrooms, chopped
4 tablespoons chopped parsley with a little chopped chervil
    if available
Leaves from a sprig of thyme
Salt and freshly ground pepper
A grating of nutmeg
4 slices of bread, crusts removed
1 garlic clove, crushed
1 leg of lamb, tunnel-boned
1 tablespoon light olive oil

Soak the dried mushrooms in hot water to cover for at least 30 minutes. Drain. Sauté the pancetta, coppa or bacon in the butter in a sauté pan for about 2 minutes, until lightly browned. Add the fennel and sauté for 2 minutes, until softened. Add the chopped and soaked mushrooms and continue to sauté until the fennel is very tender and all the liquid has evaporated from the mushrooms. Add the parsley, thyme, salt, pepper and nutmeg to season well. Meanwhile, process the bread to make breadcrumbs and add them to fennel and mushroom mixture with the garlic.

Stuff the leg of lamb with this mixture and use kitchen (cooking) thread to sew the opening, or secure with poultry pins and string. Place on a rack in a baking dish (roasting pan) and drizzle with the olive oil. Season well with salt and pepper. Roast in a preheated hot oven (220°C/425°F) for 15 minutes, then reduce the temperature to moderately hot (190°C/375°F) and continue cooking a further 45 minutes. Turn off the oven and leave the lamb to 'rest' in the oven for 10 minutes before carving and serving. Serves 8.

Roast Lamb with Borlotti Beans and Tomatoes

Fresh borlotti beans are delicious. Although they are seasonal and not readily available, some greengrocers will look out for them at the markets if you ask. If you can't get them, you can substitute fresh cranberry beans or dried haricot beans, which are the standard accompaniment to a leg of lamb in Brittany.

1 leg of lamb
2 garlic cloves, peeled and cut in slivers
Salt and freshly ground pepper
1–2 cups (9–18 fl oz) water or stock
1 kg (2 lb) fresh borlotti beans
30 g (1 oz) butter
4 golden shallots or 1 small onion, chopped
2 large ripe tomatoes, peeled (see page 130) and diced
2 tablespoons chopped parsley

*P*reheat the oven to moderately hot (190°C/375°F). Remove excess fat from the lamb. Cut a few small incisions between the skin and the flesh and insert the garlic slivers. Season the leg with salt and pepper. Place it in a baking dish (roasting pan), preferably on a rack, and put a cup (9 fl oz) of water or stock in the dish. Roast for 1¼ hours, basting every 15 minutes and adding more liquid if necessary. The flesh should be still quite pink.

Shell the beans and drop them into boiling salted water to cook for about 10 minutes or until tender. Drain. Melt the butter in a pan 20–30 minutes before the lamb is due to finish cooking. Add the shallots or onion and cook gently until softened. Add the tomatoes and beans and ½ cup (4½ fl oz) of the lamb juices from the dish. Cover and simmer gently for a further 10–15 minutes.

This leg of lamb is tunnel-boned; that is, the bone is removed without the leg being cut open. The stuffing is placed in this cavity and the leg re-formed to its original shape before roasting.

Place the lamb on a serving platter and strain any juices from the dish into a sauce boat. Toss the beans with parsley and serve separately. Serves 6–8.

If using dried haricot beans, soak 500 g (1 lb) of beans overnight in water to cover; drain. Place them in a large pan with fresh water to cover, 2 large quartered onions, a bouquet garni, a garlic clove, 1 teaspoon of salt and a few peppercorns. Bring slowly to the boil, skim and cover. Cook gently for 1¹/₂–2 hours or until the beans are tender.

Roast Lamb with Mustard and Peppercorn Crust

Some delicious combinations are created when East meets West. Here is one. Have the butcher tunnel-bone the lamb for you so that it retains its basic shape.

2 teaspoons crushed peppercorns
¹/₂ cup fresh coriander (Chinese parsley) leaves
1 teaspoon cumin
3 garlic cloves, crushed
3 tablespoons light soy sauce
1 cup (9 fl oz) red or dry white wine
1 leg of lamb about 2 kg (4 lb), tunnel-boned
2 tablespoons Dijon-style mustard
A bunch of watercress or a punnet of pea shoots

Combine half the peppercorns with the coriander leaves, cumin, garlic, soy sauce and wine in a large bowl. Add the lamb, turning it over a few times. Cover and leave to marinate in the refrigerator for several hours or overnight.

Preheat the oven to moderately hot (190°C/375°F).

Drain the lamb and tie it into a neat shape with string. Place it on a rack in a baking dish (roasting pan); pour the marinade into the baking dish with 1 cup (9 fl oz) of water. Spread the mustard evenly over the lamb and sprinkle with the remaining peppercorns. Roast for about 1¹/₂ hours, basting every now and then with the juices in the baking dish. Remove from the oven and leave to 'set' for about 15 minutes before serving.

Meanwhile, wash the watercress or pea shoots and spin dry. Pick over the watercress stems, removing the tough ones and keeping the tender sprigs. Lay these, or the pea shoots, on a serving dish and place the lamb on top. Carve the meat into thin slices to serve. Serve the pan juices separately. Serves 6–8.

Butterflied Leg of Lamb Oriental

A leg of lamb 'butterflied' (boned with the seam left open) is barbecued flat on the grill—or you can cook it under a preheated grill (broiler).

1 leg of lamb, butterflied
Juice of 1 lemon
2 garlic cloves, mashed
1 teaspoon grated fresh ginger
1 teaspoon ground cardamom
1 teaspoon ground cumin
2 teaspoons ground coriander
1/2 teaspoon ground turmeric
Pepper and salt to taste
1/2 cup (4 1/2 fl oz) natural (plain) yoghurt, beaten

Butterflied Leg of Lamb Oriental is marinated in yoghurt and exotic spices, then barbecued or grilled. This dish allows everyone meat to their own taste, from well done to pink or medium rare. I like this with lemon wedges and a Saffron Pilaf (page 176).

Lay out the leg of lamb and slash any thick portions. Combine the lemon juice, garlic, ginger and spices and rub this on all surfaces, then spread the yoghurt over the lamb and leave it to marinate in a glass dish for 1–2 hours. Lift the meat out of the marinade and place it skin side down on a greased grill 10 cm (4 in) above the glowing coals. Baste frequently with the marinade and turn occasionally; cook for about 45 minutes. (Or cook under a preheated grill, not too close to the source of heat or it will burn.) Allow to stand 5 minutes before carving. To carve, start at one end and slice across the grain. Guests may choose meat done to their own taste—well done or medium rare. Serves 6–8.

Lamb Aillade

A leg of lamb as cooked in Provence, with garlic, anchovies, rosemary and thyme.

1 leg of lamb about 2 kg (4 lb)
12 garlic cloves, 6 whole and 6 slivered
12 anchovy fillets, chopped
3 tablespoons olive oil
1 teaspoon chopped fresh rosemary
1 teaspoon chopped fresh thyme
Salt and freshly ground black pepper
3/4 cup (6 1/2 fl oz) dry white wine
2 tablespoons chopped parsley or mint

*M*ake slits in the lamb and insert a sliver of garlic and a piece of anchovy in each incision. Rub the lamb with 2 tablespoons of the olive oil, the rosemary, thyme, salt and pepper. Let it stand for 1–2 hours.

Preheat the oven to hot (200°C/400°F). Place the meat on a rack in a roasting pan and roast for 20 minutes. Reduce the heat to moderate (180°C/350°F) and cook for a further 1–1¼ hours. Heat the remaining olive oil in a frying pan (skillet) and cook the whole garlic cloves slowly for about 10 minutes or until they are soft. (Do not let the edges become crisp.) Set aside in a small bowl. Remove the lamb from the roasting pan; add the wine to the pan. Scrape up brown bits and boil the wine over high heat to reduce it by half. Add the reduced liquid to the garlic cloves. Mash well with a fork and add salt and pepper.

Slice the lamb and sprinkle with pepper. Spoon the garlic sauce over it and sprinkle with parsley or mint. Serves 6–8.

Parsleyed Rack of Lamb

Parsleyed Rack of Lamb cooked this way is perfect every time; just follow the instructions. It has a rosy pink flesh with a lemony-mustard crisp crust.

Tip
You can prepare the cutlets and coat them with herb crusts ahead, leaving only the final roasting at the last moment, which is convenient when entertaining.

3 small racks of lamb consisting of 4 cutlets each or 2 racks of
    5 or 6 cutlets
1 tablespoon Dijon-style mustard
1–2 tablespoons olive oil
¹/₂ cup chopped parsley
¹/₂ teaspoon salt
A little white pepper
Rind of 1 lemon
1 tablespoon lemon juice
1¹/₂ cups (3 oz) fresh white breadcrumbs

*T*rim the cutlets (if your butcher has not done so) by cutting away the flesh from the top of the bone and slicing the fat away, leaving about 5 cm (2 in) of bone exposed. Cut off any excess fat. Heat a frying pan (skillet) and sear the meat over a low heat for 4–5 minutes until it is golden all over. Leave to cool to room temperature. Spread the fat side with the mustard.

Preheat the oven to hot (220°C/450°F).

Mix the oil with the parsley, salt, pepper, lemon rind and juice and breadcrumbs. Toss all together lightly. Cover the fat side of the lamb with a thick, compact layer of breadcrumb mixture. Place the lamb in a baking dish (roasting pan) and roast for 10 minutes. Remove the lamb from the oven and let it stand several minutes before carving. When lamb is cooked, the juices will run clear. Cut each rack through, allowing a double cutlet per person. Serves 6.

Devilled Lamb Cutlets

Everyone who loves a grilled lamb cutlet will appreciate this devilish version.

6 drops of Tabasco sauce
1 teaspoon chilli powder
1 teaspoon salt
2 teaspoons brown sugar
1½ tablespoons Worcestershire sauce
2 tablespoons tomato sauce (ketchup)
1 tablespoon wine vinegar
4 tablespoons water
8 lamb cutlets, trimmed

*M*ix the Tabasco, chilli powder, salt and brown sugar together in a large dish. Gradually stir in the Worcestershire sauce, tomato sauce, vinegar and water. Add the cutlets and turn them to coat them thoroughly. Leave them to marinate for 2 hours.

Transfer the cutlets to a grill rack and brush with the marinade. Cook under a preheated hot grill (broiler) for 4–6 minutes on each side, depending on the thickness of the cutlets, basting frequently with the marinade. Serves 4.

Lamb Chops in Caper Sauce

2 kg (4 lb) lamb neck chops
1 teaspoon salt
2 cups (18 fl oz) water
Freshly ground pepper
1½ tablespoons plain (all-purpose) flour
2 tablespoons French capers
¾ cup chopped parsley
2 teaspoons lemon juice

*P*lace the chops in a saucepan with the salt and water and simmer gently, covered, for 1 hour or until tender. Lift the chops out onto a serving dish, season them with salt and pepper and keep them hot.

Blend the flour with a little cold water and stir it into the cooking liquid. Bring to the boil, stirring constantly, and simmer for a few minutes. Add the capers, parsley and lemon juice to taste and return the chops to the pot. Reheat gently. Serve with steamed potatoes. Serves 4–6.

Stir-Fried Lamb in Pancakes

Made in minutes. This dish can be part of a special Asian meal.

> *375 g (12 oz) lamb fillets or other trim cut lamb*
> *1 tablespoon light soy sauce*
> *2 tablespoons sugar*
> *1 teaspoon cornflour (cornstarch)*
> *3 tablespoons vegetable oil*
> *1 green or yellow capsicum (sweet pepper), halved, seeded*
>   *and cut into finger-length strips*
> *1/4 teaspoon chopped chilli (chili pepper)*
> *8–10 spring onions (scallions, green shallots), shredded*
> *2 garlic cloves, crushed*
> *3 slices of fresh ginger*
> *1 tablespoon Chinese rice wine (Shaoxing) or dry sherry*
> *Salt and freshly ground pepper*
> *Chinese Pancakes (page 255)*

*C*ut the lamb into very thin slices across the grain. Mix the soy sauce, sugar and cornflour in a bowl; add the lamb and mix well together.

Heat 1 tablespoon of the oil in a wok and stir-fry the capsicum and chilli for 30 seconds before adding the spring onion; cook for 20 seconds more. Transfer the vegetables to a bowl. Add the remaining 2 tablespoons of oil to the wok, heat with the garlic and ginger, then remove the garlic and ginger and add the meat; stir-fry for about 1 minute. Add the wine, return the vegetables to the wok and stir-fry for a further minute. Season to taste. Turn into a heated dish.

Serve with the pancakes. Guests put a spoonful of lamb on a pancake, roll it up and eat it with their fingers, like Peking duck. Little bowls of toasted peanuts, coriander (Chinese parsley) sprigs or mint leaves may be offered as extra toppings—also sliced chilli for those who like it hot. Serves 4–6.

Lamb with Dill Sauce

In Scandinavian countries you find the lamb and dill combination in many different dishes—it is a good mix.

> *750 g (1½ lb) leg or shoulder of lamb cut into 2.5 cm (1 in)*
>   *cubes*
> *2 teaspoons salt*
> *5 or 6 peppercorns*
> *A bunch of dill*
> *2 carrots, peeled and thinly sliced*
> *2 onions, peeled and thinly sliced*
> *2 parsnips, peeled and thinly sliced*
> *60 g (2 oz) butter*
> *½ cup (2 oz) plain (all-purpose) flour*
> *2 tablespoons white wine vinegar*
> *1 tablespoon sugar*
> *Salt and freshly ground black pepper*
> *1 egg yolk*
> *3 tablespoons cream (single, light)*
> *Extra dill sprigs (optional)*

Place the meat in a large flameproof Dutch oven or casserole and cover with water. Bring to the boil; remove any scum. Add the salt, peppercorns and the stalks of the dill, tied together. Cook over a slow heat until tender. Add the

Members of the onion family: golden shallots, important in French cookery, can be a pinkish colour; a sweet yellow onion, maybe Spanish or Vidalia, especially good; and garlic, by far the most pungent of the onion family.

carrots, onions and parsnips and continue cooking for 20–30 minutes until the vegetables are just cooked. Drain the meat and vegetables and keep them warm. Remove the dill stalks and reserve the stock.

Melt the butter in a saucepan. Add the flour and cook for a few minutes, but do not brown. Add the reserved stock, stirring constantly until the sauce is smooth and thick. Add the vinegar and sugar and season to taste. Mix the egg yolk with the cream in a small bowl; add this to the sauce, beating constantly. Simmer gently for 4–5 minutes, but do not boil. Add the meat and vegetables and 2–3 tablespoons of the finely chopped tops of the dill. Taste and adjust the seasoning. Serves 6.

Lamb Stew with Green Olives

This is an excellent dish for the winter months, especially for a family meal.

1 kg (2 lb) shoulder lamb
¼ cup (1 oz) plain (all-purpose) flour, seasoned with salt
*   and freshly ground pepper*
3 tablespoons olive oil
2 medium onions, peeled and chopped
1½ cups (13½ fl oz) stock or water or dry white wine
A sprig of marjoram or oregano
2 garlic cloves, crushed
2 green capsicums (sweet peppers), seeded and diced
1 celery stalk, sliced
500 g (1 lb) potatoes
⅔ cup (3 oz) pimiento-stuffed olives
4 tomatoes, peeled (see page 130) and quartered

Trim the lamb of as much fat as possible and cut it into fairly large, neat cubes. Coat them with the seasoned flour. Heat the oil in a flameproof casserole and brown the lamb cubes evenly all over. Add the onions and sauté gently until softened. Slowly stir in the stock, water or wine. Add the marjoram, garlic, capsicums and celery. Bring to a simmer, cover, and cook over a gentle heat for about 45 minutes.

Peel the potatoes and cut them into cubes or thick slices. Add them to the casserole and continue cooking until they are tender. Lastly add the olives and tomatoes and heat through gently. Serves 4–6.

Navarin of Lamb with Baby Vegetables

A forequarter of lamb, boned
1 tablespoon oil
1 tablespoon plain (all-purpose) flour
1 teaspoon sugar
3 large tomatoes, peeled, seeded and chopped (see page 130)
2 cups (18 fl oz) good beef stock (page 66)
2 garlic cloves, bruised and peeled
A sprig of rosemary
A bouquet garni (page 31)
Salt and freshly ground pepper
2 bunches each of bulbous spring onions, tiny white
*   turnips, tiny beetroot (beets)*
250 g (8 oz) slender young green beans
30 g (1 oz) butter

*R*emove excess fat from the lamb and cut the meat into large (5 cm/2 in) cubes. Heat the oil in a flameproof casserole and lightly brown the lamb cubes all over, in several lots. Remove each lot as they are browned. When they are all done, return them to the pan and sprinkle them with the flour and sugar. Stir until browned, about 3 minutes.

Add the tomatoes, stock, garlic, rosemary and bouquet garni, and season with salt and pepper. Bring slowly to the boil, reduce the heat, half cover and simmer gently for 1¹/₂ hours, adding a little more liquid if necessary.

Meanwhile, prepare the vegetables. Trim the spring onions, turnips and beetroot, leaving a little of the stem still on. Carefully scrape the turnips. Drop the spring onions into boiling salted water and simmer until tender, about 5 minutes; remove with a slotted spoon and set aside. Do the same to the turnips. Cook the beetroots in the boiling water for about 10 minutes; drain and set aside—when they are cool enough to handle, slip off their skins. Trim the stem ends of the beans, drop the trimmed beans into boiling water and cook about 5 minutes, until just tender; drain and set aside. If larger vegetables are used, peel and quarter them and cook as above.

Just before serving, melt the butter in a sauté pan, add the vegetables and cook over a gentle heat until they are heated through. Remove the rosemary and bouquet garni from the navarin and spoon it onto a serving dish, reserving some of the gravy. Scatter with the vegetables and spoon over the reserved gravy. Serve immediately. Serves 6.

Navarin of Lamb with Baby Vegetables requires good-sized pieces of lamb; the shoulder is the best cut for this classic French dish. While baby vegetables add a charm, it is good made with more mature fresh vegetables.

247

Fragrant Thai Pork Roast

Delicious roast pork loin or neck, fragrant with cumin and garlic. Cut a fresh pineapple into spears to accompany the pork. This makes something different for an informal or festive dinner, and the pork is superb cold the next day.

> *2 kg (4 lb) pork loin or rolled boned shoulder*
> *2 teaspoons ground cumin*
> *6 garlic cloves, crushed with a little salt*
> *2 teaspoons grated fresh ginger*
> *Plenty of freshly ground pepper*
> *1 pineapple*
> *4 tablespoons soy sauce*
> *3 tablespoons vinegar*
> *6 tablespoons brown sugar*
> *Coriander (Chinese parsley) sprigs to garnish*

Fragrant Thai Pork Roast is indeed a festive dish, seasoned with a generous amount of garlic, fresh ginger and cumin. It may be served at room temperature but is good cold. Fresh pineapple and steamed lemon rice complete the dish.

*R*emove the skin from the pork if the butcher has not done this; it can be baked separately in a hot oven if you want crackling. Combine the cumin, garlic, ginger and pepper and rub well into the underside of the meat. Roll up and tie at intervals. (The pork may be left flat; it should be roasted fat side up.)

Preheat the oven to moderate (180°C/350°F).

Cut the skin off the pineapple and use some of it to cover the piece of pork. Place the pork in a baking dish (roasting pan) and roast for about 1$^{1}/_{2}$ hours or until almost tender. (Unrolled pork will cook in 1 hour.) Discard the pineapple skin, then baste the meat with a mixture of the soy sauce, vinegar and sugar. Return the meat to the oven for a further 15 minutes, basting frequently.

Remove the pork to a platter, skim the fat off the juices in pan and serve these as a gravy with the meat. Meanwhile, cut the skinned pineapple into rings or spears and use to garnish the pork, along with the sprigs of coriander. Serve with plain steamed rice and follow with a mixed green salad. Serves 8–10.

Pork Chops Rosmarin

Pork chops are marinated in a herby oil to give them a gamy flavour. They are then pan-fried or grilled and served with rosemary-flavoured mushrooms and new potatoes.

6 loin or rib pork chops on or off the bone, trimmed of fat

2 garlic cloves, cut into slivers

1 tablespoon olive oil

3 tablespoons butter

375 g (12 oz) mushrooms, sliced

1 garlic clove, crushed

1 tablespoon chopped rosemary (or 1 teaspoon dried)

18 new potatoes, boiled or steamed

2 tablespoons chopped parsley

MARINADE

1/3 cup (3 fl oz) olive oil

1/4 teaspoon salt

1/4 teaspoon freshly ground pepper

1 bay leaf, crushed

A sprig of rosemary, broken

Pork Chops Rosmarin has a gamy flavour, the pork having been marinated for several hours in oil impregnated with rosemary, bay leaf and freshly ground pepper. Mushrooms, pearly white caps, receive the same rosemary flavour treatment.

*M*ake small slits in the chops with a sharply pointed knife and insert the slivers of garlic. Mix the marinade ingredients together thoroughly and marinate the pork chops in the mixture for at least 2 hours, turning them occasionally. Dry them on kitchen paper towels.

Heat the tablespoon of oil in a shallow frying pan (skillet) over fairly high heat and quickly brown the chops for 4 minutes on each side. (We are advised nowadays not to overcook pork; however, you can give the chops 10 minutes in all. They can also be cooked on a ribbed grill for the same time.) While the chops are cooking, melt the butter in a frying pan over moderate heat, and quickly sauté the mushrooms with the garlic and rosemary for about 8 minutes. When the chops are tender, arrange them on a hot serving platter with the mushrooms and sprinkle with the chopped parsley. Potatoes may be served on a separate dish. Serves 6.

Pork Chops with Apples and Cabbage. Heat 2 tablespoons of butter in a saucepan, add 1 apple and 1 onion, finely sliced, and cook gently for 3–4 minutes. Add 1/2 a green cabbage, shredded, and a small sprig of rosemary, and cook covered, tossing every now and then, about 6–8 minutes. Serve with the pork chops.

Pork Chops with Lemon and Sage

Pork is ideal to grill (broil). The fat has a chance to drain, and the excellent pork we get these days responds well to quick cooking.

> *4–6 pork loin chops, trimmed of skin and fat*
> *Olive oil*
> *4–6 sage leaves*
> *Salt and freshly ground pepper*
> *Juice of 1 lemon or lime*
> *8–10 cherry tomatoes*
> *Lemon or lime wedges for garnishing*

Pork Chops with Lemon and Sage proves once again that simplest things are often best. The sharp lemon and the pleasantly bitter flavour of sage modify the richness of pork.

Brush the pork chops with olive oil, top each one with a sage leaf and season well with pepper. Sprinkle each with the citrus juice and allow to stand for 1 hour. Place under a preheated griller (broiler) and cook for 5 minutes, until golden; turn, brush again with olive oil, and grill for a further 5 minutes. (Or grill on a preheated ribbed grill for the same time.)

Wash the tomatoes, cut a cross on top, brush with olive oil, and grill for a minute or two, just long enough to blister the skin. Arrange the pork and tomatoes on a heated serving platter, season and garnish with lemon. Serves 4–6.

Herbed Crusted Loin of Pork

> *1.5 kg (3–4 lb) loin of pork (pork loin roast)*
> *Salt and pepper*
> *2 cups (4 oz) fresh breadcrumbs*
> *Rind of 1 lemon, grated*
> *2 tablespoons chopped parsley, lemon thyme or oregano*
> *1 garlic clove, chopped*
> *1–2 tablespoons oil*

Tip
Soft herbed breadcrumbs protect the pork meat which, when trimmed of almost all the fat, could easily become dry. The crunchy crumbs are delicious served with pork, even if they do come off when the loin is being carved. Ask the butcher to chine the loin of pork to make carving easy.

Cut the skin and almost all the fat off the pork, leaving only a thin layer of fat. Cut diamond shapes into this. Combine the remaining ingredients, except the oil, and press them firmly onto the loin. Place it fat side up on a rack in a roasting pan. Drizzle the oil over the crumbs. Roast the meat in a moderate oven (180°C/350°F), allowing 25 minutes per 500 g (1 lb), until done. Carve the meat into thick cutlets. Serve on a hot platter. Serves 6–8.

Pork Fillet Piccata

500 g (1 lb) pork fillet (tenderloin)—approximately 2 fillets
Plain (all-purpose) flour seasoned with salt and pepper
2 tablespoons unsalted (sweet) butter
2 tablespoons olive oil
$1/2$ cup ($4^{1}/_{2}$ fl oz) dry white wine
3 tablespoons fresh lemon juice
2 tablespoons finely chopped fresh parsley
6 basil leaves, sliced finely
$1/2$ teaspoon chopped oregano or thyme
6 lemon slices

Trim the meat of any membrane, cut it on the bias into 12 slices and
pound them thin between 2 sheets of plastic wrap.

Dredge lightly in the flour, shaking off the excess. In a large, heavy frying pan
(skillet) heat 1 tablespoon of the butter with 1 tablespoon of the oil over
moderately high heat, add half the pork slices, and sauté them, turning them
once, for 4 minutes. Transfer them to a platter and keep them warm, covered.
Sauté the remaining pork in the remaining butter and oil in the same manner

and keep it warm and covered. Add the wine to the pan and deglaze over high heat, scraping up the brown residue, until the mixture is reduced by half. Add the lemon juice, parsley, basil and oregano, swirling to combine the mixture well. Pour the sauce over the pork, and serve immediately with steamed parsleyed rice or steamed baby new potatoes. Serves 6.

Chinese Spicy Pork in Pancakes

¹/₃ cup (3 fl oz) peanut oil
1 teaspoon grated fresh ginger
2 garlic cloves, crushed
750 g (1¹/₂ lb) pork fillet (tenderloin), cut into fine shreds
2 tablespoons Chinese rice wine (Shaoxing) or dry sherry
2 teaspoons sugar
4 tablespoons light soy sauce
1 teaspoon ground pepper
Chinese pancakes (see below)
Chinese yellow bean paste
Sliced green shallots (spring onions, scallions)

Tip
This dish is eaten like Peking Duck: the pork is rolled up in pancakes and eaten in the hand. Crisp lettuce leaves may be used in place of pancakes.

*H*eat the oil in a wok or heavy frying pan (skillet) and fry the ginger and garlic over moderate heat until softened, about 2 minutes. Add the pork, increase the heat to high and stir the mixture until the pork is brown. Add the wine, sugar, soy sauce and pepper, and continue cooking over moderate heat until the liquid is absorbed and the pork is tender and dark brown. Serve in pancakes spread lightly with bean paste and sprinkled with shallots—add a spoonful of pork, roll up, and eat in the hand. Serves 8 as a first course or part of a meal.
Chinese Pancakes. Sift 2 cups (8 oz) of plain (all-purpose) flour into a mixing bowl and make a well in the centre. Pour in ¹/₂–³/₄ cup (4–6 fl oz) boiling water, a little at a time, gradually stirring in the flour. (Use just enough water to make a soft dough.) Knead for 5–10 minutes or until the dough feels pliable and elastic, then wrap it in plastic wrap (cling film) and allow to rest for 15 minutes.

Roll out the dough to 5 mm (¹/₄ in) thickness on a lightly floured surface and cut into 8 cm (3 in) circles. Brush the tops of the circles with sesame oil and press the oiled surfaces together in pairs, sandwich fashion. Roll out each sandwich again into a slightly bigger circle, about 10 cm (4 in) across.

Lightly grease a heavy frying pan (skillet). Cook the pancakes over moderate heat for 1 minute on each side. As they are cooked, peel the sandwich apart and stack the pancakes on a warm plate until ready to serve.

Shredded Pork and Noodles in Broth

In Chinese restaurants we often see people enjoying a big bowl of soupy noodles full of delicious things. This is one of my interpretations.

3–4 Chinese dried mushrooms soaked in ¹/₂ cup (4¹/₂ fl oz)
  warm water for 30 minutes
500 g (1 lb) boned lean pork, shredded
1 tablespoon soy sauce
1 tablespoon Chinese rice wine (Shaoxing), or sherry
1 teaspoon sugar
2 teaspoons cornflour (cornstarch)
375 g (12 oz) thin egg noodles
3 tablespoons vegetable oil
4 green shallots (spring onions, scallions), cut into 2.5 cm
  (1 in) lengths
1 broccoli head, separated into florets or sliced through
Salt
4 cups (1³/₄ imperial pints) boiling chicken broth (page 68)

*D*rain the mushrooms, then squeeze dry, reserving the soaking liquid. Discard the hard stalks, then slice the caps into thin strips.

Put the pork in a bowl with the soy sauce, wine, sugar and cornflour. Stir well, then leave to marinate for about 20 minutes.

Cook the noodles in boiling water for about 5 minutes, then drain.

Heat half the oil in a wok or frying pan (skillet), add the pork, and stir-fry until it changes colour. Remove from the pan with a slotted spoon and drain.

Heat the remaining oil in the pan, add the shallots, then the mushrooms and broccoli, stir-fry until the broccoli is bright green. Add a little salt. Return the pork to the pan together with the soaking liquid from the mushrooms, bring to the boil.

Place the noodles in a large serving bowl, pour over the boiling broth, then add the pork and vegetables. Serve hot in large, deep bowls. Serves 4–6.

Shredded Pork with Peppers

This is one of the basic and best stir-fry dishes. The vegetables used may be varied—for example, use 1 cup of shredded carrot or pea sprouts or shredded green beans or snow peas in place of the capsicum. Beef may replace pork.

500 g (1 lb) fillet pork
3 tablespoons light soy sauce
2 tablespoons Chinese rice wine (Shaoxing) or dry sherry
2 garlic cloves, finely chopped
1 teaspoon grated ginger
$1/2$ cup ($4 1/2$ fl oz) vegetable oil or light olive oil
2 onions, peeled and cut into 8 lengthwise
2 red capsicums (sweet peppers), seeded and shredded
$1/2$ red chilli, seeded and chopped

Shred the pork finely. Mix the meat with the soy, wine, garlic and ginger, allowing about 30 minutes for the seasonings to be absorbed.

Heat the oil in a wok or frying pan (skillet). Add the onions and capsicums, tossing and stirring until the vegetables soften, about 2–3 minutes. Keep the heat high; add the pork with seasonings and chilli and continue frying 3 minutes longer, stirring and tossing all the while. Serve hot with steamed rice. Serves 4.

Thai Pork Fried with Garlic

3 tablespoons vegetable oil
8 garlic cloves, chopped
2 teaspoons coarsely chopped coriander (Chinese parsley) root
500 g (1 lb) pork fillet (tenderloin) or boneless loin, cut into
*   thin strips*
2 tablespoons Thai fish sauce (nam pla)
$1/2$ teaspoon freshly ground black pepper
$1/4$ cup coriander sprigs

Tip
One of the simplest dishes to make. Serve as part of a Thai or light meal. The secret is to use lots of garlic and freshly ground black pepper.

Put the oil in a wok or large frying pan (skillet) over high heat. Stir-fry the garlic just until it starts to change colour. Add the coriander root and the pork. Stir-fry over high heat for 3–5 minutes. Add the fish sauce and black pepper and stir-fry for 1 more minute. Serve hot, sprinkled with fresh coriander sprigs, accompanied by boiled rice. Serves 4.

Pork Schnitzel

Pork steaks or chops prepared bone and skin free make good schnitzels for a very quick meal. Serve with sautéed potatoes or buttered noodles and a salad to follow. Pork schnitzels are available at many meat outlets and don't have to be flattened.

Pork schnitzels are every bit as good as the familiar veal schnitzels. The crispy breadcrumb coating seals in the tender juicy thin pork steaks. Sautéed apple rings and potatoes are the perfect accompaniment.

4 – 6 pork steaks, schnitzels or sliced fillets
Plain (all-purpose) flour seasoned with salt and pepper
1 egg, beaten until frothy
2 cups (8 oz) fine dry breadcrumbs
1/2 cup finely chopped fresh parsley
2 tablespoons olive oil
30 g (1 oz) unsalted (sweet) butter
2 apples (Granny Smith, golden delicious or delicious), cut in rings
15 g (1/2 oz) unsalted butter
Lemon slices

*W*orking with one pork steak at a time, flatten it slightly between 2 sheets of plastic wrap (cling film). Dredge lightly in the flour, shaking off the excess. Dip it in the egg, letting the excess drip off, and dredge it in the breadcrumbs combined with the parsley. In two frying pans (skillets) or one large pan, heat half the oil with half the butter over moderately high heat until the fat is hot. Fry the pork in batches if you only have one pan, turning it and adding the remaining oil and butter as necessary, for 4 minutes. Transfer the pork to a heated platter as it is cooked.

While the pork is cooking, in a separate pan fry the apple rings in the butter until soft and golden and use them and the lemon slices to garnish the schnitzel. Serves 4–6.

Roast Pork with Garlic

Pork loin cooked on a bed of garlic and carrots, which is served as a sauce.

> *1 piece of loin pork (pork loin roast) weighing about 1.5 kg*
> *(3 lb)*
> *Salt*
> *2 tablespoons olive oil*
> *3 carrots, finely diced*
> *12 garlic cloves, chopped*
> *3/4 cup (6 1/2 fl oz) dry white wine*
> *Freshly ground black pepper*

*P*reheat the oven to 220°C (425°F).
Score the skin of the pork with a very sharp knife to make a grid pattern of little squares (your butcher may do this for you). Now rub the skin with salt, and oil all sides with the olive oil. Place the meat in a roasting pan and roast it for 35 minutes.

Mix the carrots and garlic together with the white wine and season with black pepper. After roasting the pork for 35 minutes, take the pan out of the oven, lift up the pork, put the carrot, garlic and wine mixture in the pan, and then replace the pork. Turn the oven down to 190°C (375°F) and cook for a further 1 1/4 hours, every now and again basting the pork with the juices in the pan.

Before carving, leave the meat to rest in its juices for 15 minutes. Accompany this dish with mashed potatoes, Brussels sprouts and the garlic and carrot sauce, having first poured off excess fat. Serves 6.

Preparing Escalopes of Veal

scalopes (scallops) of veal (*scaloppine di vitello* to the Italians) are quick to cook and delicious to eat, and they lend themselves to many easy sauces. Unfortunately they are hard to buy except at good butchers and expensive delicatessens or specialty shops. It is better and cheaper to cut your own. To do this, order a complete loin or a section of loin; this is the joint the butcher usually cuts into chops. Make sure he does no chining and doesn't chop off the bones. Cut out the cushion of lean meat, trim off all the membrane, and cut the meat into slices 2 cm (^{3}/$_4$ in) thick. They will be about 6.3 cm (2^1/$_2$ in) across and weigh about 90 g (3 oz). Place each slice between two sheets of plastic wrap (cling film) or waxed paper and flatten them with a rolling pin until they are about 10 cm (4 in) across. They are now ready for cooking, and any not required can be frozen. When packing for the freezer, place them between layers of plastic wrap and pop them into a freezer bag. Trimmings and bones can be made into a pie or fricassee and a pot of veal stock.

Escalopes of veal, on or off the bone, are a culinary delight. The veal cutlet is flattened out, dipped in egg and breadcrumbs and fried in very good butter or olive oil. This recipe has a shaving of Parmesan cheese over slivers of fine cured ham as a finishing touch.

Veal Escalopes

4 – 6 veal rib chops, escaloped

Seasoned flour

1 egg, beaten

2 cups (4 oz) fresh breadcrumbs

30 g (1 oz) butter

1 tablespoon vegetable or olive oil

4 slices prosciutto

30 g (1 oz) Parmesan, roughly grated or shaved

4 tablespoons cream (single, light)

Chopped parsley to garnish

ay each escalope between sheets of damp, greaseproof (waxed) paper or plastic wrap (cling film) and flatten with a rolling pin. Dip the meat in the seasoned flour and then in the egg, and coat with the breadcrumbs. Melt the butter and oil in a frying pan (skillet). When foaming, add the escalopes and cook for 2–3 minutes each side until brown.

Put the escalopes on a baking dish. Place a piece of prosciutto on each, cover with Parmesan, and top with a little cream. Put under a hot grill (broiler) until the cheese is melted and golden. Serve sprinkled with parsley. Serves 4 – 6.

Veal Scaloppine with Sherry Vinegar

A quick dish to make. Serve with mashed potatoes and a mixed green salad.

750 g (1¹/₂ lb) veal escalopes, pounded very thin
Plain (all-purpose) flour seasoned with salt and pepper
1 tablespoon extra virgin olive oil
¹/₂ cup (4¹/₂ fl oz) chicken stock (page 68)
1 tablespoon butter
1 tablespoon sherry vinegar
Salt and freshly ground pepper
¹/₄ cup finely chopped parsley

Tip
You can vary the vinegar in Veal Scaloppine—try balsamic, tarragon or even raspberry vinegar.

*T*rim the veal escalopes of any fat or gristle if necessary. Place the seasoned flour on a sheet of kitchen paper or plate and lightly dust the veal with the flour, shaking off any excess. In a large frying pan, heat the oil over moderately high heat and brown the veal for about 2 minutes on each side, doing so in several lots. Remove and place on a heated serving platter.

Return the pan to the heat and add the chicken stock. Let it bubble hard, scrape the pan, and allow the liquid to reduce slightly. Reduce the heat and stir in the butter and vinegar to heat through. Season with a little salt and pepper, and pour the sauce over the scaloppine. Sprinkle with parsley. Serves 6.

Veal Escalopes with Mustard Cream Sauce

Many butchers and some delicatessens sell thin veal steaks. If the steaks have not already been beaten flat, place them between two sheets of dampened plastic wrap (cling film) and beat them with a rolling pin, meat mallet or cleaver.

4 large veal steaks or 8 small veal escalopes
Plain (all-purpose) flour
30 g (1 oz) butter
1 tablespoon olive oil
¹/₂ cup (4¹/₂ fl oz) cream (single, light)
¹/₂ cup (4¹/₂ fl oz) white wine
1 teaspoon chopped fresh marjoram or ¹/₄ teaspoon dried
1 tablespoon Dijon-style mustard
Salt and freshly ground black pepper

ut large steaks in two. Pat the veal dry with kitchen paper towels and snip around the edges of each piece so that it will cook without curling. Dip both sides in flour and pat off excess.

Heat the butter and oil in a frying pan (skillet); as the foam subsides, add the veal. Sauté on fairly high heat until golden brown on both sides (do this in two batches if necessary). Remove to a heated serving dish and keep warm.

Add the cream, wine, marjoram and mustard to the pan and simmer, stirring, for 3 minutes. Season with salt and pepper. Serve the veal with the sauce spooned over. These escalopes are good with buttered noodles or rice and a green vegetable or green salad. Serves 4.

Veal Birds with Anchovies

This dish is popular in Italy; the tiny veal 'birds' with their slightly gamy taste may be reminiscent of the little birds so beloved of some Italians. Thanks to the EEC, the taking of the lovely songbirds for table use has been outlawed.

500 g (1 lb) veal, cut into thin, even slices
125 g (4 oz) mozzarella, Emmenthaler or Gruyère cheese
6–8 anchovy fillets, drained and soaked in a little milk
1 tablespoon vegetable or olive oil
³/₄ cup (6¹/₂ fl oz) white wine
2 teaspoons butter
1 teaspoon chopped parsley

Veal Birds with Anchovies. Dainty pieces of flattened veal steak are rolled around batons of cheese and anchovy, producing a gamy flavour reminiscent of the flavour of the tiny songbirds that used to be eaten in Italy.

$\mathscr{P}$ound the veal slices lightly until very thin. If large steaks are used, cut them in two. On each slice place a small finger of cheese and a halved anchovy fillet. Roll and fasten securely with toothpicks or cocktail sticks.

Heat the oil in a frying pan (skillet) large enough to hold all the birds without crowding, add the rolls and brown them on all sides. Add 2 tablespoons of the wine, cover the pan and cook the rolls quite briskly for 6–8 minutes. Remove the meat to a hot platter and keep warm. Add the remaining wine to the pan drippings and simmer for a few minutes, scraping up residue from the pan. Swirl in the butter. Add the parsley and spoon over the rolls. Serve with boiled rice or noodles and a green salad. Serves 4.

Wiener Schnitzel

I like to order veal steaks a day ahead; butchers will usually oblige by cutting good veal. You can also use veal escalopes cut from the loin (see instructions page 260). Serve this famous Viennese dish with plenty of creamy mashed potatoes or sautéed potatoes and a salad.

To make fresh breadcrumbs: Cut crusts from 6 slices of two-day-old bread, cut or tear into small pieces and process in an electric blender or food processor into crumbs. Or rub the bread through a colander.

6 veal steaks, thinly cut
Salt and freshly ground black pepper
3 tablespoons plain (all-purpose) flour
1 egg, beaten
1¹/₂ cups (3 oz) fresh breadcrumbs
Light olive oil
30 g (1 oz) butter
Lemon slices and capers for garnish

*F*latten the veal steaks between 2 sheets of plastic wrap (cling film) with a rolling pin or meat mallet until they are very thin. Trim off any sinews. Cut each steak in two or leave whole. Season with salt and pepper. Dip first into the flour, then into the beaten egg and finally into the breadcrumbs. Press the coating on with the heel of your hand. Place the breaded veal on a flat tray and chill for at least 30 minutes.

Heat sufficient oil to cover the base of a heavy frying pan (or use two pans), add half the butter and, when hot, add half the veal. Cook over a good heat about 1–2 minutes each side or until golden brown, turning three times during cooking. Repeat with the remaining veal and butter. Serve hot with slices of lemon and a few capers as garnish. Serves 4–6.

Grilled Veal Chops with Orange Butter

For this I like to use a ribbed grill pan, which does a lovely job of cooking the chops with the minimum of fat—just a brushing of olive oil. A griller (broiler) that you can trust to get good and hot does the job too.

> *1–2 tablespoons olive oil*
> *6–8 rib veal chops which have been trimmed, or 'frenched',*
> *   as for lamb cutlets*
> ORANGE BUTTER
> *60 g (2 oz) unsalted (sweet) butter*
> *½ teaspoon grated orange rind*
> *1 teaspoon grated lemon rind*
> *1 teaspoon lemon juice*
> *1 tablespoon finely chopped green shallots (spring onions, scallions)*
> *2 tablespoons chopped basil or mint leaves*
> *Salt and freshly ground pepper to taste*

*F*irst make the orange butter. Cream the butter in a small bowl and beat in the orange and lemon rinds, then the lemon juice, shallots, basil or mint leaves, salt and pepper. Shape the butter into a roll and wrap it in a piece of aluminium foil. Chill it until it is firm—this may take an hour and can be done well in advance.

Heat the ribbed grill pan or griller (broiler) and brush with the olive oil. Pat the veal chops dry and season with pepper. Cook with a moderately high heat for 5 minutes on each side, until golden and still slightly pink inside. Top each veal chop with one or two thin slices of the orange butter to serve. Serves 4–6.

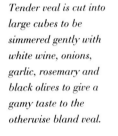

Veal with Black Olives

Delicate veal responds beautifully to the strong, robust flavours of rosemary and black olives. Serve with steamed rice and follow with a green salad.

1 kg (2 lb) lean veal, preferably from the shoulder, cut into
  4 cm (1¹/₂ in) cubes
Plain (all-purpose) flour seasoned with salt and pepper
2 tablespoons olive oil
1 garlic clove, chopped
1 onion, chopped
1 teaspoon chopped rosemary
¹/₂ cup (4¹/₂ fl oz) dry white wine
1 tablespoon tomato paste (concentrate)
1 cup (9 fl oz) stock
6 black olives, pitted and sliced
Parsley, chopped

Tender veal is cut into large cubes to be simmered gently with white wine, onions, garlic, rosemary and black olives to give a gamy taste to the otherwise bland veal.

Preheat the oven to moderate (180°C/350°F) unless you choose to cook on top of the stove. Dust the veal with the seasoned flour. Heat the oil in a heavy frying pan (skillet), add the meat and brown it on all sides. Do this in several lots if necessary. Add the garlic and onion and cook 3 minutes longer, stirring with a wooden spoon.

Add the rosemary, wine, tomato paste and enough stock to cover. Scrape up any brown crusty bits. Transfer to a casserole. Cover and cook for 1 hour or until almost tender. Add the olives and cook for a further 15 minutes. Before serving, sprinkle with the chopped parsley. Serves 6.

The dish may also be cooked on top of the stove over a gentle heat. Simmer very gently, covered, for 45 minutes.

Veal Chops with Madeira Cream Sauce

This lovely dish of lightly browned veal chops with its Madeira cream sauce is perfect with rice or noodles. A good dry sherry may be used instead of Madeira. Follow with crisp mixed green salad.

> *6 veal chops, cut thick*
> *Salt and freshly ground pepper*
> *1/4 cup (1 oz) plain (all-purpose) flour*
> *60 g (2 oz) butter*
> *1 tablespoon olive oil*
> *2 tablespoons finely chopped shallots (green or golden)*
> *250 g (8 oz) button mushrooms, sliced*
> *1/2 cup (4 1/2 fl oz) dry white wine*
> *1/2 cup (4 1/2 fl oz) cream (single, light)*
> *1/2 cup (4 1/2 fl oz) dry Madeira or sherry*

Sprinkle the chops with salt and pepper to taste. Dredge the chops on both sides in flour and shake off any excess.

Melt two-thirds of the butter and all the olive oil in a heavy frying pan (skillet) and add the chops. Cook for about 4 to 5 minutes or until the chops are nicely browned on one side. Turn and cook the other side for 5 to 6 minutes. Transfer the chops to a warm platter.

Melt the remaining butter in a saucepan and add the shallots and sliced mushrooms and cook briefly, tossing now and then. Add the dry white wine. Reduce by half and add the cream. Cook for about 1 minute. Add salt and pepper to taste.

Meanwhile, pour off the fat from the pan in which the chops cooked. Add the Madeira and cook down until almost totally reduced. Add the mushrooms in cream sauce and blend. Serve the sauce spooned over or beside the chops. Serve with rice or buttered noodles and a green salad. Serves 6.

Poultry

The plump and familiar shape of a golden roasted bird, be it chicken, duck, turkey or one of those wonderful game birds, is indeed a cheerful sight.

Apart from being roasted or baked, poultry can be cut into pieces for frying or grilling (broiling) or for use in making a casserole or fricassee, the carcass used to make stock.

I like to buy fresh free-range country poultry. Along with many chefs, I strongly believe that a bird that has spent time scratching around and pecking the ground results in a bird that tastes as it should and has had some sort of a life—the two not unrelated. Such a bird you pay extra for, but it is well worth it. It makes any meal special—and what meal isn't?

Grilled Lemon Chicken. Breasts of chicken marinated in lemon juice, onion and garlic and gently cooked on a ribbed grill. Served with a Spanish Orange and Watercress Salad and crusty farmhouse bread, it makes a lovely light meal for informal alfresco eating.

Roast Chicken Fantasia

Tip

You could cook one large chicken for four or buy small spatchcocks (Cornish hens, poussin) and allow a whole chicken for each person. A watercress salad and some crusty bread is all you need with this dish.

The name Fantasia comes from the Rome restaurant that created this lovely dish, where it is presented in its bag with great flourish. It is delicious.

> *2 roasting chickens about 1.5 kg (3 lb), excess fat removed*
> *Salt*
> *2 rashers (slices) bacon, rind removed, halved*
> *6 sage leaves*
> *4 sprigs of rosemary*
> *2 tablespoons each butter and oil*
> *12 thin slices prosciutto*

*S*eason the cavities of the chickens with salt, then place half the bacon, sage leaves and rosemary inside each cavity. Truss the chickens into a neat shape with string. Heat half the butter and oil in a frying pan (skillet) over moderately high heat and quickly brown the chickens all over. Remove from the pan, cool slightly and then cover each chicken with the slices of prosciutto.

Brush with oil two brown paper bags, place a chicken in each, and tie securely with string. If using oiled baking paper (parchment) instead of bags, wrap it loosely around the chicken, folding the edges to seal. Place the bags in an oiled pan and roast in a moderate oven (180°C/350°F) for 15 minutes. Pierce each bag in a couple of places with a sharply pointed knife and continue cooking for 1 hour longer (a large chicken will take 1 hour 15 minutes and individual small chickens 45 minutes). Remove from the oven and discard the bags, allowing any juices in the bags to drain onto a hot serving platter. Line the platter with the slices of prosciutto and arrange the chicken on top, whole or jointed. If serving a small whole chicken for each guest, the chicken can be presented in its bag at the table. Guests will enjoy opening the bag at the table. Have fresh hot plates ready to take the chicken and its juices. Serves 6–8.

Roast Chicken Fantasia is cooked 'en papillote'—sealed in paper—to capture the natural flavours and juices of a free-range country chicken. Take the bag to the table, open it and allow the guests to experience the marvellous appearance and aroma of the birds.

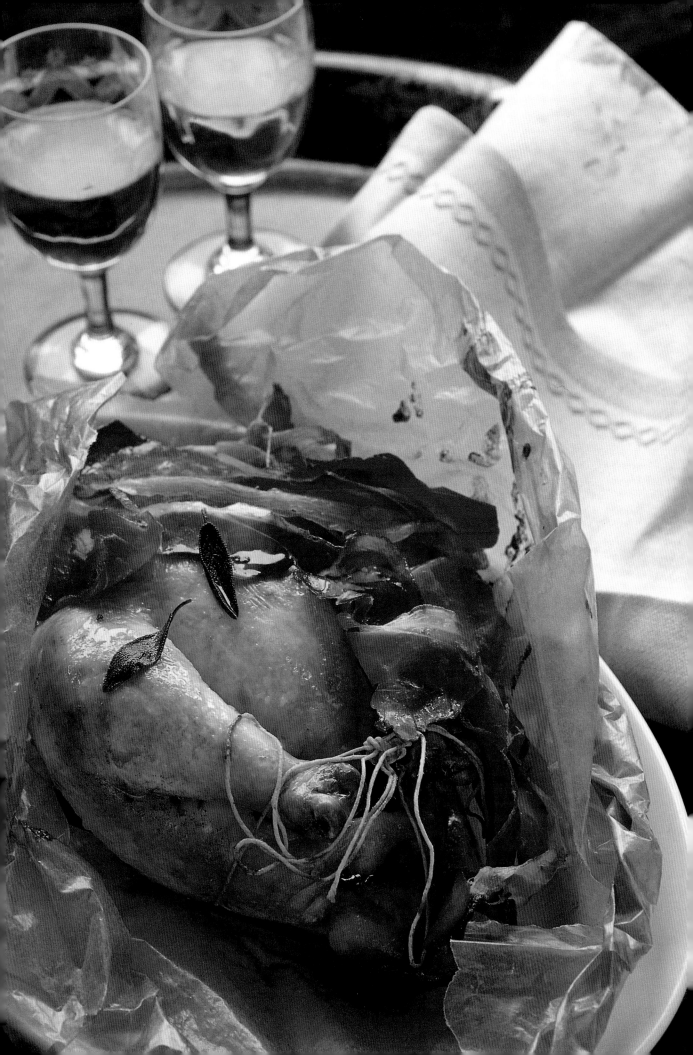

Chicken with Garlic

1 roasting chicken about 1.5 kg (3 lb) or slightly larger
Salt and freshly ground pepper
2 tablespoons olive oil
1–2 heads of garlic
A bouquet garni (comprising thyme, sage, rosemary, bay leaf)

Tip
This recipe calls for a lot of garlic. The French enjoy eating the gently braised oil-soaked cloves on crusty bread. It is surprising how mild the finished dish tastes.

*W*ipe the chicken and season it, including the cavity, with salt and pepper. Truss it into a neat shape with string. Heat the olive oil in a deep flameproof casserole dish and add the chicken, turning until golden all over. Break the heads of garlic into cloves; peel off flaky dried skins. Add the garlic cloves (you will have about 20 per head) and bouquet garni to the pot, cover and cook in a preheated moderate oven (180°C/350°F) for 1 hour.

Discard the garlic or serve it separately in a small bowl, as you prefer. Serve the chicken with a crisp salad and slices of crusty bread. Serves 4–6.

Thai Barbecued Chicken

2 kg (4 lb) chicken pieces (boneless breasts or thighs), excess
*   fat removed*
A bunch of coriander (Chinese parsley), including roots,
*   washed thoroughly*
3 garlic cloves, peeled
1–2 small red chillies (chili peppers), halved and seeded
1 teaspoon each turmeric and curry powder
1 tablespoon sugar
A good pinch of salt
3 tablespoons Thai fish sauce (nam pla)
3 tablespoons coconut cream or beaten yoghurt

Thai Barbecued Chicken is served at room temperature. The combination of fresh coriander (Chinese parsley), chilli, Thai fish sauce and coconut cream gives an exotic taste to the chicken which is best enjoyed when wrapped in a crisp lettuce leaf and eaten in the hand.

*P*at the chicken pieces dry with kitchen paper towels. Cut the coriander roots off at the stems and reserve the leaves for garnishing. Place the roots in an electric blender or food processor with the garlic, chillies, spices, sugar and salt; process to a coarse paste. Add the fish sauce and continue to blend until smooth. Place the chicken pieces in a large, shallow ceramic dish and rub them all over with the spice paste, preferably using thin rubber gloves. Leave to marinate for several hours if possible.

273

Arrange the chicken pieces on a grill and brush evenly with the coconut cream or beaten yoghurt. Grill or barbecue until the chicken is well browned and tender, turning once and basting once or twice more. Arrange on a serving platter (lined with a banana leaf if you like); garnish with the coriander leaves and accompany with cucumber pieces. You can serve it with steamed rice and crisp lettuce leaves; your guests, like Thais, may enjoy eating the chicken rolled up in lettuce leaves. Serves 6–8.

Grilled Chicken with Mustard Sauce

This is an uncomplicated dish, it will remind travellers of meals in rustic Italy or France. Grilled young chickens are set on salad greens topped with a piquant sauce. A rough country bread is all you need with this meal.

Tip
To split and flatten a chicken, cut it along the backbone and open it out with your hands, cracking the breastbone so that it lies as flat as possible.

2 small chickens about 500 g (1 lb), split and flattened
Lemon juice
Salt and pepper
2 tablespoons olive oil
SAUCE
2 green shallots (spring onions, scallions), finely chopped
2 teaspoons dry sherry
4 tablespoons chicken stock (page 68)
1 teaspoon tomato paste (concentrate)
2 teaspoons French (Dijon) mustard
Worcestershire sauce
A pinch of cayenne pepper

Season both sides of the chickens with lemon juice, salt and pepper. Brush the chickens with oil and grill (broil) very gently, starting with skin side up for about 5 minutes, then turned over, basting occasionally with oil. They will take about 20 minutes. Cut the chickens in two and place them on a heated serving dish and keep warm. They may be served on a bed of salad vegetables, to which the chicken gives a delicious taste, so there is no need to cook separate green vegetables—the gravy juices from the chicken melt into the salad.

To prepare the sauce, strain the pan juices into a small saucepan, add the shallots and cook gently until soft. Add the sherry and stock and bring to the boil. Stir in the tomato paste, mustard, a few drops of Worcestershire sauce and cayenne pepper. Garnish the chicken with watercress if not serving on salad greens, and serve the sauce separately. Serves 4.

French Roasted Chicken

Butter-roasted chicken may be delicious, but the French are clever. They roast chicken in stock, and perhaps some wine, basting it continually during the cooking. The result is a crispy skin that turns an appetising golden colour during the last 10–15 minutes, and the flesh is plump and juicy.

1 roasting chicken about 1.8 kg (3 ½ lb), necked removed
Salt and freshly ground pepper
A piece of orange rind
1½ cups (13½ fl oz) stock or half stock and white wine

*P*reheat the oven to hot (200°C/400°F). Season the chicken well with salt and freshly ground pepper. Place the piece of orange rind in the cavity. Truss the chicken and place it breast side up on a rack in a roasting pan. Pour the stock into the base of the pan and roast for 10 minutes. Reduce the temperature to moderately hot (190°C/375°F) and turn the chicken onto its side. Baste well and continue to cook, turning and basting every 15 minutes. Cook for a further 50 minutes or until the chicken is tender when a fine skewer is inserted into a thigh joint and juices run clear. Turn the chicken on its back for the last 15 minutes, until the breast is golden. Serves 4–6.

Stock. Make the stock by simmering together the neck, feet (if available) and giblets with a small onion, bay leaf, a few parsley stalks and 2 cups (18 fl oz) of water, for at least 30 minutes.

Grilled Spiced Chicken

Grilled (broiled) Spiced Chicken is perfect for informal eating, best perhaps out of doors. Seasoned with the more gentle spices and lemon juice, it has the right blend for family meals yet is interesting enough for guests.

The hot chicken 'fatigues' the salad base for the dish. It is delicious just served with a good crusty bread or one of the Arabic-Lebanese flat breads. A lovely alfresco meal.

> *1 chicken about 1.5 kg (3 lb), jointed and with neck and*
> *giblets removed, or 4–6 chicken pieces (portions)*
> *Salt and pepper*
> *2 tablespoons ground coriander*
> *1/4 teaspoon ground ginger*
> *1/2 teaspoon Mexican chilli powder*
> *1/2 teaspoon turmeric*
> *2 tablespoons olive or vegetable oil*
> *1 tablespoon lemon juice*
> *Watercress or salad greens*
> *Lemon wedges*

*W*ipe the chicken dry with kitchen paper towels, and rub the portions well with salt and pepper. Mix the spices with the oil and lemon juice in a small saucepan over very low heat.

Place the chicken on a griller rack under a preheated grill (broiler). Brush with the spice mixture. Grill, skin side up, for about 8 minutes. Turn each piece over, baste again with the spice mixture, and lower the grilling rack just a little from the source of heat. Cook for another 8–10 minutes, brushing several times with the spice mixture, then turn the pieces again and baste and cook for a further 5 minutes or until tender and the skin is golden and crackling. Place the chicken on a serving dish liberally spread with watercress, salad greens, or whatever is in season, with some lemon wedges. Serves 4–6.

Grilled Chicken with Orange

A simple family meal or an easy dish for a weekend luncheon. Use half breasts of chicken, or thighs if you prefer them, but trim off excess bones, like the backbone, which some poulterers leave on.

> *4–6 chicken pieces (half breasts or thighs)*
> *1 tablespoon olive oil*
> *Juice of ¹/₄ lemon*
> *Salt*
> *1 small onion, peeled and thinly sliced*
> *1 tablespoon sherry*
> *2 large oranges*
> *Parsley or watercress*

*B*rush the chicken pieces with the oil and squeeze half the lemon juice over. Sprinkle with salt. Place under a preheated moderate griller (broiler), skin side up, and grill (broil) for about 8 minutes to let the skin brown, brushing frequently with oil. Turn each piece over and grill for another 8 minutes, then turn them again and grill for a few minutes more until the skin is golden and bubbling.

Meanwhile, with a small sharp knife or vegetable peeler, cut strips of rind off one orange and slice them into julienne strips. Marinate the rind and the onion slices in the sherry. Peel the oranges, removing all pith, and cut into thin slices.

Place the chicken on a heated platter. Strew the marinated orange rind and onion on top of the chicken. Surround with oranges slices, garnish with parsley or watercress. Serve with boiled new potatoes. Serves 4–6.

Chicken Saltimbocca

Traditionally made with thin veal steaks in Italy, where *saltimbocca* means 'jump into the mouth' because it's so quick to prepare. A simple green salad goes very well with this dish; use a selection of salad greens, including a little arugula (rocket) or watercress.

4 chicken half-breast fillets
60 g (2 oz) piece of Parmesan cheese
8 slices prosciutto
8 sage leaves
60 g (2 oz) butter
Freshly ground pepper
$^1/_2$ cup (4$^1/_2$ fl oz) dry white wine

Chicken Saltimbocca was inspired by the much-loved Italian veal dish of the same name. 'Saltimbocca' literally means 'jump into the mouth', which refers to its being very quick to cook and eat, and suggests that it should not be left hanging about.

Split each half breast through into two to make 8 thin chicken-breast steaks. Place a thin slice of Parmesan cheese in the centre of each and top with a slice of prosciutto. Place a sage leaf in the centre and carefully secure it with a wooden cocktail stick or toothpick.

Melt the butter in a large frying pan (skillet), add the chicken steaks and brown quickly on both sides for a few minutes. Season with plenty or freshly ground pepper. Arrange on a warm serving dish and keep warm. Add the wine to the pan and scrape the base well; a small nut of butter may be swirled in for a richer sauce. Pour the sauce over the saltimbocca and serve immediately. Serves 4.

Grilled Lemon Chicken

I like to grill chicken breasts on the bone, as it helps to keep the good shape; you can detach the breast from the bone after it is cooked. This is one of the simplest and best ways to cook chicken breasts.

Juice of 1 large lemon
$^1/_2$ small onion, grated
1 garlic clove, crushed with a little salt
Freshly ground white pepper
1–2 tablespoons olive oil
4 half breasts of chicken, skin removed
1 lemon, sliced or cut in wedges

ombine the lemon juice, grated onion, crushed garlic, pepper and oil. Marinate the chicken breasts in this mixture for at least an hour. Place them under a preheated grill (broiler) for 15–20 minutes, turning halfway through cooking until the juices run clear when the chicken is pierced with a fine skewer. If you have a ribbed grill pan, heat the pan and place the chicken, rounded side down, on the pan. After 3 minutes reduce heat the cook for another 7 minutes. Turn and cook the other side for 7–10 minutes. Serve with lemon slices or wedges. Serves 4.

Green Peppercorn Chicken is at its best freshly grilled (broiled) so that the skin is crisp and golden and the flesh moist and full of flavour from the pungent green peppercorn butter. Serve warm, on or with crisp salad greens.

Green Peppercorn Chicken

Green peppercorns in small cans labelled *poivre vert* are available from specialty food shops and large supermarkets. They are little berries from the same trees as the black peppercorn but are canned in their soft, undried state and have a more vibrant flavour than black peppercorns.

4 large chicken breasts, boned
1 garlic clove, crushed with a little salt
1 tablespoon green peppercorns, crushed
30 g (1 oz) butter, softened
Lemon juice

Tip
Crush peppercorns
with the back of a
spoon.

*D*ry the chicken breasts with kitchen paper towels. Combine the garlic and peppercorns with the butter and lemon juice to make a smooth paste. Spread the mixture on both sides of the chicken and push a little between the flesh and the skin. Leave to stand for several hours. Put the chicken in a shallow roasting or broiling pan and place under a preheated grill (broiler).

Cook skin side up for 5 minutes. Turn the chicken and cook for a further 10–15 minutes, turning once or twice and finishing skin side up, until the chicken is tender and the skin crisp and golden. Serve with fluffy boiled rice and a crisp salad or green vegetable. Serves 4.

Chicken Breasts with Capers and Lemon

Chicken breasts can be found anywhere; make a special effort to find the salted capers—they really do make a difference—and the lemon gives the dish a tart, fresh flavour. Boneless chicken thighs are good cooked this way.

4 half breasts of chicken, skin and bones removed
Plain (all-purpose) flour seasoned with salt and pepper
1 tablespoon capers (salted if possible)
30 g (1 oz) plus 2 teaspoons butter
Grated rind and juice of 1 large lemon
Salt and freshly ground pepper

*W*ipe the chicken dry with paper towels and dust with the seasoned flour. Soak the capers in a little water if using the dried, salted ones.

Heat the 30 g (1 oz) of butter in a large frying pan (skillet). Add the chicken breasts and fry gently on each side until they are cooked and golden brown, about 10 minutes. Remove the chicken to a heated serving dish. Add the 2 teaspoons of butter to the pan, then the capers (chopped into pieces if they are large) and the lemon rind and juice. Stir well to deglaze the pan, season with salt and pepper and pour over the chicken breasts. Serve with sautéed or boiled new potatoes and follow with a green salad. Serves 4.

281

Basque Chicken

Basque Chicken is just what one would expect from Spain. It is colourful in its lavish use of bright red or green capsicums (sweet peppers) and ripe tomatoes. And it is flavoursome; a bouquet garni, wine and good olive oil see to that. A great way to treat chicken.

Lavish use of capsicums (sweet peppers) and tomatoes is a characteristic of the Basque cuisine—and with capsicum and tomato so rich in vitamin C, this dish is good for any health program.

> *1 roasting chicken about 1.5 kg (3 lb), jointed and with neck*
> *and giblets removed, or 6 chicken pieces (portions)*
> *2 tablespoons olive oil*
> *Salt and pepper*
> *A bouquet garni (see page 31)*
> *$1/2$ cup ($4^1/_2$ fl oz) dry white wine*
> *1 onion, peeled and chopped finely*
> *1 green or red capsicum (pepper), seeded and cut into strips*
> *2 medium tomatoes, skinned, seeded and chopped*

*D*ry the chicken with kitchen paper towels. Slowly brown the chicken pieces in 1 tablespoon of the oil in a heavy saucepan. When brown, transfer to a flameproof casserole, season with salt and pepper and add the bouquet garni and wine. Put the remaining oil in the pan and cook the onion until soft but not brown. Add the capsicum, cook for about 5 minutes and add the tomatoes. Season with salt and pepper and add this sauce to the chicken in the casserole. Cook over a gentle heat for 20–30 minutes or in a slow oven (150°C/300°F) for 1 hour. Accompany with rice pilaf. Serves 4–6.

282

Poached Chicken Breasts

A poached chicken breast is one of the most useful and versatile foods to have on hand. It's great for salads and sandwiches, for dieters, and for use in many family dishes.

2 cups (18 fl oz) water, lightly salted
Peppercorns
1 small bay leaf or 1 teaspoon dried tarragon
1 small onion, sliced
4 half breasts of chicken or 4 breast fillets

*I*n a frying pan with a lid, or in a wide saucepan, bring to the boil the salted water, peppercorns, bay leaf or dried tarragon and onion. Add the chicken, cover, and reduce the heat. Poach for 8–10 minutes. Turn off the heat and allow to cool in the stock. Store in the refrigerator in a covered container with some of the strained liquid. Remove skin and any bones before serving. Serves 4.

Chicken in Plum Sauce

Chinese enjoy warm salads served in lettuce cups. The crisp lettuce is a perfect wrap for the tasty filling. It suits the casual eating we all seem to favour today.

500 g (1 lb) chicken fillets, finely chopped
2 tablespoons light soy sauce
2 tablespoons Chinese plum sauce
Salt and freshly ground pepper
1 teaspoon sugar
1 teaspoon cornflour (cornstarch)
2 tablespoons rice wine or dry sherry
3 tablespoons vegetable oil
5 Chinese dried mushrooms, soaked and sliced
8 water chestnuts, chopped
2 tablespoons water
1 large cos (romaine) or iceberg (crisphead) lettuce, washed
and crisped
6 tablespoons Chinese plum sauce for garnish

ombine the chopped chicken with 1 tablespoon of the soy sauce, the 2 tablespoons of plum sauce, salt and pepper to taste, the sugar, cornflour and 1 tablespoon of the rice wine or sherry. Mix well and let stand for 30 minutes.

Heat the oil in a wok and stir-fry the mushrooms for 30 seconds. Add the chicken mixture and water chestnuts quickly; stir-fry, separating the chicken pieces, for 1 minute. Add the remaining rice wine and soy sauce and the water, and cook for a further 1 minute. Turn into a bowl.

Guests spoon some of this mixture into lettuce cups, spoon a little plum sauce over, then fold the lettuce over to eat in the hand. Provide finger bowls or paper napkins. Serves 4–6.

Lemon Pepper Chicken

This delicious chicken is good with crusty bread and a mixed green salad. To get a coarse pepper, loosen the screw on your pepper mill so that it just holds together—enough to give you a coarse grind.

> *4 chicken marylands (legs and thighs) or half breasts*
> *$1/4$ cup ($2^1/4$ fl oz) lemon juice*
> *2 garlic cloves, chopped*
> *4 green shallots (spring onions, scallions), chopped*
> *4 thyme sprigs*
> *1 bay leaf*
> *$1/2$ cup ($4^1/2$ fl oz) olive oil*
> *Rind of 2 lemons, grated*
> *2 teaspoons fresh black pepper, coarsely ground*

ut the marylands at the joint and trim any excess backbone skin and fat off the thighs. (If preferred, the marylands can be left whole.) In a large ceramic or glass bowl whisk together the lemon juice, garlic, shallots, thyme and bay leaf; add the oil in a thin stream. Place the chicken in the mixture, and turn to coat well. Marinate for 2 hours, turning the chicken several times.

Arrange the chicken, skin side up, on a rack or roasting pan; sprinkle it with the lemon rind and pepper and salt to taste. Roast in an oven preheated to 220°C (425°F) for 25–30 minutes or until the juices run clear when a thigh is pierced with a fine skewer. Serves 4.

Chicken Tonnato

The perfect lunch dish for a spring day. You can prepare the dish the day before and chill it in the refrigerator. This will allow the full flavour to develop. Keep it in a covered container. Don't add the garnish until presenting the dish.

Chicken Tonnato is a great dish for informal entertaining. With the chicken breasts poached and the tuna mayonnaise sauce made, it can be dressed on a bed of mixed salad greens at the last moment, or the chicken and sauce may be combined and left to develop full flavour.

185 g (6 oz) can tuna in oil
6 anchovy fillets
1 egg yolk
1 tablespoon lemon juice
1 cup (9 fl oz) olive oil
1–2 tablespoons chicken stock, if necessary
Freshly ground pepper
6–8 cold cooked chicken breast fillets (see page 283), if large,
   cut in two
Capers, black olives and lemon wedges to garnish

Put the tuna (with oil), anchovies, egg yolk and lemon juice in a food processor or electric blender and process, using an on/off action, until evenly combined. Add the oil in a steady stream and process until a thickish mayonnaise consistency. If necessary, thin the mixture to a coating consistency with a little chicken stock. Season with pepper. Arrange the cooked chicken on a platter. Spoon the sauce over the chicken. Scatter over capers and olives, and add lemon wedges to squeeze. Accompany with crusty French bread and a good green salad and perhaps some boiled new potatoes. Serves 8–10.

285

Warm Chicken Liver, Mushroom and Spinach Salad

A lovely example of the trend in warm salads, this salad makes a delicious entrée.

1 bunch spinach or watercress sprigs
12 button mushrooms, thinly sliced
2 teaspoons sugar
1 teaspoon vinegar (balsamic, sherry or malt)
125 g (4 oz) bacon, rind removed
250 g (8 oz) chicken livers, trimmed and cut in two
1–2 tablespoons brandy
Salt and freshly ground pepper

*W*ash the spinach leaves and tear them into large bite-size pieces. Toss them with the mushrooms, sugar and vinegar in a salad bowl. Cut the bacon into thin strips and cook in a frying pan (skillet) in its own fat until browned and crisp. Remove the bacon from the pan and set aside.

Pat dry the chicken livers and add them to the hot pan. Cook in the bacon fat, shaking the pan frequently, for about 2 minutes, until the livers are brown on the outside and still slightly pink inside. Return the bacon to the pan. Add the

Warm Chicken Liver, Mushroom and Spinach Salad is very much a dish of today. The warm chicken livers and bacon strips are poured flaming onto the fresh salad. You may select greens of your choice; a few arugula leaves are a good addition.

286

brandy and ignite it when it has heated. Pour the chicken livers and bacon, still flaming, over the mushrooms and spinach. Toss and season well with freshly ground pepper and a little salt. Serve while still warm. Serves 6 for an entrée, 4 for a light lunch.

Chicken Livers and Mushrooms

A quick snack with toast or a light meal for two with rice or noodles.

> *15 g (¹/₂ oz) butter*
> *2 teaspoons vegetable or olive oil*
> *375 g (12 oz) chicken livers, trimmed and cut into small pieces*
> *125 g (4 oz) mushrooms, sliced*
> *1 tablespoon chopped onion*
> *¹/₂ teaspoon salt*
> *A pinch of paprika*
> *Parsley, chopped finely*

*H*eat the butter and oil in a heavy frying pan (skillet) and sauté the livers, mushrooms and onion over high heat for 4 minutes, stirring occasionally. Add the salt, paprika and parsley. Serve with rice or noodles and a tossed salad. Serves 2.

Tip
To prepare chicken livers for cooking, remove all the fibres with a sharp knife. Be sure to cut away the green bile spots that are sometimes left on, as the bile will make everything it touches taste very bitter. Cook livers quickly over a high heat to seal in the juices. If overcooked, they will become tough and dry.

Rice Portuguese

This makes a savoury accompaniment to roast chicken or quail.

> *1 onion, peeled and chopped*
> *90 g (3 oz) butter*
> *2 cups (10 oz) long-grain rice*
> *3 cups (27 fl oz) chicken stock (page 68), hot*
> *2 tomatoes, peeled, seeded and diced (see page 130)*
> *1 capsicum (sweet pepper), seeded and diced*

*F*ry the onion gently in half the butter until a golden colour. Add the rice and cook, stirring, over medium heat until the rice is coated with the butter. Add the hot stock, tomatoes and capsicum. Bring to the boil, reduce heat, then cover with a lid and cook about 18 minutes. As soon as it is cooked, carefully fork in the remaining butter. Serves 4–6.

Quail Portuguese

A beautifully simple meal for guests—or family. Allow 2 quails per serve for hearty appetites.

Quail Portuguese is quickly and simply prepared. A thin piece of orange rind, a dash of wine, salt and freshly ground pepper are the only seasonings. The roasted quails are served on a bed of just-cooked well-flavoured rice.

6–8 quails
Rind of 1 orange, thinly peeled
Salt and freshly ground pepper
30 g (1 oz) butter
1/2 cup (41/2 fl oz) dry white wine or orange juice
1 quantity Rice Portuguese (see preceding recipe)

Dry the quails, put a piece of orange rind in each, and season with salt and pepper. Tie each one neatly with string so that they will keep their shape during cooking. Place them in an ovenproof casserole with the butter and wine or orange juice, cover and cook in a very hot oven (240°C/475°F) for 20 minutes.

Turn the Rice Portuguese onto a serving dish, untie the quails and set them on top of the rice. Swirl the juices in the casserole to mix well, and spoon them over the rice. Serves 4–6.

Duckling with Ginger and Pears

This may seem an unusual recipe—by using dry ginger ale—but it makes a great sauce and is a fresh taste with the ginger and pears.

2.5 kg (5 lb) duckling
5 cm (2 in) slice of fresh ginger, peeled and cut in three
3 teaspoons ground ginger
Salt and pepper
30 g (1 oz) butter
2 bottles (285 ml size) or 21/2 cups (22 fl oz) dry ginger ale
2 teaspoons sugar
2 large pears, peeled, quartered, cored and sliced
1 tablespoon natural (plain) yoghurt or crème fraîche

Remove all excess fat from the inside of the duck and wipe the outside. Rub 1 piece of the ginger around the cavity of the duck and place it inside. Truss the duck. Cut another piece of ginger into thin slices and then into needle-fine strips. Make small holes in the skin of the duck with a trussing needle and

push ginger strips under the skin. Mix 2 teaspoons of the ground ginger with salt and pepper and rub well into the skin of the duck.

Melt the butter in a large heavy-based frying pan (skillet). Place the duck in the pan, breast side down. Brown on all sides. Cut the remaining piece of ginger into 2 or 3 pieces and place them in a roasting pan with $1^1/_2$ cups (13 fl oz) of the ginger ale. Put in the duck, breast side up. Cook in a hot oven (220°C/425°F) for 15 minutes.

Skim fat off the surface of the liquid in the roasting pan. Lower the temperature to 190°C (375°F) and cook the duck for 1 hour or until cooked. Twenty minutes before the end of cooking time, place the remainder of the ginger ale in a wide-based saucepan with the sugar and the remaining ground ginger. Bring to the boil. Arrange the pear slices in a single layer in the dry ginger ale. Poach gently until tender but not soft. When the duck is cooked, remove trussing string and keep the duck warm.

Remove all the fat from the roasting pan and strain the remaining liquid into an electric blender or food processor. Add a few poached pear slices (about half a pear) and the yoghurt. Blend into a smooth sauce. Reheat in a saucepan, but do not boil; adjust seasoning. Garnish the duck with pear slices and serve the sauce separately. Serves 4.

Roast Duckling with Green Peppercorn Sauce

For those who enjoy duck but want a change from the usual cherries or orange. Green peppercorns, herbs and vinegared onion make a superb sauce and seem to add to the richness of duck while cutting the fat.

> *2.5 kg (5 lb) duckling*
> *2 cups (18 fl oz) duck stock (see next page)*
> *Salt and pepper*
> *1 small onion, finely chopped*
> *4 tablespoons red wine vinegar*
> *1 teaspoon chopped fresh tarragon*
> *1 teaspoon chopped fresh thyme*
> *2–3 tablespoons green peppercorns*
> *1 teaspoon chopped fresh basil or oregano*
> *2 teaspoons French (Dijon) mustard*
> *2 tablespoons chopped parsley*

emove the neck and giblets of the duckling and reserve them for the stock. Remove excess fat from the duckling. Wipe it with a damp cloth inside and out and season with salt and pepper. Place breast side up on a rack in a roasting pan with $1/2$ cup ($4^1/2$ fl oz) of the stock and roast in a moderately hot oven (190°C/375°F), basting occasionally, for $1^1/2$ hours or until the duckling is cooked.

Put the onion, vinegar, tarragon and thyme in a small saucepan. Boil, uncovered, stirring until all liquid has evaporated. Add the peppercorns, basil, mustard and the remaining duck stock. Boil, uncovered, until reduced slightly. Set aside. Remove the duckling from the roasting pan and keep warm. Spoon or siphon as much fat as possible from the pan and pour the remaining liquid into the green peppercorn sauce. Stir in the parsley.

Cut the duck into serving pieces and spoon over a little of the sauce. Serve the remaining sauce separately. Serves 4.

Duck stock. Heat a little oil in a saucepan and brown the neck and giblets of the duck. Pour off all fat and add $2^1/2$ cups (22 fl oz) of water and a bouquet garni. Simmer for 1 hour. Strain before using.

Roast Duckling with Green Peppercorn Sauce makes a change from the usual orange, cherry and pear flavourings. Duckling never tasted so good; the combination of fresh herbs, red wine vinegar and green peppercorns is just right for the rich flavour of the bird.

291

Luncheons and Suppers

Having a luncheon for family or friends should be an easygoing affair. It can be relaxing and pleasurable, particularly at weekends when we have time to sit and enjoy each other's company, the weather—sunshine or cosy fire depending on the season—and of course the food. Suppers before or after the movies or theatre or a sporting event, or perhaps a visit to a museum or art gallery, call for the same kind of light-hearted food.

Pasta with a good sauce is one of my stand-bys. So too is gnocchi in all its forms. I often have a quiche or flamiche at the ready—just to be finished off at the last moment. A simple salad and fruit for dessert is all you need.

If you are into casual luncheons and suppers as a way of keeping up with family and friends, don't stop at the recipes in this chapter; look at the chapter on vegetarian cooking for ideas, also the poultry and fish chapters, for they include many of my no-fuss recipes for today's easy-living style.

Fettuccine with Mussels and Prawns in Tomato Sauce is a dish that is hard to resist. The fresh shellfish, if hard to find, may be replaced by what is available—clams, pipis, scampi, or even rings of calamari. The pasta used could be tagliatelle, linguini or bucatini.

Savoury Quiche

A favourite weekend luncheon in my home is a freshly baked quiche. Warm from the oven and accompanied by a fresh green salad, it is a perfect meal to enjoy in the garden. It is also a favourite picnic food. Today's healthy recipes are lighter on fats and cream than traditional quiches.

The flan case (shell) can be prepared ahead—the pastry made and the tin lined and stored in the refrigerator. The custard can be mixed and the filling prepared and kept covered in the refrigerator. It then becomes a simple matter of assembling the quiche and putting it in the oven.

Flan Case (Shell)

This shortcrust pastry is the basic one I use for quiche, flans or simple savoury tarts. It is just enough for a 20–23 cm (8–9 in) flan or tart case.

> *1¹/₂ cups (6 oz) plain (all-purpose) flour*
> *A pinch of salt*
> *90 g (3 oz) butter*
> *2¹/₂ tablespoons iced water*

S ift the flour and salt into a bowl. Rub in the butter lightly and evenly until the mixture resembles breadcrumbs. Sprinkle the water evenly over the flour mixture, stirring with a spatula or knife to form a dough; add more water if necessary. Knead lightly on a floured board, wrap and chill for 30 minutes or until required. Roll out on a lightly floured board to fit a 20–23 cm (8–9 in) fluted flan ring. Press the pastry well into the flutes, being careful not to stretch it. Using a sharp knife, cut the pastry level with the top of the flan ring. Chill while preparing the filling.

Risen brioche dough, leeks shredded and lightly cooked, a custard of cream and eggs and you are ready for one of the great dishes of France, Leek Flamiche.

Herb Quiche

You may vary the herbs used in this quiche, but parsley should always be the main one.

30 g (1 oz) butter
2 medium onions or 8–10 spring onions (scallions, green
*   shallots), finely chopped, or 2 leeks, sliced*
¹/₂ cup (4¹/₂ fl oz) cream (single, light)
¹/₂ cup (4¹/₂ fl oz) milk
2 eggs
1 tablespoon snipped chives
1 tablespoon chopped fresh tarragon or chervil
1 tablespoon chopped watercress
2 tablespoons chopped parsley
Salt and pepper
1 flan case (opposite page)

*M*elt the butter in a heavy-based saucepan and fry the onions or leeks until softened. Place the cream, milk and eggs into a mixing bowl and beat together until well combined. Stir in the onions, herbs and seasonings. Spoon this mixture into the flan case. Bake in a moderately hot oven (190°C/ 375°F) for 30–40 minutes or until the custard is set. Serves 6–8.

Spinach Quiche

A quiche for those on a low-fat regime using ricotta and natural yoghurt. It has good flavour with spinach and basil.

500 g (1 lb) spinach, tough stalks removed
30 g (1 oz) butter
1 small onion, finely sliced
1 flan case (opposite page)
1 egg and 1 egg yolk
250 g (8 oz) low-fat ricotta
¹/₃ cup (3 fl oz) non-fat natural (plain) yoghurt
Salt and freshly ground black pepper
1 tablespoon chopped fresh basil

*W*ash the spinach well under running water, and shake off excess. Place it in a saucepan, cover partly and simmer for 4–5 minutes. Press the spinach between two plates to remove all liquid. Chop finely (a food processor may be used) and set aside. Melt the butter in a saucepan, add the onion and cook for 2–3 minutes until soft but not coloured, then add the spinach. Cook over high heat to remove any moisture, place in a bowl and allow to cool.

Prick the base of the flan case with a fork and bake blind (see page 346) in a hot oven (220°C/425°F) for 10 minutes.

Beat the egg and egg yolk together, add the ricotta cheese and yoghurt, and mix well. Season to taste with salt and pepper. Add the spinach and the chopped basil; stir to combine. Bake in a moderately hot oven (190°C/375°F) for 30 minutes or until golden. Serves 6–8.

Leek Flamiche

Leek Flamiche is one of the best vegetable pies of France, at its best in a rich brioche dough and served still warm. I have made this filling in a pastry shell following the technique used for a quiche, and that too is very good. A salad and a glass of wine is all else that is needed.

60 g (2 oz) butter

3 medium leeks, trimmed, washed and sliced

1/2 quantity of brioche dough (page 320), risen and chilled, or a double quantity flan case (page 294)

1 1/4 cups (11 fl oz) cream (single, light)

2 eggs and 1 egg yolk

3 bacon rashers (slices) (optional)

Salt, freshly ground black pepper and a little grated nutmeg

1 egg, beaten, for glaze

Tip

To prepare leeks for cooking, trim the root ends and remove any coarse outer leaves, cut off some of the green tops and make a slit from the top to where the white begins, then wash thoroughly under cold running water; flick out any sand or grit. Slice the leeks across into 1 cm (1/2 in) slices.

*I*n a heavy frying pan (skillet) melt the butter and add the leeks with salt and pepper to taste. Cover tightly and cook gently for 20 minutes until soft without colouring. Remove the leeks and fry the bacon rashers if they are being used. Take two-thirds of the dough and press it into a buttered 25 cm (10 in) cake tin, preferably with a loose base. Spread the cooked and slightly cooled leeks over the dough with the fried bacon, if using. In a bowl, lightly whisk the cream with the eggs and yolk, adding seasonings; pour the mixture over the leeks.

Take the remaining third of the dough and roll it out into a rectangle. Cut it into strips and lay them over the flamiche in a lattice, pressing down at the ends. Trim the edges and brush the strips with a beaten egg glaze. Lightly cover the flamiche and leave it to rise in a warm place for 30 minutes. Bake in a preheated hot oven (200°C/400°F) for 45 minutes or longer, until the crust is golden and the filling has set. Serves 6.

Leek Filo Pie

6 medium-sized leeks, trimmed, washed and sliced
1 egg
125 g (4 oz) feta cheese
Salt and pepper
6 sheets filo pastry
3 tablespoons olive oil

Simmer the leeks in a little lightly salted boiling water for 8 minutes. Drain and refresh under cold running water. Drain again. Leave until cold.

Place the egg and the feta cheese in an electric blender or food processor and blend until smooth. Combine with the cold leeks. Season to taste, but do not add too much salt as feta is a salty cheese.

Stack the filo between two dry tea towels with another dampened tea towel on top. Brush a 20 cm (8 in) shallow square cake tin or round pie dish with 1 teaspoon of the oil. Brush 1 sheet of filo lightly with oil, fold in half and brush lightly with oil again; line the tin or dish with it. Place two more sheets of filo, each lightly brushed with oil, on top, overlapping them and allowing the ends to hang over the sides. Add the leek filling and spread it evenly. Top with the remaining filo, folded in half and lightly brushed with oil. Brush the top with oil. Tuck the overhanging ends inside, enclosing the filling completely.

Bake in a moderately hot oven (190°C/375°F) for 45 minutes or until the filo is golden. Serves 6.

Grilled Vegetable Platter. An assortment of vegetables can be roasted on a ribbed grill or over a charcoal grill. Serve with bruschetta or toasted country bread.

Aigroissade

In France one of the best-loved dishes is a pot of vegetables served with a rich garlicky mayonnaise sauce. Great for weekend entertaining out of doors.

250 g (8 oz) green beans
250 g (8 oz) snow or sugar peas (mangetout)
250 g (8 oz) carrots
250 g (8 oz) zucchini (courgettes)
1 can (440 g, 15^1/$_2$ oz) chickpeas (garbanzos), drained
1 cup (9 fl oz) Sauce Aïoli (see next page)
2 hard-boiled eggs, finely chopped

*W*ash, trim and cut the vegetables into short lengths, then cook, separated, in boiling water until just tender. Drain and combine the vegetables with the chickpeas and reheat.

Turn into a serving dish and fold through the Sauce Aïoli. Sprinkle with the chopped hard-boiled eggs. Serve warm or cold. You can use Lebanese flat bread, or pitta, for serving; cut in two, open out like a pocket and fill with the prepared vegetables. Serves 4.

Sauce Aïoli. Crush 4 garlic cloves with 1 teaspoon of salt. Beat in 1 egg yolk, then $^{1}/_{4}$ cup ($2^{1}/_{4}$ fl oz) of olive oil, drop by drop, and 1 tablespoon of lemon juice. Beat in a further $^{3}/_{4}$ cup ($6^{1}/_{2}$ fl oz) of olive oil a little at a time, taste and adjust the seasoning.

Tuscan Beans with Sage uses the small white cannellini beans that have to be soaked overnight and cooked for several hours. Not exactly a last-minute notion dish, unless you use canned cannellini beans, which is not the same thing. Serve as a vegetarian dish; good also with spicy sausages.

Tuscan Beans with Sage

350 g (12 oz) dried white cannellini beans
Salt
1 bay leaf
1 onion, stuck with 4 cloves
$^{1}/_{2}$ cup ($4^{1}/_{2}$ fl oz) olive oil
3 garlic cloves, chopped
6 sage leaves
300 g (10 oz) peeled Italian tomatoes (fresh or canned),
*   chopped*

*S*oak the beans overnight in cold water. Bring 8 cups ($3^{1}/_{2}$ imperial pints) of water to the boil, add a little salt, the bay leaf, onion and the drained beans. Bring quickly back to the boil, then turn down the heat to minimum and simmer for about 3 hours.

Heat the oil and fry the garlic until it begins to change colour. Add the sage and the drained beans. Stir gently with a wooden spoon to coat the beans with oil. Add the tomatoes and simmer gently for another 15 minutes. Serves 6.

Green Pasta Salad

Tip
Be careful when you
flake tuna, as it can
easily become mushy.

350 g (12 oz) green tagliatelle (or fettuccine)
185 g (6 oz) can good quality tuna
2 small onions, finely sliced
4 ripe tomatoes, peeled (page 130) and quartered
2 hard-boiled eggs, quartered
A handful of black olives, pitted
Vinaigrette dressing (page 188) to taste
Parsley, chopped

Cook the pasta in plenty of rapidly boiling salted water until *al dente* (tender but still firm). Drain well and cool. Flake the tuna with a fork. Mix with the cooked pasta, onions, tomatoes, eggs, olives and vinaigrette dressing. Sprinkle with chopped parsley. Serves 4.

Variation. Green pasta salad takes on a festive air when made with fresh shellfish. Prepare the salad but omit the tuna and eggs—replace them with a mixture of seafood: scallops, prawns (shrimp) or squid (calamari). Allow about 250 g (8 oz) each of cooked prawns, squid (see page 211) or scallops (poached in salted water)—all marinated in vinaigrette for 20–30 minutes.

Fettuccine with Creamy Tomato Sauce

The creamy tomato sauce is delicious on its own with the pasta. As an alternative, try folding through fine strips of ham, prosciutto or salami.

3 ripe tomatoes, peeled, seeded and chopped (see page 130)
A sprig of oregano or 6 fresh basil leaves
1 cup (9 fl oz) cream (single, light)
45 g (1¹/₂ oz) butter
Salt and freshly ground black pepper to taste
375 g (12 oz) fettuccine

In a wide, shallow saucepan cook the tomatoes with the oregano for 10 minutes. Rub through a coarse sieve or blend in a food processor and then sieve.

Return the tomatoes to the pan, add the basil leaves (if oregano was not used) and a little salt, and simmer gently for about 3 minutes. Pour the cream into a wide saucepan and heat gently. Stir in the butter and cook gently for a few minutes to reduce. Remove the basil leaves from the tomato purée and stir into the cream and butter mixture. Season to taste with salt and pepper.

Meanwhile, cook the fettuccine in a large saucepan of boiling salted water, then drain and add to the sauce, stirring gently. Serve immediately. Serves 4–6.

Fettucine with Mussels and Prawns in Tomato Sauce

Do try to get small mussels; they are sweeter and more delicate than those large green-lip mussels, which really are too strong for this dish.

> *1 kg (2 lb) fresh mussels*
> *6 tablespoons olive oil*
> *1 small bay leaf*
> *¼ cup (2¼ fl oz) water*
> *1 kg (2 lb) ripe tomatoes, peeled, seeded and chopped*
> *10 basil leaves or fresh sprigs*
> *Salt and freshly ground black pepper*
> *1 large garlic clove*
> *500 g (1 lb) raw prawns (shrimp), shelled and deveined*
> *½ cup (4½ fl oz) white wine*
> *375 g (12 oz) fettuccine*

Scrub the mussels and place them with 2 tablespoons of oil, the bay leaf and water in a large pan with a tight-fitting lid. Cook over a high heat, shaking the pan frequently, until the mussels open. Cool slightly, then remove the mussels from their shells. Discard any unopened mussels.

Heat about 2 tablespoons of olive oil in a saucepan, and add the tomatoes, with any juice, and half the basil leaves. Simmer for 10 minutes, stirring from time to time, until the sauce is thick. Remove the basil and season with salt and pepper. In a small saucepan heat the remaining oil and fry the garlic with the prepared prawns. Stir-fry for about 3 minutes until the prawns have turned pink. Add the wine and cook briskly for a minute or so, then add the mussels and the tomato sauce. Heat together gently.

Meanwhile, cook the fettuccine in a large saucepan of salted boiling water until just tender; this will only take a few minutes. Drain, return to the pan, and add the mussels and sauce. Toss over a gentle heat for a minute before serving in heated serving bowls. Scatter with the remaining basil leaves which have been snipped into shreds with scissors. Serves 4–6.

Fettuccine Nero and Saffron with Clams

750 g (1¹/₂ lb) fresh clams in shell or 1 can clams (vongole)
185 g (6 oz) each black (noir) and saffron or tomato fettuccine
 or a double quantity of plain fettuccine
6 tablespoons olive oil
6 spring onions (scallions, green shallots) or shallots, chopped
1 garlic clove, chopped
¹/₄ teaspoon chopped red chilli
¹/₂ cup (4¹/₂ fl oz) dry white wine
Freshly ground black pepper
1 tablespoon chopped parsley

Fettuccine Nero and Saffron with Clams is a pasta dish made more intriguing when you can find fresh pasta flavoured with exotic ingredients: black squid ink for the 'nero' and golden saffron for that inimitable colour. The clam sauce itself is simple but so good— it's what makes this dish.

*I*f using fresh clams, let them soak under running water for an hour to remove all traces of sand. Drain and heat the clams in a large covered saucepan for about 4 minutes. Leave 12 or 16 clams in the shell and remove the rest from their shells. Strain the liquor from the pan and reserve this along with the clams.

Cook the pasta in a large saucepan of boiling salted water until cooked *al dente*. Drain. Heat the olive oil in a large saucepan and gently cook the spring onions or shallots and garlic without colouring. Add the chilli and wine and all the clams (fresh or canned) with the reserved juice and fettuccine: stir for a minute over moderate heat. Season with freshly ground pepper and parsley, and serve immediately. Serves 4.

Pasta with Uncooked Tomato Sauce

A fresh-tasting uncooked cold sauce with steaming hot pasta is winning favour with people who enjoy good food a bit different. This recipe makes enough sauce for 500 g (1 lb) of pasta.

3 large tomatoes, peeled, seeded and chopped (see page 130)
3 garlic cloves, finely chopped
¹/₂ cup packed fresh basil leaves, sliced
125 g (4 oz) Neufchâtel (cream) cheese, diced
¹/₂ cup (4¹/₂ fl oz) olive oil (preferably extra-virgin)
2 tablespoons red-wine vinegar
Salt and freshly ground black pepper to taste

*I*n a large bowl combine all the ingredients and let the sauce stand, covered, at room temperature for at least 1 hour. Just before serving, in a saucepan of boiling salted water cook your pasta until it is *al dente*, drain it well, and add it to the sauce. Toss the pasta well with the sauce. Serves 4.

Tagliatelle all'Amatriciana

This is one of the most famous of all pasta dishes. It comes from the little village of Amatrice in the Sabine country near Rome. Try to buy pecorino cheese and pancetta bacon for the authentic Italian touch.

Tip
Soak a dried chilli in hot water for 5 minutes before removing the seeds.

2 tablespoons vegetable or olive oil
250 g (8 oz) pancetta (unsmoked bacon) or bacon rashers
  (slices), cut into 2.5 cm (1 in) pieces
1 small dried chilli, seeded and chopped finely, or a pinch of
  cayenne pepper
1 small onion, chopped
500 g (1 lb) tomatoes, peeled, seeded and chopped (page 130)
Salt and freshly ground black pepper
500 g (1 lb) tagliatelle (or fettuccine)
1 cup (4 oz) grated pecorino or Parmesan cheese

*H*eat the oil in a heavy frying pan (skillet). Add the bacon and cook until brown and crisp. Remove from pan, drain and set aside.

Add the chilli and onion to the pan and sauté until the onion is softened. Stir in the tomatoes, season with salt and pepper, and simmer the sauce for 10 minutes.

While the sauce is cooking, drop the pasta into plenty of rapidly boiling salted water and cook until *al dente*. Drain. Place the pasta in a large shallow serving dish. Add the reserved bacon to the sauce and pour it over the pasta. Sprinkle with the grated cheese and serve at once. Serves 4–6.

Fried Hokkien Noodles

There are numerous variations on this basic Chinese combination of noodles, bean sprouts and garlic. Fresh Hokkien noodles are available from Chinese food stores, but if unavailable use the plump Italian *bucatini* pasta, which should be cooked *al dente*. Garlic is an intrinsic part of this dish, as you can see by the amount used; in fact, Chinese chefs might be inclined to add more.

500 g (1 lb) fresh yellow Hokkien noodles
3 tablespoons vegetable or olive oil
250 g (8 oz) raw prawns (shrimp), shelled, with shells and
*   heads reserved*
1 cup (9 fl oz) fish stock (page 68; also available packaged)
*   or water*
6–8 large garlic cloves, crushed
2 eggs, lightly beaten
250 g (8 oz) bean sprouts, rinsed and trimmed
250 g (8 oz) barbecued pork or cooked chicken, sliced or
*   diced finely*
Salt and freshly ground black pepper to taste
GARNISH
Fresh red chillies, seeded and finely sliced
4 green shallots (scallions), cut into short lengths
A few stalks of tender celery, finely chopped

Tip
Rinse bean sprouts before using them, and if you have time on you hands nip off the root ends to give the sprouts a better look.

*I*n a bowl, pour over the noodles enough boiling water to cover. Leave to stand for a few minutes, then drain and set aside.

Heat 1 tablespoon of the oil in a wok and stir-fry the prawn shells and heads for a few minutes. Add the fish stock or water and bring to the boil. Cover and simmer for about 5 minutes, then pour through a strainer and discard the shells. In the resulting broth, poach the prawns until pink. Strain and reserve the stock; set the prawns aside. Rinse the wok.

Heat the remaining oil in the wok and fry the garlic gently until aromatic. Raise the heat, and pour in the beaten eggs. Stir constantly for 1 minute, then add the drained noodles, bean sprouts and the reserved prawn stock; there should be about $^1/_2$ cup ($4^1/_2$ fl oz). Stir-fry over high heat for a minute, then add the prawns and pork or chicken with salt and pepper to taste. Continue to stir-fry for a few more minutes and serve on a platter finished with the garnish ingredients. Serves 4–5.

Fusilli with Smoked Trout Salad

Smoked trout and eel are both specialties that we enjoy with crisp toast or in salads. Combined with pasta and greens and a very flavoursome dressing, this makes a good first-course salad.

> *250 g (8 oz) fusilli (corkscrew pasta)*
> *1 smoked trout or a 15–20 cm (6–8 in) length of smoked eel*
> *8 sun-dried tomatoes, halved if large*
> *12–16 small black olives*
> *1 small red onion, sliced*
> *Salad greens, prepared and crisped*
> *1 lemon, cut into wedges*
> DRESSING
> *2 teaspoons Dijon mustard*
> *6 tablespoons extra virgin olive oil*
> *2 teaspoons balsamic vinegar*
> *1 tablespoon mayonnaise*
> *1 tablespoon fruit chutney*

Fusilli with Smoked Trout Salad was created by a small-town chef using the local smoked eel, which is particularly good. Try this salad with smoked eel or trout or any choice smoked fish. The dressing is unusual but full of flavour.

Bring a large saucepan of salted water to the boil, add the pasta and cook for 8–10 minutes, until *al dente*, or firm to the bite. Drain, refresh under cold running water, drain.

Skin the smoked trout or eel, remove fillets from the backbone and break into pieces. Put into a bowl with the sun-dried tomatoes, olives and onion.

To prepare the dressing, put the mustard in a small bowl or soup plate, gradually beat in the olive oil to make a thickish emulsion, then beat in the vinegar and add the mayonnaise and fruit chutney. Toss the fusilli in the dressing and allow to stand until needed.

To assemble the salad, spread 4 dinner plates with the mixed salad greens. Combine the fusilli with the smoked fish, tomatoes, olives and onion. Mix gently and pile lightly onto the greens. Add 2 lemon wedges to each plate. Serves 4.

Mussel and Potato Salad

This is a festive salad, serve it as a light luncheon dish for weekend entertaining.

VINAIGRETTE

4 tablespoons fresh lemon juice

2 teaspoons Dijon-style mustard

Salt and pepper

3/4 cup (6 1/2 fl oz) olive oil

1 tablespoon chopped fresh basil leaves

1/2 teaspoon dried tarragon, crumbled

3 tablespoons chopped parsley

SALAD

750 g (1 1/2 lb) new potatoes, quartered lengthwise

2 kg (4 lb) small mussels

2–3 celery stalks, thinly sliced

1 cup (6 oz) cooked peas

1 cup cherry tomatoes, halved

8 green shallots (spring onions, scallions), chopped

Salt and freshly ground pepper

Crisped lettuce leaves for lining the serving platter

*I*n a bowl whisk together the lemon juice, mustard, and salt and pepper to taste; add the oil in a stream while beating, and whisk until the vinaigrette is emulsified. Whisk in the basil, tarragon and parsley.

A Chinese ladle is a very useful utensil— here used for lifting steamed vegetables into iced water.

In a steamer set over boiling water, steam the potatoes, covered, for 8–10 minutes or until they are just tender, and transfer them to a large bowl. Toss the potatoes with ¹/₂ cup (4¹/₂ fl oz) of the vinaigrette and let them cool.

Scrub the mussels well in several changes of water, scrape off the beards, and rinse the shells. In a large pan, steam the mussels in 1 cup (9 fl oz) of water, covered, over moderately high heat for 5 to 7 minutes or until they are opened, then transfer them with a slotted spoon to a bowl and let them cool.

Discard any unopened mussels and remove the mussels from the shells, reserving 8 shells for garnish. To the potatoes add the mussels, celery, peas, tomatoes, ¹/₄ cup of the shallots, the remaining vinaigrette, and salt and pepper to taste, and toss the salad well. Line a large platter with the lettuce leaves and mound the salad in the centre; arrange the reserved mussel shells around the salad and sprinkle the salad with the additional shallots. Or arrange on 6 dinner plates. Serves 6.

Capellini with Wine and Clam Sauce

This is one of those great 'out of the pantry' dishes—a dish of good, robust flavours which is made in a matter of minutes.

>   *290 g (10 oz) can of clams*
>   *5 golden shallots or green shallots (spring onions, scallions),*
>   *finely chopped*
>   *1 large garlic clove, crushed*
>   *¹/₂ small chilli, seeded and finely sliced*
>   *¹/₄ cup (2¹/₄ fl oz) olive oil*
>   *1 cup (9 fl oz) dry white wine*
>   *Salt and freshly ground pepper*
>   *3 tablespoons chopped parsley*
>   *375 g (12 oz) capellini (vermicelli) or linguine*

Drain the clams, reserving ¹/₂ cup (4¹/₂ fl oz) of the juice. Sauté the shallots, garlic and chilli in the olive oil until softened, about 5 minutes. Add the wine and the reserved clam liquid and bring to the boil. Simmer for about 5 minutes until reduced and thickened slightly. Add the clams, salt to taste and freshly ground pepper. Stir in the parsley.

Meanwhile, boil the capellini in a large pan of boiling salted water until done to the bite (*al dente*). Drain thoroughly and toss with the clam sauce in a heated serving bowl. Serves 4.

Parisian Gnocchi au Gratin

$2^1/_2$ cups (22 fl oz) milk

125 g (4 oz) butter, cut into pieces

$^1/_2$ teaspoon salt

A good pinch of nutmeg

2 cups (8 oz) plain (all-purpose) flour

6 eggs

1 cup (4 oz) grated Parmesan cheese

2 cups (18 fl oz) Mornay Sauce (see following)

30 g (1 oz) butter, melted

MORNAY SAUCE

3 cups (27 fl oz) milk

A slice of onion

A blade of mace or a pinch of nutmeg

$^1/_2$ bay leaf

45 g ($1^1/_2$ oz) butter

2 tablespoons plus 2 teaspoons plain (all-purpose) flour

Salt and white pepper

$^1/_2$ cup (2 oz) grated Parmesan cheese

Parisian Gnocchi au Gratin is one of my favourite light luncheon dishes. I have given the recipe enough for 6 to 8 people, as I find it a great dish for entertaining. Much of the preparation can be done ahead. Everyone seems to appreciate this light and delicate dish.

*H*eat the milk in a heavy saucepan with the butter, then add the salt and nutmeg. Sift the flour onto a square of greaseproof (waxed) paper, and when the milk boils and all the butter has melted, tip in the flour, all at once, stirring rapidly. When the mixture leaves the sides of the pan to form a ball around the spoon as you beat, remove from the heat and allow to cool slightly.

Beat in the eggs, one at a time, which can be done by hand, using a wooden spoon and strong arm, or with an electric beater or in a large food processor using the plastic blade. When the mixture is smooth and shiny, it is ready. Lastly, beat in $^3/_4$ cup (3 oz) of the grated Parmesan cheese.

Spoon the dough into a piping bag fitted with a 1–2 cm ($^1/_2$–1 in) plain round nozzle. Have ready a large pan of boiling salted water and next to it a large wire rack covered with a tea towel. Press the mixture out of the bag and cut off 3 cm ($1^1/_4$ in) lengths with a sharp knife or scissors, letting the pieces drop into the boiling water. Cook for about 5 minutes, until they are all floating on the surface of the water. Lift them out with a slotted spoon and arrange them on the wire rack. This amount should be cooked in three lots. You can prepare to this stage well ahead and store the cooked gnocchi in the refrigerator, covered.

Cover the base of two large ovenproof shallow dishes with several tablespoons of Mornay Sauce and arrange the gnocchi on top in one layer. Cover with the rest of the sauce; top with the remaining Parmesan and the melted butter. Put in a preheated hot oven (200°C/400°F) for about 15 minutes, until the gnocchi have souffléed a little and are bubbling in the sauce and the top is golden. Serves 6–8.

Mornay Sauce. Heat the milk gently with the onion, mace and bay leaf in a covered pan, about 5 minutes. Cool, then strain into a bowl. Rinse out the pan and use it to melt the butter. Remove from the heat and blend in the flour. Stir in the milk and return to the heat. Bring slowly to the boil, stirring constantly, and simmer gently for 3 minutes. Season to taste and stir in the grated Parmesan.

Spinach and Cheese Gnocchi. These tender light dumplings of ricotta and Parmesan cheese flavoured with quickly cooked spinach may be served simply with melted butter and a topping of Parmesan cheese or on a bed of tomato sauce.

Spinach and Cheese Gnocchi

A small bunch of spinach
375 g (12 oz) ricotta
1 teaspoon salt
Freshly ground pepper
3 egg yolks
5 tablespoons grated Parmesan cheese
Plain (all-purpose) flour
60 g (2 oz) butter, melted

Wash the spinach and chop the leaves finely, discarding the stalks. Cook the spinach until just tender. Drain well, and process in an electric blender or food processor using an on/off action. Mix together the spinach, ricotta, salt and pepper, egg yolks and 3 tablespoons of the Parmesan cheese. Drop the mixture by spoonfuls into a little flour spread on greaseproof (waxed) paper. Shape into small balls or egg shapes using two dessertspoons, one to pick up the mixture, the other to gently scoop it off. (This is best done straight into the simmering water.) Bring a large saucepan or frying pan (skillet) of lightly salted water to the boil, drop in the gnocchi and simmer gently—they are cooked as soon as they float to the top. Remove the gnocchi with a slotted spoon to a hot serving dish. Pour the melted butter over and sprinkle with the remaining Parmesan cheese. Serves 4.

Spinach Gnocchi with Tomato Sauce. Prepare gnocchi as above. Heat 1 quantity of Fresh Tomato Sauce (page 184). Spoon the sauce onto 4 plates, top with gnocchi and a sprinkling of Parmesan cheese, and spoon a little melted butter over each.

Gnocchi with Butter and Cheese

Use semolina (farina), a useful cereal made from high-grade wheat, or the fine yellow corn meal sold in some Italian shops as polenta for making this easy gnocchi recipe. Serve the little squares or rounds of gnocchi topped with Gruyère cheese, lightly grilled under a hot grill (broiler), or top them with a freshly made tomato sauce. Either way they make a light but satisfying luncheon or supper when accompanied by a good salad. Small portions can accompany a roast or grilled (broiled) chicken or meat.

> *1 onion, peeled and cut in half*
> *1 bay leaf*
> *3³/₄ cups (1³/₄ imperial pints) milk*
> *³/₄ cup (4 oz) semolina (farina) or corn meal (polenta)*
> *1¹/₂ teaspoons salt*
> *Pepper to taste*
> *2 tablespoons grated Parmesan cheese*
> *30 g (1 oz) butter*
> *¹/₂ teaspoon dry mustard (mustard powder)*
> *A fresh grating of nutmeg*
> *90 g (3 oz) Gruyère cheese, shredded*

Gnocchi with Tomato Sauce belongs to the tribe of light and tender little shapes so beloved of the Italians. This dish calls for a fine semolina cooked to a porridge, cooled in a slab, cut out and finished in a fresh tomato sauce. Superb.

Put the onion in a thick, heavy saucepan with bay leaf and milk. Bring slowly to the boil, remove the onion and bay leaf and add the semolina, salt and pepper. Cook, stirring, over a low heat for 15–20 minutes or until very thick. Remove from the heat, stir in the Parmesan cheese, half the butter, the mustard and nutmeg.

Spread the porridge-like mixture out on an oiled baking tray (sheet) to an oblong slightly less than 1 cm (¹/₂ in) thick. Cool. When cold, cut into squares with a knife or rounds with a cookie cutter.

Arrange the gnocchi, slightly overlapping, in a lightly greased, shallow ovenproof dish. Sprinkle with shredded Gruyère cheese. Melt the remaining butter and sprinkle it over the top. Bake in a moderate oven (180°C/350°F) for 15 minutes, then place under a hot grill (broiler) until the top is brown and crisp. Serve immediately, while still bubbling. Serves 6.

Gnocchi with Tomato Sauce. Prepare gnocchi as described above. When cool, cut out and arrange in a flat, buttered ovenproof dish. Spoon over a cup of Fresh Tomato Sauce (page 184) and sprinkle with Parmesan cheese. Bake in a moderate oven (180°C/350°F) for 30 minutes.

Home Baking

Good things from the oven—a batch of biscuits, a beautiful cake, a fragrant fruit tart, a loaf of special bread—cheer the spirits as nothing else does.

The English look forward to afternoon tea with fresh orange cake. Coffee and a wedge of freshly baked, still warm Gâteau de Pithiviers has made many a cherished break in France. Spicy apple cake has been the choice in Germany. In Spain a lovely teacake is made with olive oil. In New York, Linda's Orange Cake wins acclaim. The Scots cannot do without their breakfast baps, and Proust waxed lyrical over madeleines, the 'seashell cake so strictly pleated outside and so sensual within'.

Hazelnut crescents have appeared at generations of weddings. Shortbread sablés and brandy snaps lift fruit and creamy desserts. Cheese biscuits or gougères to nibble with drinks, a Greek cake for picnics—the list of treats is endless.

Today good things from the oven have come into their own again. A new generation of cooks is discovering that home-baked is still the yardstick of quality. On top of everything else, home baking lets you explore new cooking skills, which is in itself a joy.

Madeleines, the little seashell cakes, make afternoon tea time a special delight. A bowl of luscious ripe strawberries seems just right for the occasion. Tea, freshly brewed and a pot of steaming hot water allows the hostess to pour tea to every guest's preference.

Brioche Dough

Brioche dough is rich in butter and eggs. It can be used in various ways and with various fillings. It makes superb small breads and can be flavoured with candied or dried fruits. It can be kneaded with grated cheese and baked in loaf tins (pans) to make a spectacular sandwich bread (see Le Gannat, page 323); enjoy it warm and fresh or later toasted. It is fabulous for enclosing roasts, smoked sausage and other meats to be baked 'en brioche'. In France it is used as a base for a flamiche, a type of savoury flan (see Leek Flamiche, page 296). For afternoon tea see the recipe for Brioche Fruit Loaf (page 323). As each of these recipes uses a half quantity of Brioche Dough, plan to make two at the one time.

Brioche Fruit Loaf is just one of the breads that can be made with a rich brioche dough. The dried and candied fruit can be of your choice. You may knead it through the dough or have it form a twirl pattern.

4 cups (1 lb) plain (all-purpose) flour
7 g ($^1/_4$ oz) dry yeast or 15 g ($^1/_2$ oz) compressed yeast
1 teaspoon salt
1 tablespoon caster (superfine) sugar
6 medium-sized eggs, beaten
$^1/_4$ cup (2$^1/_4$ fl oz) lukewarm water
250 g (8 oz) unsalted (sweet) butter, softened
Beaten egg to glaze

Sift the flour, dry yeast, salt and sugar into a large bowl. Make a well in centre and pour in the eggs and the lukewarm water (with the compressed yeast previously dissolved in it, if compressed yeast is being used). Mix to a smooth dough, first with a wooden spoon and then with your hand.

Turn the dough onto a floured board and knead, lifting it up and slapping it down until it is smooth and elastic. Sprinkle with more flour as necessary. Alternatively, the dough can be kneaded using an electric mixer with a dough hook for 5 minutes or in a large food processor fitted with plastic blades. Turn the dough into a lightly oiled bowl, cover loosely with plastic wrap (cling film), then a towel, and leave to rise in a warm place for 1$^1/_2$ hours, until doubled in bulk.

Knock down the dough in the bowl and, with your hand or a dough hook, gradually work in the softened butter. Turn into a cleaned, oiled bowl, cover again as before and refrigerate for at least 4 hours or overnight.

The dough should be shaped while it is still chilled and firm. After shaping, it should rise again, be brushed with beaten egg and baked in a hot oven (200°C/400°F).

Brioche Fruit Loaf

Dried apricots, pitted prunes and almonds or walnuts can replace the fruit here.

> *¹/₂ quantity Brioche Dough (page 320)*
> *90 g (3 oz or ¹/₂ cup) sultanas (golden raisins)*
> *¹/₄ cup (1¹/₂ oz) currants*
> *1 tablespoon chopped candied (crystallised) peel*
> *2 tablespoons halved glacé (candied) cherries*
> *1 tablespoon sugar*
> *Milk to glaze*

*B*utter a loaf tin 23 × 13 × 10 cm (9 × 5 × 4 in). Knock down the chilled brioche dough and turn out onto a lightly floured board. Press out to a thick rectangle and scatter the surface with the fruits and sugar. Knead lightly just to mix, or simply fold over to enclose the fruits, and turn at once into the buttered loaf tin. Cover with a tea towel and leave to rise for 15 minutes in a warm place. Brush with milk and bake in a preheated hot oven (200°C/400°F) for 40–45 minutes until golden. Turn out to cool on a wire rack. Serve sliced.

Le Gannat

An excellent cheese brioche for a luncheon or supper bread with soup, or for a picnic sandwiched with cream cheese.

> *¹/₂ quantity of Brioche Dough (page 320)*
> *1 cup (4 oz) grated or finely diced Gruyère (Swiss) cheese*
> *Salt, freshly ground pepper and a pinch of cayenne*
> *Beaten egg or milk to glaze*

*K*nock down the dough and knead lightly. Spread it out slightly with the palms of your hands and sprinkle with the cheese and seasonings. Knead just enough to mix thoroughly. Shape the dough to fit a 23 × 13 × 10 cm (9 × 5 × 4 in) loaf tin, or a deep cake tin, which has been buttered.

Cover loosely with plastic wrap (cling film), then a tea towel, and leave in a warm place for 45 minutes or longer until the dough has risen to the top of the pan. Brush with the beaten egg or milk and bake in a preheated hot oven (200°C/400°F) for 35 minutes or until browned and sounds hollow when tapped with the knuckles. Turn out onto a wire cooling rack to cool.

Le Gannat is a savoury loaf made from a basic brioche dough. Grated Gruyère cheese is kneaded through the dough. Slice it and enjoy it with or without butter. It keeps well and towards the end can be toasted.

Linda's Orange Cake

Linda is a New York friend, and this is her family cake that is made for special occasions. When I gave the recipe in my weekly pages in *New Idea* magazine, it was an instant success. It has even turned up in one or two top restaurants.

1 cup caster (superfine) sugar
4 eggs, separated
1 cup plain (all-purpose) flour
2 teaspoons baking powder
125 g (4 oz) butter, melted
Grated rind and juice of 1 orange
³/₄ cup (6 ¹/₂ fl oz) orange juice
Extra 2 tablespoons caster (superfine) sugar
CHOCOLATE ICING
125 g (4 oz) dark (semi-sweet) chocolate
1 teaspoon instant coffee
1 tablespoon boiling water
1 tablespoon (dairy) sour cream

Lightly grease a 23 cm (9 in) round cake tin and preheat the oven to moderate (180°C/350°F).

Beat the cup of caster sugar and the egg yolks until thick and creamy. Sift the flour and baking powder and fold into the beaten egg yolks. Fold in the cooled melted butter, the rind and juice of the orange, then the egg whites which have been beaten until they stand in peaks.

Place the mixture in the prepared cake pan and bake for 40 minutes. Remove from the oven and turn out onto a cake cooler (wire rack) while you combine the ³/₄ cup of orange juice and the 2 tablespoons of caster sugar, stirring briskly until the sugar is dissolved.

Replace the cake in the cake tin and, while it is still warm, spoon over the sweetened orange juice. Leave until cold—the cake will absorb the juice—then turn it out onto a flat plate and spread top and sides with the prepared chocolate icing. Serve as a dessert with a bowl of unsweetened whipped cream. The cake may be decorated with fresh berries or redcurrants.

Chocolate icing. Place the chocolate in a bowl and stand it over hot water. Dissolve the coffee in the boiling water, add to the chocolate and stir until smooth. Remove from heat and stir in the sour cream. When smooth, spread over the cake.

Gougères Bourguignonnes

A specialty of the French Burgundy area, these savouries are often served with a glass of local wine. I like to serve them with pre-dinner drinks. You can make a batch, freeze them on their trays unbaked, then transfer them to a suitable container and store frozen. Bake as required.

> *2¹/₄ cups (1 imperial pint) milk*
> *Salt, pepper and grated nutmeg to taste*
> *155 g (5 oz) butter, cut into small pieces*
> *2¹/₄ cups (9 oz) plain (all-purpose) flour, sifted*
> *1 teaspoon salt*
> *8 small or 7 large eggs*
> *300 g (10 oz) Gruyère (Swiss) cheese, of which 250 g (8 oz) is*
> *   grated, the rest cut into small dice*
> *Beaten egg for brushing*

*P*reheat the oven to very hot (220°C/425°F). Butter 2 baking trays (sheets). Place the milk, salt, pepper and nutmeg with the butter in a saucepan. Bring to the boil, ensuring that the butter has melted by the time the milk boils. Remove from the heat and add the flour and salt, all at once. Incorporate quickly and thoroughly with a wooden spoon and continue beating until the mixture balls around the spoon and leaves the sides of the pan.

Remove from the heat and allow to cool a minute or so before beating in the eggs, one at a time. Beat each egg gradually into the mixture before proceeding with the next. This step can be done with an electric mixer or food processor. Stir in the grated Gruyère, then spoon small balls of the mixture onto the buttered baking trays. Push a piece of diced cheese into each puff, brush with little beaten egg and bake for 20 minutes until risen and golden. Serve piping hot. Makes about 28.

Brushes for gilding pastry, brushing marinades on foods, or glazing fruit tarts. Brushes should be washed in warm soapy water, then rinsed, flicked dry and left to air. Rinse brushes used for eggs in cold water before washing.

Brandy Snaps

60 g (2 oz) butter
¹/₃ cup (3 oz) caster (superfine) sugar or brown sugar
¹/₃ cup (4 oz) golden syrup
¹/₂ cup (2 oz) plain (all-purpose) flour
1 teaspoon ground ginger
Grated rind of ¹/₂ lemon
1 cup (9 fl oz) cream, whipped

Tip
These crisp, lacy rolled wafers, when filled with cream, should be stored in an airtight container and refrigerated for 1 hour before serving.

*P*reheat the oven to moderate (180°C/350°F). Put the butter, sugar and golden syrup into a pan and heat gently until the butter has melted. Remove from the heat and cool until lukewarm. Sift in the flour with the ginger and stir in with the lemon rind.

Butter 3 baking trays (sheets) and drop teaspoonfuls of the mixture, 3 or 4 on each tray, allowing 10 cm (4 in) between each for spreading. Bake one tray at a time for approximately 10 minutes. When the brandy snaps are golden brown, remove them from the oven, let them stand for a few moments, then ease them one at a time from the tray with a broad-bladed knife or metal spatula. Working quickly, wrap each brandy snap lightly round the greased handle of a wooden spoon; keep the smooth side of the biscuit to the handle of the spoon. Once set, slip off onto a rack to cool.

Continue with the remaining mixture, alternating trays. One tray should be in the oven while you are curling the snaps from the tray before.

An hour or two before serving, pipe the whipped cream into each end of the wafers. Makes 24.

Hazelnut Crescents

One of the most beautiful biscuits—I made them for my wedding aeons ago and again for my daughter's wedding.

1¹/₄ cups (5 oz) plain (all purpose) flour
2 tablespoons caster (superfine) sugar
125 g (4 oz) butter
¹/₂ cup (2 oz) finely chopped hazelnuts or walnuts
1 egg yolk
Extra caster sugar

$\mathscr{S}$ift the flour into a bowl, stir in the sugar and rub in the butter until the mixture resembles coarse breadcrumbs. Mix in the nuts and stir in the egg yolk to make a dough. Cover and refrigerate for 30 minutes.

Preheat the oven to moderate (180°C/350°F). Butter 2 baking trays. Take about 2 teaspoons of dough at a time, roll into 5 cm (2 in) lengths and shape into crescents. Place on the baking trays and bake for 12 minutes or until lightly coloured. Remove the crescents and dredge them with the extra caster sugar while still warm. Cool on a wire rack. Makes about 35.

Guavas, pink-fleshed and sweet, make the most wonderful jelly and a thick paste that is so good on a cheese plate. Almonds and hazelnuts complete the picture.

Shortbread Sablés

1¹/₂ cups (6 oz) plain (all-purpose) flour
¹/₂ cup (2 oz) custard powder or cornflour (cornstarch)
¹/₂ cup (3 oz) icing (confectioners') sugar, sifted
A pinch of salt
185 g (6 oz) unsalted (sweet) butter
Vanilla essence (extract) to taste
Extra icing sugar for dusting

Tip
These shortbreads may be made several days ahead and stored in an airtight container until required.

$\mathscr{S}$ift the flour, custard powder, icing sugar and salt together. Rub the butter in with the tips of your fingers, add the vanilla, then lightly work the mixture to a firm dough. Shape into a round, flatten it out slightly, and wrap in greaseproof (waxed) paper. Leave to rest in the refrigerator for 1 hour.

Preheat the oven to moderate (180°C/350°F) and lightly butter baking trays (sheets). Roll the pastry out to 5 mm (¹/₄ in) thickness on a lightly floured board. Stamp out rounds, ovals or heart-shapes or cut out small triangles, and bake on the trays for about 20 minutes or until lightly coloured. Cool on a wire rack and store in an airtight container. Dust with the extra icing sugar before serving. Makes about 36.

Lemon Shortbreads

Little shortbread biscuits with a fresh lemon, buttery flavour—these are light, delicate and perfect with a cup of tea or coffee. Or use them as a dessert biscuit.

> *250 g (8 oz) butter*
> *Rind of 1 lemon, peeled thinly and finely chopped*
> *1 cup (6 oz) sifted icing (confectioners') sugar*
> *2 cups (8 oz) plain (all-purpose) flour, sifted*

*P*reheat the oven to moderate (180°C/350°F) Beat the butter and lemon rind until creamy. Add the icing sugar and beat well. With a metal spoon stir in the sifted flour. Take level teaspoons of the mixture and roll them lightly into balls. Place them on ungreased baking trays (sheets) and press down well with a fork dipped in cold water to prevent sticking. Fork the biscuits out using gentle strokes in the one direction. Bake for 10–12 minutes or until lightly coloured. Cool and store in an airtight container. Makes about 48.

Cheese Biscuits

Cheese Biscuits, homemade, have to be one of the most appreciated nibbles to enjoy with drinks. The same basic dough may be baked as discs pressed out using a biscuit (cookie) press or cut into straws. Don't forget the charm of straws held in neat little rings.

Crisp, delicate and perfect at a drinks party. Keep a roll of unbaked dough on hand in the freezer and slice and bake when needed.

> *30 g (1 oz) Gruyère (Swiss) cheese, grated*
> *90 g (3 oz) Cheddar cheese, finely grated*
> *185 g (6 oz) butter*
> *1¹/₂ cups (6 oz) plain (all-purpose) flour*
> *1 teaspoon paprika*
> *¹/₄ teaspoon pepper*
> *1 teaspoon salt*
> *2 tablespoons grated Parmesan cheese*

*C*ream the Gruyère and Cheddar cheeses and butter until soft. Sift the flour, paprika, pepper and salt, then stir this into the creamed mixture together with the Parmesan cheese. Mix well and form into a roll, 4 cm (1¹/₂ in) in diameter. Wrap in plastic wrap (cling film) or aluminum foil and refrigerate for 1 hour. Cut into thin discs and bake on ungreased baking trays (sheets) in a preheated moderate oven (180°C/350°F) for 10–12 minutes. Cool on wire racks. Store in airtight containers. Makes approximately 100 biscuits.

Variations

Using a biscuit press. The mixture may be put into a biscuit press fitted with a fancy nozzle. Press the mixture onto ungreased bakings trays and bake for 12–15 minutes.

Sesame cheese straws. Add a tablespoon of toasted sesame seeds to the mixture. The mixture can be rolled out and cut into straws 8 × 6 mm (3 × ¹/₄ in). Form a few straws into rings, securing the ends. These can be used to hold a bundle of straws, making an attractive presentation. Bake for 10–12 minutes.

Baps

Tip
If refrigerating overnight, remove and warm slightly before final kneading and shaping into buns.

Some of the best breakfast rolls are the Scottish baps. They should be eaten no later than 15 minutes out of the oven. They are split, buttered and eaten whole, often with some good Ayrshire bacon in the centre. The dough was originally left to rise all night, involving kitchen activity late in the evening. The dough may be left to rise slowly overnight in the refrigerator.

> *4 cups (1 lb) plain (all-purpose) flour*
> *1 teaspoon salt*
> *³/₄ cup (6¹/₂ fl oz) water*
> *¹/₂ cup (4¹/₂ fl oz) milk*
> *60 g (2 oz) butter*
> *15 g (¹/₂ oz) compressed yeast or 7 g (¹/₄ oz) dried yeast*
> *1 teaspoon sugar*

$\mathcal{S}$ift the flour with the salt into a large warmed bowl. Heat the water, milk and butter until the butter has melted without boiling. Cool to lukewarm.

Sprinkle the compressed yeast with the sugar and leave for a few minutes until the yeast becomes liquid, then stir it (or the dried yeast) into the milk and butter mixture. Make a well in the centre of the flour and pour in the liquid. Stir in a little of the flour from the side until the centre has the consistency of a thick batter. Cover with a folded tea towel and place in a warm place to sponge. When bubbles have formed, mix in all the flour.

Turn onto a floured board, and knead until the dough is smooth and elastic, about 5 minutes. Place in a clean, greased bowl and turn dough over so that the top surface is lightly greased. Cover with a tea towel and leave in a warm place for about 2 hours or until well risen and doubled in bulk, or leave in the refrigerator overnight. Knock down the dough and turn it onto a floured board. Knead lightly, divide the dough into 12 pieces and shape each into a round ball.

Flatten to half the thickness and press a hole in the centre of each with the thumb. Place on a greased baking tray (sheet), cover and allow to prove (rise) in a warm place for about 15 minutes. For floury baps, brush them with milk and dust thickly with extra sifted flour. Bake in a preheated hot oven (200°C/400°F) for 12–15 minutes or until pale golden. Serve hot or warm with butter. Makes 12 generous rolls.

Madeleines

These famous little teacakes are traditionally baked in shell-shaped tins (pans) which come in several sizes. The vanilla may be replaced by a teaspoon of finely chopped orange or lemon rind; both flavours are lovely. Perfect for afternoon teas or evening coffee, or serve with fruit as a dessert cake.

To clarify butter:
Slowly heat the butter in a small saucepan. When it has melted, remove it from the heat and let it stand for a few minutes, then pour the clear yellow liquid into a cup, leaving the sediment in the pan. Allow to cool.

> *185 g (6 oz) unsalted butter, clarified*
> *2 eggs*
> *³/₄ cup (6 oz) caster (superfine) sugar*
> *1 teaspoon vanilla essence (extract)*
> *1 cup (4 oz) plain (all-purpose) flour*
> *1 tablespoon rum (optional)*
> *Icing (confectioners') sugar for dusting*

𝒫reheat the oven to hot (200°C/400°F). Butter the madeleine tins and dust them with flour. If using teflon tins this is not necessary.

Melt the butter, clarify and let it cool. Beat the eggs and sugar until thick and light, using a hand whisk and a bowl set over a pan of gently simmering water (or use an electric mixer). Remove from the heat (if using that method) and continue to beat until cooled. Add the vanilla and fold in the flour, the cooled butter and rum, if using, mixing only until everything is blended. Three-quarters fill each tin with the batter and bake for 8 minutes, until pale golden. Turn out onto wire racks to cool. Dust liberally with icing sugar. Makes about 32 cakes.

Lemon Tea Ring

1¹/₂ cups (6 oz) plain (all-purpose) flour
1 cup (7 oz) sugar
1 teaspoon baking powder
¹/₄ teaspoon salt
125 g (4 oz) butter
2 eggs, beaten
¹/₂ cup (4¹/₂ fl oz) milk
Grated rind of 1 lemon
¹/₂ cup (2 oz) chopped walnuts
Juice of 1 lemon mixed with ¹/₄ cup (2 oz) sugar

*B*utter a 20 cm (8 in) ring tin or a 23 × 13 × 8 cm (9 × 5 × 3 in) loaf tin. Line the base with greaseproof (waxed) paper and grease again. Preheat the oven to moderate (180°C/350°F).

Sift the flour, sugar, baking powder and salt together into a bowl. Rub in the butter with your fingertips. Mix the beaten eggs and milk together and stir in, then fold in the lemon rind and walnuts.

Pour the mixture into the prepared tin and bake until firm to the touch and a straw or fine skewer inserted into the centre comes out clean—about 50 minutes for a ring, 1 hour and 20 minutes for a loaf. When the cake is cooked, pour the lemon juice and sugar over the top. Allow to cool in the tin.

Orange Cake

A simple but good recipe for orange cake is in every keen cook's repertoire. It has so many uses: sliced for afternoon tea; toasted when it adds interest to many desserts; pan-fried and topped with ice cream for dessert.

125 g (4 oz) butter
Grated rind and juice of 1 medium orange
³/₄ cup (6 oz) caster (superfine) sugar
2 eggs, separated
2 cups (8 oz) self-raising flour
A pinch of salt
2–3 tablespoons milk
Sifted icing (confectioners') sugar

*P*reheat the oven to moderate (180°C/350°F). Brush a 20 cm (8 in) ring tin or a 20 × 10 × 8 cm (8 × 4 × 3 in) loaf tin with butter and dust lightly with flour.

Cream the butter with the orange rind and sugar until light and fluffy. Add the egg yolks one at a time, beating well after each. Sift the flour with the salt and fold it into the creamed mixture alternately with the strained orange juice and the milk, beginning and ending with flour. Beat the egg whites until stiff peaks form, and gently fold in. Spoon the mixture into the prepared tin, and bake for 35–40 minutes or until a fine skewer inserted in the centre comes out clean. Turn out onto a wire rack and, when cool, dust with the sifted icing sugar.

German Apple Cake

Make this for morning or afternoon teas, for picnics, or serve it warm for dessert.

60 g (2 oz) butter
¹/₃ cup (3 oz) caster (superfine) sugar
1 egg
1 cup (4 oz) self-raising flour, sifted
¹/₄ cup (2¹/₄ fl oz) milk
4 medium apples, peeled, quartered and cored
Juice of 1 lemon
Sugar
Cinnamon

Tip
While the original recipe calls for apples, you can use sliced fresh peaches, nectarines, plums or pears; these fruits should be sliced just before arranging on the batter, as they tend to discolour if left too long.

*P*reheat the oven to moderate (180°C/350°F). Cream the butter with the sugar. Add the egg and beat well. Add half the flour and beat to combine. Add the milk and the remaining flour alternately (this will make a thick mixture). Spread the mixture over the bottom of a greased 23 cm (9 in) springform tin. Cut the quartered apples into thin slices but not all the way through to the core. Put the apples in a bowl as you are preparing them and squeeze over the lemon juice. Place the drained apples, cored side down, on the cake. Bake for 1 hour. While still warm, sprinkle with sugar and cinnamon.

Banana Date Cake

Tip
It is helpful to know
that three large
bananas make about
1¹⁄₂ cups of mashed
banana.

4 cups (1 lb) plain (all-purpose) flour
4 teaspoons baking powder
1¹⁄₂ teaspoons mixed spice
1 teaspoon salt
¹⁄₄ teaspoon bicarbonate of soda (baking soda)
1¹⁄₃ cups (10 oz) caster (superfine) sugar
1 cup (4 oz) chopped walnuts or pecans
2 eggs
1 cup (9 fl oz) milk
60 g (2 oz) butter, melted
1¹⁄₂ cups mashed banana
1 cup (5 oz) chopped dates
Icing (confectioners') sugar for dusting

*Banana Date Cake is
a great family cake. It
keeps well, travels well
to picnics or to school,
and is good to have on
hand.*

*B*utter a 9-cup ring or Bundt tin generously. Dust lightly with flour. Preheat the oven to moderate (180°C/350°F). Sift the flour, baking powder, spice, salt and soda together into a large bowl. Stir in the sugar and nuts.

Beat the eggs lightly. Stir in the milk, melted butter, mashed banana and dates and combine well. Add the liquid ingredients to the flour mixture. Stir until combined; do not overbeat. Turn the batter into the prepared tin and smooth the top. Bake for 1 hour and 10 minutes or until cooked when tested with a cake tester or fine skewer. Leave it in the tin for 10 minutes. Turn out onto a wire rack and cool. Dust the top with a little sifted icing sugar.

Spanish Teacake

In Spain cakes have always been made with Spanish olive oil. I like to use a light olive oil, although any good olive oil can be used. The flavour will permeate the cake ever so gently.

2 cups (8 oz) self-raising flour
1 cup (7 oz) caster (superfine) sugar
1–2 teaspoons caraway seeds
3 eggs, well beaten
¹⁄₂ cup (4¹⁄₂ fl oz) milk
1 cup (9 fl oz) olive oil

reheat the oven to moderate (180°C/350°F). Grease a 20 cm (8 in) round cake tin and line the base with greased greaseproof (waxed) paper. Sift the flour into a large bowl and stir in the sugar and caraway seeds. Gradually beat in the eggs, milk and olive oil, mixing until well combined.

Pour the mixture into the prepared tin and bake 1¼ hours or until a fine skewer inserted comes out clean. Cool on a wire rack and serve cut into wedges.

Greek Orange and Semolina Cake

This cake will keep in the refrigerator for at least a week if well wrapped in aluminium foil; it also freezes well. Allow it to reach room temperature before serving, either plain with tea or coffee or with cream as a dessert. I find it an excellent cake for picnics.

> *125 g (4 oz) butter*
> *½ cup (4 oz) caster (superfine) sugar*
> *1 tablespoon grated orange rind*
> *2 eggs*
> *2 tablespoons orange-flavoured liqueur or brandy*
> *1 cup (6 oz) semolina*
> *1 teaspoon baking powder*
> *1 cup (3½ oz) ground almonds*
> SYRUP
> *½ cup (4 oz) caster (superfine) sugar*
> *1 cup (9 fl oz) orange juice*

reheat the oven to hot (200°C/400°F). Grease and line a 20 cm (8 in) round or square cake tin. Cream the butter with the sugar and orange rind until light and fluffy. Add the eggs, one at a time, beating thoroughly after each addition. Stir in the brandy. Combine the semolina, baking powder and almonds and fold lightly into the creamed mixture.

Turn the mixture into the prepared cake tin. Place in the preheated oven, then immediately lower the oven temperature to moderate (180°C/350°F). Bake for 30 minutes or until a fine skewer inserted in the centre comes out clean. Remove the cake from the oven, pour the prepared syrup over the hot cake and allow it to cool in the tin. Turn onto a serving plate and serve with tea or coffee or as a dessert with whipped cream.

Syrup. Place the sugar and orange juice in a saucepan, bring to the boil and boil briskly for 5 minutes. Cool slightly before pouring over the cake.

Olive Quick Bread

2¹/₂ cups (10 oz) plain (all-purpose) flour

2 tablespoons baking powder

1 tablespoon sugar

A pinch of salt

1–2 tablespoons chopped mint (optional)

2 large eggs

¹/₃ cup (3 fl oz) olive oil

²/₃ cup (6 fl oz) milk

¹/₂ cup (3 oz) black olives, pitted and chopped

Greek Orange and Semolina Cake is a really useful cake. It is moist—orange syrup is poured over the hot cake as it comes from the oven—and can be served as a dessert cake with whipped cream, taken to a picnic, or served with coffee.

Preheat the oven to moderate (180°C/350°F). Butter a loaf tin (pan) 20 × 10 × 10 cm (8 × 4 × 4 in). Sift the flour with the baking powder, sugar and salt into a large bowl. Stir in the mint. In a small bowl lightly beat the eggs and stir in the olive oil and milk to mix. Make a well in the centre of the flour, add the liquid and the olives and stir until the batter is just mixed.

Turn into the loaf tin and bake for 1¹/₄ hours, until a skewer or tester inserted comes out clean. Turn out onto a wire rack to cool.

Gâteau de Pithiviers

2 sheets of frozen puff pastry

1 egg, beaten with 1/2 teaspoon salt (for glaze)

Caster (superfine) or icing (confectioners') sugar for sprinkling

ALMOND FILLING

125 g (4 oz) butter

1/2 cup (4 oz) caster (superfine) sugar

1 egg and 1 egg yolk

125 g (4 oz) blanched almonds, freshly ground

1 tablespoon plain (all-purpose) flour

2 tablespoons rum

Gâteau de Pithiviers, a much-loved pastry of France. Motoring through France, we reached the village square of Pithiviers at noon one Sunday, just as the villagers were coming out of church and collecting their freshly baked pastries for lunch. We joined them and, to my delight, got the recipe for this spectacularly good pastry.

Prepare the almond filling: Cream the butter in a bowl. Add the caster sugar and beat until soft and light. Beat in the egg and egg yolk. Stir in the almonds, flour and rum; don't beat the mixture at this point, or the oil will be drawn out of the almonds.

With a sharp knife and using a cake tin as a guide, cut out a 25 cm (10 in) round from each sheet of pastry. Set one round on a baking tray (sheet) and mound the filling in the centre, leaving a 2.5 cm (1 in) border. Brush the border with the egg glaze. Lay the remaining round on top and press the edges together firmly. Scallop the edge of the gâteau by pulling it in at regular intervals with the back of a knife. Brush the gâteau with egg glaze and, working, from the centre, score the top in curves like the petals of a flower; don't cut through to the filling. Chill for 15–20 minutes. Preheat the oven to very hot (220°C/425°F).

Pierce a few holes in the centre of the gâteau to allow steam to escape. Sprinkle it with the fine sugar and bake for 20–25 minutes or until puffed and brown on the top. Lower the oven temperature to hot (200°C/400°C) and continue baking for 15–20 minutes or until firm, lightly browned on the sides and glazed with melted sugar on top. If the sugar has not melted by the time the pastry is cooked, grill (broil) it quickly until shiny. Cool the gâteau on a rack. Serve slightly warm or at room temperature. Serves 8.

Fresh Fruit Tarts

1 sheet ready-prepared and rolled puff pastry

1 egg, separated

³/₄ cup (3 oz) ground almonds

¹/₂ teaspoon vanilla essence (extract) or 1 teaspoon brandy

2 tablespoons caster (superfine) sugar

2 ripe peaches or plums or nectarines, sliced

Fresh Fruit Tarts, something I make in a trice when I haven't planned a dessert, using ready-rolled sheets of puff pastry, some ground almonds, and any fresh fruit in season.

Preheat the oven to hot (200°C/400°F). Butter a baking tray (sheet). Lay the sheet of pastry on a lightly floured board and cut it into two oblongs of the same size. Fold one of the oblongs in two lengthwise and cut a smaller oblong out of the folded side so that the remaining pastry, when unfolded, will form a 1 cm (¹/₂ in) frame. (The unwanted smaller oblong can be saved and used for biscuits like Parmesan Twists; see page 58.)

Brush the edge of the uncut oblong of pastry with water; set the frame of pastry on top, pressing it down gently. Brush the frame with the egg yolk beaten with a tablespoon of water. Mix the egg white with the ground almonds, vanilla

or brandy and 1 tablespoon of the caster sugar, and spread this paste on the base of the pastry within the frame.

Arrange the sliced fruit on the paste. Sprinkle the fruit and pastry frame with the remaining sugar. With the help of a spatula, place the tart on the buttered baking tray and bake for 15–20 minutes. Serve warm, cut into 4–6 slices.

Plum Soufflé Tart

When they are in season, use halved ripe plums—or apricots—for this lovely French tart.

> *1 quantity Rich Shortcrust Pastry (page 345)*
> *2 eggs, separated*
> *$^1/_3$ cup (3 oz) caster (superfine) sugar*
> *2 tablespoons plain (all-purpose) flour*
> *$^3/_4$ cup (6$^1/_2$ fl oz) milk*
> *Vanilla essence (extract)*
> *425 g (15 oz) can plums, halved and pitted*
> *Icing (confectioners') sugar, sifted*
> *Plum jam*

Tip
This quantity of pastry and filling is also sufficient for 8 individual tartlets. Egg rings placed on a baking tray (sheet), or 8 cm (3 in) tartlet cases are ideal.

Roll out the pastry to line a 20 cm (8 in) flan (quiche) ring. Prick the base lightly and chill for about 15 minutes. Bake blind (see page 346) in a moderately hot oven (190°C/375°F) for about 15 minutes until the pastry is set. Cook for a further 5 minutes after removing the beans. Allow to cool slightly before filling and baking further. Increase oven heat to hot (200°C/400°F).

Beat the egg yolks with the sugar until the mixture forms a ribbon into the bowl when the beater is lifted. Add the flour and mix well. Bring the milk to the boil and pour it into the egg-yolk mixture, beating well until blended. Add the vanilla and return the mixture to the saucepan. Cook gently, stirring constantly, until thickened. Remove from heat, and beat the mixture until lukewarm.

Whisk the egg whites until stiff but not dry, and fold them gently into the custard. Pour into the prepared flan case. Drain the plums and arrange them on the filling, rounded side down. Bake in the preheated hot oven for 20 minutes. Reduce the heat to moderate (180°C/350°F) for a further 20 minutes or until golden brown. Remove the tart from the oven and dust with the icing sugar. Heat a little plum jam and brush each plum with it. Serve warm or at room temperature. Serves 6–8.

Desserts

I particularly enjoy freshly prepared desserts such as fruit pies, rice puddings and baked apples, but they must be freshly cooked and still warm. Ice-creams and cold desserts, beautiful moulded Bavarian creams, soft and rich custards as a sauce or baked or as a base for floating islands have, justifiably, many fans. There is much to be said for tender, light and delicate pastries and fruits whether fresh, poached or used in puddings or little French tarts.

Fruits make the best and most delicious desserts. Serve them in the simplest way possible—an orange peeled, sliced, macerated in a little sherry, reshaped and decorated with a few strawberries or slices of kiwi fruit and a fresh leafy sprig from the garden is the kind of dessert you get at expensive health resorts.

While a large proportion of recipes in this chapter make use of fresh fruit, there are some revamped oldies, like bread and butter pudding and baked custard, but they are given new life with new ingredients—a touch of whisky, no less.

There aren't many short cuts to making good desserts, but there are a few. Bought puff pastry, perhaps; the food processor, a definite yes. Care with choice and use of ingredients really shows in the end result. The almond macaroons you make yourself, the tender buttery pastry—these are as important as blemish-free strawberries or perfumed peaches.

Caramel Oranges is an old nursery favourite that has found its way into many a top restaurant menu. A glaze of hot golden caramel, poured over chilled sliced or sometimes re-formed oranges, crisps immediately. Enjoy the firm toffee or refrigerate and allow the caramel to dissolve into a sauce.

Baked Apples

6 large cooking apples
4 tablespoons honey
1 teaspoon cinnamon
Rind of ¹/₂ lemon, grated
6 dates or 6 tablespoons dried fruit
³/₄ cup (6 ¹/₂ fl oz) boiling water

*W*ash the apples and core them, leaving the base of each intact. Cut the skin around the centre of each apple in a scallop design, to prevent the skin bursting. Combine the honey, cinnamon and lemon rind. Fill the core of each apple with a date or a tablespoon of dried fruit, and top with the honey mixture. Place in a small baking dish and pour in the water. Cover with aluminium foil or greaseproof (waxed) paper and bake in a moderately hot oven (190°C/375°F) for 30–40 minutes, until tender without breaking. Remove from heat and baste several times with the pan juices. Serve hot or chilled. Serves 6.

Bread and Butter Pudding with Whisky

10–12 slices of white bread, crusts, removed
Butter
1 cup (5 oz) seedless sultanas (golden raisins)
¹/₄–¹/₂ cup (2–3 oz) currants (optional)
6 eggs, lightly beaten
¹/₂ cup (4 oz) caster (superfine) sugar
¹/₂ cup (4 ¹/₂ fl oz) whisky
1 teaspoon vanilla essence (extract)
5 ¹/₂ cups (2 ¹/₂ imperial pints) milk

*P*reheat the oven to slow (150°C/300°F). Butter the bread slices and cut each into four triangles. Arrange half in a large buttered 8-cup deep pie or baking dish and scatter with the sultanas and currants. Top decoratively with the remaining bread triangles.

Beat the eggs with the sugar and stir in the whisky and vanilla. Scald the milk, add to the beaten eggs and pour the hot liquid over the bread. Soak for about 15 minutes, then place in a pan half-filled with hot water and bake in the preheated oven for 1–1¹/₄ hours until risen and golden. Serves 6.

Rich Shortcrust Pastry

This quantity of pastry makes enough for one 20–23 cm (8–9 in) flan or tart.

1 ¹/₂ cups (6 oz) plain (all-purpose) flour
A pinch of salt
125 g (4 oz) unsalted (sweet) butter, cut into small pieces
1 tablespoon caster (superfine) sugar
1 egg yolk
1 tablespoon water

*S*ift the flour and salt into a large bowl. Add the butter and rub it into the flour with the fingertips until the mixture resembles breadcrumbs. Do not overdo this, as the butter will be blended more thoroughly later. Stir in the sugar.

Make a well in the centre. Mix the egg yolk with the water and combine it quickly with the flour and butter mixture, using a knife. Press the dough together with the fingers.

Turn out onto a floured board and knead lightly until smooth. Roll into a ball. Brush off excess flour. Wrap in greaseproof (waxed) paper and chill for 20–30 minutes before using.

Food processor alternative. Have the butter ready well-chilled, or even better, frozen. Fit the metal double-bladed knife. Sift the flour and salt into the bowl. Cut the butter into small pieces and add to the flour. Process for 15–20 seconds, turning the motor on and off until the mixture resembles fine breadcrumbs. Add the sugar and egg yolk and sprinkle over the water. Process for about 20 seconds or until the pastry clings together and forms a ball. Lightly knead the mixture together to form a smooth dough. Chill and use as required.

Rich Shortcrust Pastry is easily mastered. Light handling and 'resting' are two essential steps.

Prune and Almond Tart

A delicious French tart, using best-quality dessert prunes. A more exotic flavour can be achieved by first soaking pitted prunes in a good cognac or brandy for 30 minutes. The tart may be dusted with sifted icing (confectioners') sugar.

1 quantity Rich Shortcrust Pastry (page 345)
12–14 large dessert prunes, pitted
½ cup (4½ fl oz) white wine
12–14 almonds, blanched (skinned)
2 eggs
½ cup (4 oz) caster (superfine) sugar
3 tablespoons ground almonds
2 tablespoons extra thick (double, heavy) cream

Tip

Baking 'blind' means baking a pastry case (shell) without a filling. First prick the pastry with a fork, then cover the base with a piece of greaseproof (waxed) paper, baking parchment or a kitchen paper towel and weight it down with a layer of dried beans. When the pastry is cooked, remove the beans and paper. The beans can be kept and used over and over again.

*R*oll out the pastry to fit a 23 cm (9 in) round or square flan tin, preferably with a loose base. Prick the pastry base with a fork, chill for 15 minutes, then bake 'blind' (see tip, left) in a moderately hot oven (190°C/375°F) for 15 minutes. Remove beans and paper and continue to bake for a further 5 minutes.

Meanwhile, soak the prunes in the white wine for 30 minutes. Insert a whole almond in each. Beat the eggs and sugar in a bowl until thick and mousse-like. Add the ground almonds and cream and combine well. Arrange the prunes in the half-baked pastry case (shell). Spoon over the almond mixture and bake in a preheated hot oven (200°C/400°F) for 10 minutes. Reduce the heat to moderate (180°C/350°F) and bake for a further 30–35 minutes until golden brown. Serve warm or cold. Serves 8.

Almond Cream and Pear Tart

1 quantity of Rich Shortcrust Pastry (page 345)
90 g (3 oz) unsalted (sweet) butter
⅓ cup (3 oz) caster (superfine) sugar
2 medium eggs
1 teaspoon brandy or cognac
¾ cup (3 oz) ground almonds
4–6 ripe pears, depending on size
¼ cup (3 oz) apricot jam
1 tablespoon water
A squeeze of lemon juice

Tip
Use a teaspoon or a
melon baller to scoop
out the cores of half
pears.

*R*oll out the pastry to fit a 23 cm (9 in) round or square flan tin. Prick the base with a fork, chill for 15 minutes, then bake 'blind' for 15 minutes in a moderate oven (180°C/350°F). Remove the beans and paper and cook another 5 minutes. Meanwhile, cream the butter and sugar until light and fluffy, and beat in the eggs one at a time. Stir in the brandy and almonds. Spread into the prepared pastry case (shell). Peel the pears, halve and core them, and slice them across thinly. Lift the pear halves with a spatula and arrange them over the almond cream, fanning the slices out yet retaining the pear shape. Heat the jam with the water and lemon juice, rub it through a sieve and brush over the pears.

Bake in a preheated moderately hot oven (190°C/375°F) for about 45 minutes or until the almond cream is browned and the pastry well cooked. Serves 8.

Citrus Tart

1 cup (4 oz) plain (all-purpose) flour
¼ cup (1 oz) ground almonds
75 g (2½ oz) butter
⅓ cup (2 oz) icing (confectioners') sugar, sifted
1 egg yolk
A few drops of vanilla essence (extract)
A pinch of salt
Eggwash made with 1 egg yolk and ½ teaspoon milk
4 eggs
¾ cup (6 oz) sugar
Grated rind and juice of 2 lemons and 1 orange
½ cup (4½ fl oz) cream (double, whipping), lightly whipped
2 additional lemons

*S*ift the flour with the ground almonds and make a large well in the centre. Into the well put the butter, icing sugar, egg yolk, vanilla and salt and work these ingredients with the fingertips of one hand to a soft paste. Gradually draw in the surrounding flour and almond mixture and knead lightly to form a dough. Wrap and chill for 1 hour.

Roll out the dough to line a 23 cm (9 in) flan ring; press the sides in well and trim the edge. Lightly prick the base and chill for 15 minutes. Bake 'blind' (see page 346) in a preheated, hot oven (200°C/400°F) for 15 minutes. Remove from the oven, lift away the paper and beans and brush the pastry case (shell) with the egg wash. Return to the oven for a further 5 minutes.

Beat the eggs and sugar in a bowl until smooth, and stir in the lemon and orange rind and juice, then stir in the cream. Pour the mixture into the pastry case. Peel the 2 lemons, removing all the pith. Detach the segments and arrange them around the top of the tart. Bake in a moderate oven (180°C/350°F) for about 45 minutes. Leave to cool for several hours before serving. Serves 8.

Italian Baked Stuffed Peaches

2 tablespoons sugar
2 egg yolks
45 g (1¹/₂ oz) butter, cut into small pieces
90 g (3 oz) amaretti biscuits, crushed
6 medium just-ripe peaches, halved and pitted
²/₃ cup (6 fl oz) white wine or water

*I*n a bowl mix together the sugar, egg yolks, butter and amaretti crumbs. Scoop out a little pulp from each peach half, chop finely and mix with the other ingredients in the bowl. Use this to stuff each peach half.

Arrange the peach halves in a buttered shallow ovenproof dish, pour around the white wine or water—it should be just enough to cover the base of the dish. Bake in a moderate oven (180°C/350°F) for about 30 minutes or until tender. Serve warm with cream. Serves 6.

Italian Baked Stuffed Peaches is a feature in many Italian restaurants in the summertime when fresh ripe peaches are in season. The peaches combine well with the little almond macaroons, which are moistened with egg and often a little wine to make a lovely topping for the fragrant fruit.

Demerara Meringues

185 g (6 oz) demerara sugar
3 large egg whites

$\mathscr{S}$pread the sugar out on a baking tray (sheet) and place in a cool oven (100°C/200°F) for an hour or so to dry out. Leave to cool and place in an electric blender or food processor and grind the sugar fairly finely.

Beat the egg whites until they form soft peaks, then beat in half the sugar until the mixture is thick and shiny. Using a large metal spoon, gently fold in the remaining sugar. To do this, cut gently down and through the mixture and lift some mixture up and over on to the top, repeating until whites and sugar are lightly mixed. It is not necessary to mix thoroughly; if the mixture is overworked, the air cells in the meringue will break down.

To shape meringues, use 2 damp dessertspoons. With one, scoop up a heaped spoonful of mixture; with the other, scoop the meringue out on to a baking tray (sheet) lined with baking paper (parchment or waxed), to form a half-egg shape. If necessary, neaten the shape with a knife dipped in cold water. Repeat until all the mixture is shaped. This should make 16 meringues.

Dredge the tops with a little extra demerara sugar and bake in a preheated very slow oven (120°C/250°F) for 1 hour or longer until firm. Gently lift each meringue, press its base while still warm to make a hollow (this will take some of the filling) and return to the oven for a further 30 minutes until crisp and dry. Leave to cool in the turned-off oven. An hour before serving, sandwich meringues together in pairs in one of the following two ways.

Demerara Meringues —the moist, brown demerara sugar gives the meringues an intriguing flavour. The meringues may be joined together with whipped cream or, better still, a rich chestnut and chocolate filling.

Demerara Meringues with Chestnut and Chocolate

$^{1}/_{4}$ cup (2 oz) sugar
$^{1}/_{3}$ cup (3 fl oz) milk
220 g (8 oz) canned unsweetened chestnut purée
60 g (2 oz) dark (semi-sweet) chocolate, cut into small pieces
$^{1}/_{2}$ cup (4$^{1}/_{2}$ fl oz) cream (single, light)
1 quantity Demerara Meringues (as above)
Thick cream (double, heavy) for serving
Pieces of marron glacé and syrup or shaved dark chocolate

351

issolve the sugar in the milk over a gentle heat. Add the chestnut purée and chocolate and stir over heat until smooth. If lumpy, rub through a sieve. Leave to cool completely. Whip the light cream and fold it into the chestnut purée. Spread a good scoop of this mixture on the base of one meringue, top with another meringue and place on a plate. Serve with a dollop of thick cream alongside and scatter with marron glacé and syrup or shaved chocolate. Serves 8.

Demerara Meringues with Passionfruit Sauce

Tips

Make sure the bowl you select for beating egg whites is perfectly clean and dry.

Meringues may be made ahead and kept in airtight containers. Make up with cream (or other filling) an hour before guests arrive and keep them in the refrigerator; this firms the cream.

Meringues always turn out better when the weather is dry.

¼ cup (2 ¼ fl oz) water
2 tablespoons sugar
Pulp of 6 passionfruit (purple granadillas)
1 cup (9 fl oz) cream (single, light)
A little extra sugar to taste
Vanilla essence (extract) to taste
1 quantity Demerara Meringues (page 351)

n a small pan heat the water and sugar together until a light syrup is formed. Stir the syrup into the passionfruit pulp and set aside.

Whip the cream until stiff and add the extra sugar and vanilla to taste. Spread a spoonful on the base of one meringue and top with another. Repeat with the remaining meringues and cream. Leave for an hour. To serve, place on serving plates and spoon around the passionfruit sauce. Spoon just a little passionfruit sauce across the cream filling of each meringue sandwich. Serves 8.

Rolled Pavlova

The light, airy marshmallow of the pavlova has intrigued the world of sweet lovers. When a rolled version came along, it seemed a bonus. Passionfruit, raspberries and/or strawberries provide the necessary tartness.

4 egg whites
A pinch of salt
⅔ cup (5 oz) caster (superfine) sugar
1 teaspoon cornflour (cornstarch)
1½ teaspoons white vinegar
½ teaspoon vanilla essence (extract)

FILLING

300 ml (10¹/₂ fl oz, 1¹/₄ cups) cream, whipped to soft peaks
Pulp of 6 ripe passionfruit (purple granadillas) or 250 g (8 oz)
  raspberries and/or strawberries, lightly washed and hulled
Icing (confectioners') sugar to dust

$\mathscr{H}$eat the oven to moderate (180°C/350°F). Line a 26 cm × 30 cm (11 in × 12 in) Swiss roll tin (jelly roll pan) with baking paper (parchment). Beat the egg whites with the salt until stiff peaks form. Beat in three-quarters of the sugar, 2 tablespoons at a time. Gently fold in the remaining sugar, cornflour, vinegar and vanilla and spoon the mixture into the prepared pan. Smooth over the surface.

Bake for 12–15 minutes or until set on the top and springy to the touch. Turn out onto a cake cooler covered with a clean tea towel sprinkled generously with caster sugar and leave 5 minutes. Carefully remove the paper. Roll up gently from a long end, using the tea towel to assist the rolling. Leave for 30 minutes or until cool.

Fold the whipped cream through the passionfruit pulp, raspberries or sliced strawberries. Unroll the pavlova and spread with the cream filling. Roll up and place seam side down on a serving plate. Refrigerate at least 30 minutes and dust with icing sugar to serve. Surround with the remaining strawberries, if using, or serve with a berry coulis. To serve, cut into thick slices. Serves 8.

Berry coulis. Crush 125 g (4 oz) strawberries or raspberries and push through a sieve. Add 1 tablespoon icing (confectioners') sugar and a squeeze of lemon juice.

Chocolate Roulade

Of all the desserts my daughter Suzanne makes, this is the one that we like the best. Just a word about the recipe: it does not contain flour and is light as air; it's really a chocolate soufflé omelette.

3 large eggs, separated
¹/₂ cup (4 oz) caster (superfine) sugar
2 tablespoons cocoa, sifted
1 teaspoon vanilla essence (extract)
³/₄ cup (6¹/₂ fl oz) cream, whipped
250 g (8 oz) fresh strawberries or raspberries (optional)
1 tablespoon each icing (confectioners') sugar and cocoa,
  sifted and mixed

*L*ine a 30 cm × 25 cm (12 in × 10 in) Swiss roll tin (jelly roll pan) with greaseproof (waxed) paper, and grease the paper with melted butter, or use baking paper (parchment). Set the oven temperature at moderate (180°C/350°F).

Beat the egg yolks with a whisk or an electric beater until they are thick and creamy. Gradually beat in the sugar. Fold the cocoa into the egg-yolk mixture with the vanilla essence.

Beat the egg whites until soft peaks form and gently fold them into the cocoa mixture. Pour at once into the prepared tin and bake for 15 minutes, until the cake has drawn away from the sides and feels springy when gently touched in the middle.

Have ready a tea towel or sheet of greaseproof (waxed) paper liberally sprinkled with caster sugar. Turn the cake out onto the towel and carefully peel away the base paper. While it is still warm, roll it up, with the towel, and leave on a wire rack to cool.

When completely cold, unroll and spread with the whipped cream. Scatter over sliced strawberries or raspberries if they are being used, reserving several whole perfect ones for decoration. Re-roll the cake, place it seam side down on a serving plate, and chill it for 30 minutes. Just before serving, dust the roulade with a little icing sugar and cocoa and garnish with the reserved fruit. Serves 6–8.

Cardamom Bavarian Cream

Dainty cream desserts are always welcome. This one has an intriguing spicy flavour which is complemented by the raspberry sauce.

> $1^1/_2$ cups ($13^1/_2$ fl oz) milk
> 2 cinnamon sticks
> 6 cardamom pods, crushed
> 4 egg yolks
> $^3/_4$ cup (6 oz) caster (superfine) sugar
> A pinch of salt
> 1 tablespoon gelatine, softened in $^1/_4$ cup ($2^1/_4$ fl oz) cold water
> $1^1/_2$ cups ($13^1/_2$ fl oz) cream, whipped until stiff
> Raspberry sauce (see below)
> Whipped cream

Scald the milk with the cinnamon and cardamom and cool. Beat the egg yolks with the sugar and salt until thick and lemon-coloured; place in a heavy saucepan with the milk and stir over low heat until the mixture coats the back of the spoon. Add the softened gelatine, and stir until it has dissolved. Remove the cinnamon sticks and cardamom pods. Cool, then chill until the mixture begins to set. Fold in the cream. Pour into a 6-cup (1.5 litre, $2^1/_2$ pint) mould rinsed with cold water, or 6 individual moulds. Chill for at least 5 hours. Unmould carefully onto a chilled plate. Serve with raspberry sauce and a dollop of whipped cream. Serves 6.

Raspberry sauce. Gently heat 250 g (8 oz) of raspberries—fresh or frozen—with $^1/_2$ cup (4 oz) of sugar and the juice of half a lemon, lightly mashing the fruit. Purée in an electric blender or food processor, then push through a sieve. Strawberry sauce may be made the same way.

Pears in Citrus Sauce

6 large pears
4 tablespoons honey
³/₄ cup (6¹/₂ fl oz) water
Juice of 2 oranges
Rind of 1 orange
Juice of 1 lemon

Peel the pears, leaving the stalks (stems) on. Place them in an ovenproof dish. Combine the remaining ingredients in a small saucepan and heat gently until the honey has become quite fluid. Pour this sauce over the pears and cover the dish. Cook in a moderate oven (180°C/350°F) for 1 hour or until the pears are tender. Serve warm or chilled. Serves 6.

Baked Pears in Red Wine

Pears in Citrus Sauce, fresh tasting and a translucent gold, is among the loveliest of fresh fruit desserts. Baked Pears in Red Wine becomes a rich red mahogany when baked slowly in red wine. Always choose firm but ripe pears; hard pears never seem to soften in the cooking.

¹/₂ cup (4 oz) sugar
1 cup (9 fl oz) light dry red wine such as pinot noir
A strip of lemon rind
1 small cinnamon stick
8 small pears of even size, or 6 large pears
1 teaspoon arrowroot (optional)

Peel the pears, but do not remove the stalks (stems); if the pears are large, cut them in two and scoop out the core. In a saucepan, dissolve the sugar in the wine, add the lemon rind and cinnamon stick, and bring to the boil for 1 minute. Place the pears in an ovenproof casserole dish and pour over the wine syrup. The pears should just fit so that they all stand up nicely, which gives them a better shape when cooked.

Cover the casserole and bake in a moderate oven (180°C/350°F) until tender, about 1 hour. (If the pears are very firm they may take up to 2 hours.) Remove and strain the syrup. Reduce if necessary to make 1 cup (9 fl oz). The syrup may be thickened with arrowroot mixed with a little water; add to the syrup, and stir until almost boiling and quite clear.

Arrange the pears in a serving dish and spoon over the wine sauce. They are served cold and may be accompanied by a bowl of whipped cream. Serves 6–8.

Orange Jellies

Rind of 1 orange, thinly peeled
Rind, thinly peeled, and juice of 1/2 lemon
1/3 cup (3 oz) sugar
1 1/4 cups (11 fl oz) hot water
3 tablespoons gelatine
Enough oranges to make 2 1/2 cups (22 fl oz) of orange juice,
*   halved; juice extracted and strained*
Extra sugar or lemon juice

Tip
Halve the oranges for juicing as evenly as possible to make cups in which to set the orange jelly.

𝒫ut the orange and lemon rind, lemon juice, sugar and half the water into a saucepan and warm over gentle heat for 10 minutes to infuse. Dissolve the gelatine in the remaining hot water and stir it into the ingredients in the saucepan. Strain and cool. Stir in the orange juice, taste and add a little more sugar or lemon juice if needed.

Meanwhile, gently scrape the inside of the orange shells to remove the membrane and some of the pith and arrange the shells to sit upright on a tray that will fit in the refrigerator. Pour the orange jelly into the shells and chill until set. To serve, cut each orange half in half again, carefully cutting through the rind and the jelly. Arrange the orange jellies on a pretty dessert stand and decorate with citrus leaves if available. Serves 6–8.

Fresh Mango in Lime Syrup

Pawpaw (papaya) can also be prepared this way. Look for fresh limes; if you can't get them, use lemons, which offer a similar tang.

1/2 cup (4 1/2 fl oz) water
Rind of 1 lime, cut into julienne strips
1/3 cup (3 oz) sugar
1/4 cup (2 1/4 fl oz) lime juice—squeezed from 1 or 2 limes
3 mangoes, peeled and sliced

ℐn a small saucepan bring the water to the boil, then drop in the julienned lime rind. Add the sugar, stir until dissolved, then allow the syrup to boil for 3 minutes. Lastly, stir in the lime juice. Arrange the mango slices decoratively in a shallow serving bowl. When the syrup is cool enough, pour it over the mango slices. Leave to macerate for an hour or so before serving. Serves 6.

Caramel Oranges

When oranges are at their peak, serve them chilled and topped with a thin crunchy golden toffee.

> *6–8 large oranges*
> *1 cup (7 oz) sugar*
> *²/₃ cup (6 fl oz) cold water*

*U*sing a swivel-bladed vegetable peeler, thinly pare several strips of rind from one orange and cut them into shreds. Drop into boiling water for 1 minute, drain and set aside. Peel the oranges, removing all the pith. Cut across into slices, removing any seeds, and reshape the oranges, or arrange slices, overlapping, on a serving dish; chill.

Put the sugar and cold water in a heavy saucepan and heat, stirring, until the syrup begins to colour, then drop in the shredded rind and cook for 3–4 minutes to glaze. Remove the rind with a slotted spoon and continue to cook the syrup, rotating the pan frequently so that it will colour evenly, until it is a rich caramel brown. Remove the pan from the heat and, protecting your hand with a cloth, top the fruit with glazed rind and pour over a little caramel. Chill in the refrigerator. The toffee will stay crisp for a short time, then it will melt to a lovely caramel sauce. Enjoy the oranges either way. Serves 6–8.

Tip
Offer a bowl of mascarpone (Italian cream cheese), for those who like a touch of cream with the Caramel Oranges, and a plate of crisp biscuits.

Caramel Oranges in its rich golden caramel sauce is one of the simplest and best ways of serving a fruit dessert. Rich, thick mascarpone can be offered for those who like cream.

Ice-Cream Alexander

Alexander was my father, whisky was his tipple, and he loved ice-cream. He never grew tired of this sweet-treat. Here is the recipe for an individual serving of this delicious, simple dessert.

> *Best vanilla ice-cream, homemade or commercial*
> *1¹/₂ teaspoons freeze-dried instant coffee granules*
> *1 tablespoon whisky or Drambuie*
> *2 crisp dessert biscuits (tuiles, cigarettes russes)*

*P*ut 2 generous scoops of ice-cream in a glass coupé. Sprinkle over the coffee granules and the whisky. Serve with the crisp biscuits.

Lemon Parfait

This is a lovely dessert, one that can be prepared ahead and which cuts and presents very easily for entertaining.

Lemon Parfait with a passionfruit sauce is one of the most refreshing desserts after a rich meal. It is a frozen ice-cream and when set in a loaf tin can be cut in thick slices. Any light fruit sauce could be used; see, for example, the raspberry sauce served with Cardamom Bavarian Cream.

> *¹/₂ cup (4 oz) sugar*
> *5 tablespoons water*
> *4 egg yolks*
> *Rind of 1 lemon, grated*
> *2 tablespoons lemon juice*
> *1¹/₄ cups (11 oz) cream, whipped*
> *Passionfruit sauce (page 392) and thick (double, heavy) cream*
>   *for serving*
> *Mint sprigs for decoration*

*D*issolve the sugar in the water over a gentle heat. Boil the syrup about 5 minutes. Set aside. Now beat the egg yolks with the lemon rind for a moment or so. Gradually add the hot syrup in a thin stream, whisking all the time. Continue whisking until it has doubled in bulk. Whisk in the lemon juice. Fold in the whipped cream. Pour into a small loaf tin lined with baking paper (parchment) and leave to set in the freezer for 8 hours.

Unmould and serve cut into slices. Accompany each serving with passionfruit sauce and a dollop of thick cream (you can also add a crisp dessert biscuit). Decorate with mint sprigs. Serves 6.

Rosie's Baked Ricotta

This recipe is an adaptation of a sweet from the Middle East, where wonderful honeys are prized. Rosemary Penman gave me the recipe after it became a hit on her television program; thus the title. She uses a strong Tasmanian leatherwood honey but recommends also an orange blossom honey.

Tips
Prepare breadcrumbs in a food processor or by rubbing bread through a colander.

Toast almonds under a hot griller (broiler) or use a heavy saucepan over a gentle heat, tossing the almonds to prevent scorching.

2 teaspoons butter
2/3 cup (1 1/2 oz) fresh breadcrumbs
300 g (10 oz) fresh ricotta
1 cup (12 oz) Tasmanian leatherwood or other strong honey
1 teaspoon vanilla essence (extract)
3 eggs, well beaten
90 g (3 oz) unblanched almonds, toasted and chopped
  roughly
1/4 cup (2 1/4 fl oz) orange juice (blood orange if available)

Preheat the oven to moderate (180°C/350°F). Lightly butter a 20 cm (8 in) round cake tin (preferably springform) and coat it with breadcrumbs.

Place the ricotta in a mixing bowl. Use a fork to mix in 2/3 cup of the honey and vanilla essence; add the eggs gradually, then the almonds, mixing in lightly. Fill the prepared cake tin with the mixture and bake until just set in the middle, about 30–40 minutes. Allow to stand for 10–15 minutes. Turn out onto a serving dish.

Heat the remaining honey and mix with the orange juice; drizzle this over the ricotta when serving. If using leatherwood honey, you may prefer to drizzle it over the dessert without the addition of the orange juice. Serve warm or cold; it is delicious both ways. Serves 6–8.

Baked Goat's Cheese

Serve this as a cheese course and dessert combined. It is delicious.

250 g (8 oz) goat's cheese
2 Granny Smith apples
3 tablespoons chopped walnuts
1 tablespoon virgin olive oil
A few choice salad greens for garnish

*C*ut the cheese into 6 slices. Cut top and bottom ends off the apples, remove the cores, and cut each apple across into 3 thick slices. Top each apple slice with a cheese slice, and sprinkle over the chopped walnuts. Place on a baking tray (sheet).

Bake in a moderately hot oven (190°C/375°F) for 15 minutes. The apples will be warmed through but still have a crunch, the cheese soft, and the nuts toasted. Serve on individual plates with a little oil poured over each and some salad greens for garnish. Serves 6.

Sweet Cream Cheese Mould with Fresh Summer Fruits

250 g (8 oz) unsalted cream cheese or cottage cheese or ricotta
300 ml (10¹/₂ fl oz, 1¹/₄ cups) cream (single, light)
2 tablespoons caster (superfine) sugar
2 egg whites
Extra cream to serve (optional)

Tip
If this mixture were set in heart-shaped pierced china moulds it would be called 'coeur à la crème'. It is easy to improvise your own perforated cheese drainer by piercing holes either in a small cake tin or in cottage cheese or other plastic tub containers.

*R*ub the cheese through a sieve and beat in the cream. Stir in the sugar; it should not be too sweet. Whisk the egg whites until they are stiff but not dry and fold them into the cheese mixture. Wet a piece of muslin (cheesecloth) and use it to line a perforated mould. Turn in the cheese mixture, stand the mould on a deep plate or saucer and cover lightly. Leave it in the refrigerator to drain overnight. Turn the sweet cream cheese out just before serving. If you like, you can pour over some pouring cream.

Serve with soft summer fruit—fresh strawberries or raspberries—or hot sliced peaches sprinkled with vanilla sugar and baked. Serves 4–6.

Cook it Light

Since the terms nouvelle cuisine *and* cuisine minceur *were coined and the Heart Foundation symbol made an impact, we have been taking a greater interest in more varied and lighter meals. We have also been taking more interest in our physical well-being. Much as we love our food, we certainly don't want to negate the morning's work-out in the gym, the brisk walk in the park or the determined jogging by eating food that will undo all that good work.*

Nutritionists, chefs and food writers have addressed this problem collectively with their skills and knowledge. The message is clear:

Eat less fat and dietary cholesterol.

Eat less salt and less sugar.

Eat more foods high in carbohydrates and fibre.

Drink less alcohol.

Eat a greater variety of foods.

Let me tell you, it is enjoyable and rewarding to put these guidelines into practice. There should be no feeling of deprivation. Cooking and eating will remain one of life's greatest pleasures so long as you work with a variety of fresh, colourful and quality ingredients. This chapter will set you on the right path.

Ricotta dessert served with an array of wonderful fruits. From the top, clockwise: pomegranate, Fijian pawpaw (papaya), tamarillos (tree tomatoes), raspberries, guavas and strawberries.

Roasted Tomato and Basil Soup

Roasting gives tomatoes an extra depth of flavour, just as it does capsicum, transporting an ordinary tomato soup into something quite special.

Roasted Tomato and Basil Soup garnished with fine strips of red basil. Roasting gives the tomatoes an extra depth of flavour. The tomatoes should be ripe and red—if possible, tree ripened. So many tomatoes come to us picked green, they remain hard and never seem to ripen and soften.

> *750 g (1¹/₂ lb) tomatoes, halved and seeds scooped out*
> *1 tablespoon olive oil*
> *1 garlic clove, crushed*
> *2 tablespoons chopped fresh basil*
> *A pinch of sugar*
> *2¹/₂ cups (22 fl oz) chicken stock (chilled, to remove all fat)*
> *Freshly ground pepper*
> *4 basil leaves, freshly cut*

Preheat the oven to moderate (180°C/350°F). Place the tomato halves cut side down on a lightly greased baking tray (sheet). Roast for 20 minutes, then remove them from the oven and slip off the skins. Chop the flesh finely, saving all the juices.

Heat the oil and add the tomatoes, garlic and chopped basil. Add the pinch of sugar and simmer gently for about 5 minutes. Add the chicken stock and reserved juices and cook a further 5 minutes. Serve immediately with a sprinkling of basil to garnish. Alternatively, cool the soup, place it in the refrigerator, and serve it chilled. Serves 6.

Pan-Fried Cherry Tomatoes

> *24–30 cherry tomatoes, depending on size*
> *2 tablespoons light olive oil*
> *1 garlic clove, chopped*
> *1 tablespoon chopped parsley*
> *6 fresh basil leaves, shredded*
> *Salt and a fresh grinding of pepper*

Wash and stem the tomatoes. Heat the oil in a frying pan (skillet), add the tomatoes, garlic and parsley and cook the mixture over a moderate heat for about 2–3 minutes or until the tomatoes are heated through. Take care not to allow the skins to split. Just before serving, toss in the basil and season with salt and pepper. Serves 4–6.

Mini Lamb Topside Roast

The new mini-roasts of lamb are a boon to small households or for entertaining. They can be cooked on top of the stove or in the oven. They are always tender, juicy, flavoursome and healthy. Most butchers will understand the cutting of small mini-roasts from the lamb topside or round, but you had best give a day's warning. These cuts average 375 g (12 oz).

1 trim lamb topside or boneless round roast
2 tablespoons chopped herbs (mainly parsley with a little
  oregano or thyme)
1 teaspoon honey
1 teaspoon lemon juice
A pinch of mustard
1 tablespoon olive oil

Mini Lamb Roasts are a new concept in trim lamb. These roasts are fillets cut from the neck or leg, either topside, chump or rump, into bone and fat free cuts. When tied into a neat shape, they are suitable for roasting or pan frying as a roast. They average around 375g (12 oz), which is plenty for two adults.

Open the little topside roast and spread it with herbs. Roll it into a neat shape and fix it with a metal skewer or tie it with string. Mix the honey, lemon juice and mustard and rub the mixture into the meat. Let it stand for 30 minutes, turning in the mixture several times.

In a small, heavy saucepan, frying pan or flameproof casserole, brown the meat in the oil on all sides. Put a lid on the pan and cook over moderate heat, covered, for no longer than 7–10 minutes. Remove the roast from the heat and put it in a warm place, covered with aluminium foil, for no longer than 10 minutes while you're finishing off the vegetables. This standing time allows the juices to settle, making slicing easier and giving a juicy result.

Serve the lamb in thick slices and pour over any of the juices in the pan, if you like. Serve with steamed herbed potatoes, green beans or steamed spinach and pan-fried tomatoes. Serves 2.

Tender pink slices of a lamb mini-roast served with a green vegetable in season, this time lightly steamed spinach and baby turnips.

Orange Lamb Kebabs

The flavour of orange with soy may seem unusual, but the finished kebabs, served with a rice pilaf followed by a green salad, make an excellent meal.

1 kg (2 lb) shoulder of lamb, boned
1 garlic clove, peeled and crushed with salt to a smooth paste
A large pinch of salt
$^1/_2$ cup (4$^1/_2$ fl oz) orange juice
2 tablespoons soy sauce
2 oranges
2 green capsicums (sweet peppers)

Orange Lamb Kebabs call for well-trimmed cubes of lamb; a shoulder cut is best for this. The fresh taste of juicy orange slices is lovely with the lamb.

Trim the lamb of excess fat and cut into large cubes. Combine the garlic with the orange juice and soy sauce in a bowl and marinate the lamb cubes in this mixture for at least 2 hours covered with plastic wrap (cling film).

Peel the oranges, removing all pith; halve and cut them across into thick slices. Halve the capsicums, remove the seeds, and cut the flesh into squares the same size as the meat cubes.

Drain the lamb cubes, reserving the marinade. Arrange the lamb, orange slices and capsicum squares alternately on skewers. Brush with the marinade and place the kebabs under a preheated grill (broiler). Turn them frequently and brush them with marinade every few minutes. Cook for about 10 minutes or until the meat is tender. Serve with rice pilaf or plain boiled rice. Serves 4–6.

Pan-Roasted Loin of Lamb with Fresh Coriander Chutney

Tip
To test the doneness of roast lamb without actually running a skewer into it, press it with the back of a spoon. If the meat is still quite rare it will feel soft and spongy; if it is well done it will feel firm; medium rare will be between these two, still a little soft and spongy without being too firm. This takes a little experience at first, but after a while you will be able to judge very well.

Ask your butcher to bone a loin of lamb and cut away the skin and membrane, leaving only the eye and the tenderloin. Expensive but good.

1 large loin of lamb, boned and trimmed
1 garlic clove, cut into thin slivers
Freshly ground pepper
1 teaspoon each butter and olive oil
1 quantity Sauté of Ratatouille Vegetables (page 134)
Lemon Rice (page 177)
1 quantity Coriander Chutney (page 187)
Mint or coriander (Chinese parsley) sprigs as garnish

Make several slits in the lamb and insert the garlic slivers. Season all over with freshly ground pepper.

In a heavy flameproof roasting pan or large frying pan (skillet) heat the oil and butter and, when sizzling, add the lamb. Brown all over, turning frequently, for about 8 minutes. Test for doneness. Remove the pan from the heat and cover the meat in the pan entirely with aluminium foil. Leave the meat to 'set' for 10 minutes.

To serve, cut the lamb diagonally into 1 cm (¹/₂ in) slices. Divide among 4 warmed plates. Spoon the ratatouille onto the plates, serve with the rice and spoon the coriander chutney near the meat slices. Garnish with mint or coriander sprigs and follow with a green salad. Serves 4.

White Cooked Chicken

The Cantonese have a special way with chicken. They know that the white meat of a chicken is easily overcooked; it becomes fibrous when the meat shrinks, contracts and separates from the juices. They call their dish white cooked chicken or white chop chicken, and once you prepare it you'll know why. The chicken is white, it gets chopped up, but best of all it is succulent and juicy and lends itself to many variations when it is served with one of a multitude of sauces. A bonus is the light stock that is left; it is just right for Chinese soups. White chicken is best made with a fresh free-range chicken and not one that has been frozen; it makes a great difference in taste and texture.

> *1.5 kg (3 lb) fresh chicken*
> *1 teaspoon salt*
> *2 green shallots (spring onions, scallions), chopped*
> *¹/₄ cup (2¹/₄ fl oz) peanut (groundnut) oil*
> *Extra salt*

Wash the chicken with warm water to bring it to room temperature. Pat dry with a kitchen paper towel.

Place the chicken in a saucepan or large pot into which it just fits. Add enough water to cover. Take the chicken out. Add the salt and shallots and bring to the boil. Lower the chicken into the saucepan and bring back to the boil. Cook for 5 minutes. Cover the pan and remove it from the heat. Let the chicken steep for 2 hours.

Lift the chicken out, rinse it under cold water, drain and pat dry. Brush the chicken with the peanut oil. Generously sprinkle the extra salt over the whole

Pan-Roasted Loin of Lamb with Fresh Coriander Chutney. The meat is an expensive cut, the tender long fillet removed from its surrounding bone and fat off the loin of lamb. It can be cooked in minutes to tender perfection. A special-occasion dish, served here with Sautéed Ratouille of Vegetables and Creamy Mashed Potato.

Tip
When preparing White Cooked Chicken, never cook the chicken until the meat falls off the bone. That is why it is much better to steep rather than simmer the chicken, because you are less likely to overcook it. The cold water rinse helps stop the chicken from further cooking and also helps to crisp the skin. The chicken may be cooked a little ahead of time.

chicken. When cool, chop the chicken into 5 cm × 2 cm (2 in × 1 in) pieces. It is best to chop it just before serving, so that the juices stay in the meat. If on a low-fat program, remove the skin.

Serve the chicken cold with oyster sauce or fresh ginger sauce.

Oyster sauce. Combine 4 tablespoons of commercial oyster sauce, 2 tablespoons of chicken stock and 1 teaspoon of sugar in a small saucepan, and heat the mixture until the sugar dissolves. Pour the sauce over the white cooked chicken.

Fresh ginger sauce. Shred 6–8 spring onions (scallions) on the diagonal and place them with 2 tablespoons of finely chopped ginger (the ginger should be very young, fresh and free of fibres) and 1 tablespoon of salt in a heatproof bowl. Heat 4 tablespoons of vegetable oil and pour it over the ginger and spring onions and steep for 10 minutes. Spoon the sauce over the white cooked chicken.

Coriander Chicken

Coriander Chicken is a dish that exemplifies the Chinese skill at cooking chicken. A cold-water rinse crisps the skin, a texture Chinese appreciate. The chicken is topped with shreds of ginger, green shallots (spring onions, scallions) and coriander (Chinese parsley). Boiling oil, soy and sesame oil are poured over. The fragrance is amazingly good.

1 White Cooked Chicken (preceding recipe)
6–8 green shallots (spring onions, scallions), shredded
1 tablespoon peeled and finely shredded fresh ginger
2–3 tablespoons sesame seeds, toasted
1 cup coriander (Chinese parsley) sprigs
4 tablespoons peanut (groundnut) or vegetable oil
2 tablespoons light soy sauce
2 teaspoons sesame oil

*A*rrange the chopped white cooked chicken on a plate. Top with the shallots, shredded ginger (the shreds should be very fine and free from fibres), sesame seeds and coriander. Just before serving, heat the oil, soy sauce and sesame oil and pour over the chicken. Serves 6.

Steamed Chicken Breasts

A useful recipe to learn, as there are so many uses for cooked chicken.

1 onion or 1/2 leek, sliced
1/2 carrot, cut into ribbons with vegetable peeler
4 half-breasts of chicken
4 springs of oregano or a sprinkling of dried tarragon
A light sprinkling of salt

374

*M*ake a bed of the onion or leek and carrot on a steaming rack or an expanding steamer. Set the chicken breasts on this, and sprinkle with the herbs and salt.

Bring a small saucepan of water to the boil, lower in the steamer with the chicken, cover and gently steam for 15 minutes or until the juices run clear when the chicken is pierced with a fine skewer. Remove skin and bones when ready to serve. The chicken may be served warm with a simple sauce or used cold in salads, as well as in many other ways.

Fish (steaks, fillets or small fish) can be steamed in the same way, but cooking time will be much shorter. Check with a sharp pointed knife after 4 minutes for fine fish; 6 minutes is average.

Thai Grilled Chicken

1 kg (2 lb) boneless chicken thighs
MARINADE
6–8 coriander (Chinese parsley) roots, stems and tops
3–4 garlic cloves
1 teaspoon freshly ground pepper
1 teaspoon sugar
2 teaspoons ground turmeric
4 tablespoons vegetable oil
TO SERVE
Boiled rice, crisp lettuce cups and chunks of Lebanese
   (Continental) cucumber

*W*ash the coriander well and shake it dry. Cut off the roots and 5 cm (2 in) of the green stems; roughly chop. Reserve tops. Place in an electric blender or food processor with the remaining marinade ingredients and process to make a thick purée.

Coat the chicken pieces with marinade and let them stand for 1 hour.

Line a grill rack with aluminium foil, spread the thighs smooth side up on foil and grill (broil) them under moderate heat for about 10 minutes. It shouldn't be necessary to turn the chicken, but check that the underside is cooked.

Serve with the rice, lettuce cups, cucumber and coriander tops. For casual meals the chicken can be sliced and put into the lettuce cups with a cucumber wedge, rolled up and eaten in the hand. A hot Thai chilli sauce can be offered to give that Thai heat—just a touch. Serves 4.

Stir-Fried Pork in Lettuce Cups

A lovely light way of enjoying lean pork. It is stir-fried and served and eaten in crisp lettuce cups. The little packages are eaten from the hand. Very informal but very delicious.

1 large iceberg lettuce, washed and chilled

375 g (12 oz) lean minced (ground) pork

230 g (8 oz) can water chestnuts, chopped

2 tablespoons light vegetable oil

1/4 teaspoon salt

2 teaspoons light soy sauce

1 teaspoon sesame oil

A little freshly ground pepper

1/2–3/4 cup (41/2–61/2 fl oz) chicken stock (page 68)

1 tablespoon cornflour (cornstarch) mixed with 3 tablespoons water

Chinese plum sauce (optional)

Stir-fried Pork in Lettuce Cups is derived from a popular Chinese dish made with pigeons. It is quick, easy and delicious served with Asian plum sauce in crisp lettuce cups made into a parcel to eat with the fingers.

377

eparate the leaves of the lettuce. Cut larger leaves with scissors into neat cup shapes and select small cup-shaped leaves; place them in iced water to crisp. Combine the pork and the water chestnuts. Heat the vegetable oil in a wok or sauté pan, add the pork mixture and stir-fry for a few minutes. Sprinkle with the salt, soy sauce, sesame oil and pepper and stir-fry until the pork is no longer pink. Add the stock and simmer, covered, for 3–4 minutes. Stir in the blended cornflour and cook, stirring, until thickened.

Place the mixture in a bowl or on a serving dish. Drain the lettuce cups and dry them. Each diner places 2 tablespoons of pork and a little plum sauce into a lettuce cup, folds it over and rolls it up to enclose the filling. Serves 6.

Gingered Chicken on Skewers

The Japanese keep slim and relatively free from heart disease by eating dishes like this fat-free skewered chicken. If you like the flavour but want a change, try marinating whole chicken breasts in the oriental marinade; grill (broil) them under moderate heat, about 5 minutes on each side, and brush with the marinade during cooking.

Gingered Scallops on Skewers is an adaptation of a Japanese recipe for chicken. The warm food is served on a bed of greens, this time one of the Japanese spicy leaves. Green pea shoots or watercress may be used.

> *4 chicken half-breasts or fillets*
> *¹/₄ cup (2¹/₄ fl oz) light soy sauce*
> *¹/₄ cup (2¹/₄ fl oz) dry sherry*
> *1 tablespoon sugar*
> *2 tablespoons finely chopped green ginger*
> *125 g (4 oz) water chestnuts*
> *4 green shallots (spring onions, scallions), cut into short lengths*

emove skin and bone from the chicken. Cut the breasts into squares of about 2 cm (³/₄ in). Combine the soy sauce, sherry, sugar and ginger in a bowl and add the chicken. Cover and marinate for about 20 minutes.

Thread the chicken meat alternatively with water chestnuts and shallot lengths on bamboo skewers which have been soaked in warm water for at least 30 minutes. Cook under a preheated hot griller (broiler) for about 10 minutes, turning and brushing with the soy mixture, or until chicken is cooked. Serve on a bed of greens. Serves 4.

Gingered Scallops on Skewers

Prepare as above, using 375 g (12 oz) of fresh scallops instead of the chicken. These will cook in 5–6 minutes.

Mustard Chicken in Yoghurt

4 chicken half-breasts, boned
Salt and freshly ground pepper
1 tablespoon olive oil
4 teaspoons French mustard
1 small carton (200 g, 7 oz) non-fat natural (plain) yoghurt
4 teaspoons grated Parmesan cheese

Tip
By removing the skin, which contains much of a chicken's fat, and using low-calorie but flavourful yoghurt, this is a good way of serving chicken to dieters or those on a low-fat program. Serve it with a salad.

Preheat the oven to hot (200°C/400°F). Remove the skin from the chicken breasts and cut each into halves lengthwise. Season with salt and pepper. Place the chicken in a shallow ovenproof dish in one layer. Drizzle with olive oil. Cover with aluminium foil and bake for about 20 minutes. Remove from the oven and increase the oven temperature to very hot (230°C/450°F).

Remove the foil and spread each chicken piece with 1 teaspoon of mustard, then cover with yoghurt. Sprinkle 1 teaspoon of cheese on each and return to the oven. Cook uncovered for a further 10 minutes, or until light golden. Serve with a salad. Serves 4.

Lamb and Apricot Pilaf

Fat-free cubes of lamb are cooked with spices and fruit, then layered with rice to make a fragrant pilaf.

Lamb and Apricot Pilaf is very much a dish of today, yet it is centuries old. A small amount of lamb flavours long-grain rice with gentle spicing and the sweet taste of dried raisins and apricots. The long-grain Basmati rice from the Punjab is my choice of rice.

1 onion, finely chopped
1 tablespoon olive oil
500 g (1 lb) lean lamb, cubed
Salt and ground black pepper
1/2 teaspoon cinnamon
2 tablespoons raisins
1 cup (4 oz) dried apricots
1–1 1/2 cups (8 oz) long-grain rice

In a heavy flameproof casserole or saucepan, fry the onion gently in the oil until soft and golden. Add the meat, turning until it is brown all over. Season with salt, pepper and cinnamon. Add the raisins and apricots and cook a few minutes longer. Add water to just cover, place the lid on the pot and simmer for about 1 hour, until the meat is very tender and has absorbed the flavours of the fruit. Remove the lid and increase the heat to reduce the sauce if necessary.

380

Cook the rice in boiling salted water for about 10 minutes, until not quite tender; drain. In a heavy, flameproof casserole arrange alternate layers of rice and meat, starting and ending with rice. Cover and steam gently for about 10 minutes, until the rice is tender and has absorbed some of the sauce. Serve hot. Serves 4.

Chicken and Rice Soup

Chicken and Rice Soup is known to travellers in South-East Asia. There are many versions, all with claims to be good for whatever ails you. It is eaten for breakfast or late supper—indeed, any time of the day, between meals or at any mealtime.

There are many versions of this soup-cum-porridge throughout China and South-East Asia. It is eaten at any time of the day from breakfast to supper. It is considered good for whatever ails you when you are off colour, and as an antidote for a hangover. It is one of my favourite dishes, especially with the assortment of garnishes that really pep up the simple rice base.

2 cups (10 oz) long-grain rice
8 cups (3¹/₂ imperial pints) water
2 chicken half-breasts or 3 thighs
GARNISHES
1 tablespoon peeled and finely cut fresh ginger
1 tablespoon dried prawns, fried in a little oil until crisp
*6 golden shallots or 1 onion, cut into thin slices and fried
     gently in a little oil until crisp*
2 garlic cloves, finely sliced and fried gently until crisp
A few sprigs of coriander
1 chilli, finely sliced
Soy sauce
Sesame oil

 ash the rice well. Bring the water to the boil, drizzle in the rice, and cook over a gentle heat for about 40 minutes until the rice grains are broken and the resulting porridge has a thick consistency. For the last 15 minutes, put the chicken on top of the rice in the pan and allow the rice to finish cooking and the chicken to cook.

Remove the chicken and tear the flesh into shreds, discarding any bones and skin. Return the chicken to the rice. If the rice gets too thick, add a little chicken stock or water. Serve in soup bowls and offer the garnishes in small dishes. Everyone can season their own soup to taste. Serves 6.

Steamed Vegetables

A collapsible steamer is a most worthwhile investment. It allows the cooking of a wide variety of vegetables at one time, and as steamed vegetables cook quickly and don't lose any of their goodness in the water, their flavour is more intense.

Simply prepare the vegetables as usual, place them in a steamer over boiling water in the base of a saucepan or wok, and cover with the lid. It is important that none of the vegetables sit in water; there should be sufficient room between water and food for the steam to form and rise up through the vegetables.

Start with the firmest vegetables, and add the softer ones progressively according to the length of cooking time each requires. As a guide, sliced carrot, pumpkin or small new potatoes take about 15 minutes, beans take 8 minutes and zucchini (courgettes), snow peas (mangetout), spinach or cabbage take about 5 minutes. Best of all is a selection of perfect baby vegetables, carefully chosen and prepared.

Serve with a dab of butter or a squeeze of lemon juice or a sprinkling of freshly chopped herbs and a grinding of pepper.

Butternut Squash with Cumin

This is a delicious salad. It makes an excellent meal for vegetarians.

> *1½ teaspoons cumin seeds*
> *½ cup loosely packed mint leaves*
> *½ cup (4½ fl oz) orange juice*
> *¼ cup (2¼ fl oz) lemon juice*
> *½ red salad onion, sliced*
> *1 tablespoon sugar*
> *Pepper and salt*
> *750 g (1½ lb) butternut squash or other winter squash*
> *1 large green or red capsicum (sweet pepper), cut into dice*
> *¼ cup (1 oz) chopped roasted peanuts (groundnuts)*

P eel the squash, cut in half lengthwise, discard the seeds and strings and cut the flesh crosswise into slices. Place in a steamer set over boiling water and steam for 5 minutes or until it is barely tender. Allow to cool. In a large shallow platter, place slices of squash in overlapping layers.

In a small frying pan, toast the cumin seeds over moderate heat until they are very fragrant, being careful not to let the seeds burn. Transfer them to a plate and when cool crush them between two sheets of greaseproof (waxed) paper or in a mortar with a pestle. Finely chop the mint leaves and combine them in a small bowl with the orange and lemon juice, onion, half the cumin powder, sugar, and pepper and salt to taste. Add the diced capsicum, mix well and spoon over the squash. Sprinkle with the peanuts and the remaining cumin powder. Serves 6.

Vegetable Spaghetti with Fresh Peas

Vegetable spaghetti (spaghetti squash) looks like a long melon with a smooth skin like a marrow and a colour similar to that of a rockmelon (cantaloupe). This fascinating and delicious vegetable has a surprising centre after being boiled and split—a mass of thready flesh, like a tangle of spaghetti.

> *1 vegetable spaghetti (spaghetti squash)*
> *1–2 tablespoons butter, melted, or extra virgin olive oil*
> *1 tablespoon grated Parmesan cheese*
> *2 cups (12 oz) fresh peas, cooked until tender and drained*
> *Freshly ground pepper*

Push a skewer into the vegetable spaghetti to make a hole; this helps the centre to cook more quickly. Boil in a large pan of salted water for 40–50 minutes, depending on the size. Test with a skewer to see if the inside is tender. Drain and cool for a few minutes, then split it in half to reveal the strings of flesh inside. The seeds are removed at this stage. Turn the strings of flesh out into a serving bowl, using a large fork to help pull them away from the sides.

Add the butter or oil to the vegetable spaghetti, together with the cheese and peas. Season well with freshly ground pepper and toss together using two forks. Serves 6.

Grilled Chicken Salad with Balsamic Vinegar

Balsamic vinegar is no longer a mystery to good cooks. It adds its pungent, magical flavour to many dishes. Take care, though, not to be heavy-handed with it; a small amount is all that is needed.

4 half-breasts of chicken
Freshly ground pepper
2 tablespoons extra virgin olive oil
2 teaspoons balsamic vinegar
A selection of salad greens, e.g. watercress, arugula (rocket),
   radicchio, butterhead or mignonette lettuce and green pea
   shoots
¹/₄ cup (1 oz) toasted walnuts or pecans

DRESSING
¹/₄ teaspoon Dijon mustard
1 teaspoon champagne vinegar, sherry vinegar or wine vinegar
1 teaspoon balsamic vinegar
4 tablespoons virgin olive oil

Grilled Chicken Salad with Balsamic Vinegar, still warm and fragrant from the grill (broiler), is served on a bed of greens. These may be a mesclun selection, watercress or arugula, or, as shown here, green pea shoots. The toasted nuts are optional. Steamed new potatoes make a good accompaniment.

℞emove any excess fat from the chicken breasts, leaving the skin and bone intact (remove the skin for a low-fat regime). Season with freshly ground pepper and brush with the olive oil and vinegar. Leave to marinate for 1 hour, turning the chicken several times.

Lift out the chicken, reserving the marinade. Have ready a preheated grill (broiler) or ribbed grill pan and cook the chicken until tender—about 5 minutes on each side. Remove the chicken from the heat and, as soon as it has cooled enough to handle, cut the flesh in one piece from the bone. Slice each one across in medium thick slices, or leave it whole if you prefer.

Have ready the salad greens, washed and dried thoroughly and torn into serving-size pieces; pea shoots can be left whole. Toss in the prepared dressing (see below) and arrange on a serving plate or 4 dinner plates. Arrange a sliced half-breast on the greens, top with the toasted walnuts. Add the reserved marinade to the pan and let it sizzle, scraping up the pan drippings. Drizzle this over the chicken. Serves 4.

Dressing. Place the mustard and vinegars in a bowl. Whisk well and slowly add the olive oil, whisking all the time. Season with salt and pepper.

Roasted Capsicum and Tomato Tians

Look for yellow and red capsicums (sweet peppers). Failing the yellow, select firm green ones. This dish, which is best served cold, needs plenty of crusty bread to mop up the delicious juices. I use individual soufflé dishes to prepare it. Serves as a first course or luncheon dish.

3 large red capsicums (sweet peppers)
2 large yellow capsicums
2 large garlic cloves, crushed with a little salt
¹/₄ cup (1 oz) freshly grated Parmesan cheese
2–4 tablespoons fresh breadcrumbs
1 cup basil leaves, shredded roughly
2 sweet salad onions, sliced finely
4–6 ripe red tomatoes, sliced
Salt and freshly ground pepper
1–2 tablespoons olive oil

Char, skin and seed the capsicums as described on page 108. Cut them into 2 cm (³/₄ in) strips and toss them with the crushed garlic. Combine the Parmesan cheese and breadcrumbs with a little of the shredded basil. Sprinkle a little breadcrumb mixture in each of 6 large ramekins or individual soufflé dishes, using half in all. Layer 2 strips of red capsicum and one of yellow in the base to come up the sides of each dish and continue to layer the sliced onion, tomato, remaining capsicum strips, and shredded basil until filled.

Season with salt and pepper, top with the remaining half of the breadcrumb mixture and drizzle with oil.

Bake in a moderately hot oven (190°C/375°F) for about 20 minutes. Remove from the oven and cool before chilling for several hours and serving. Serves 6.

These long egg or plum tomatoes have been sun-ripened on the vine to a bright, blazing red. They will have a full, sweet flavour. The deep purple, almost black, capsicums are one of the newest strains of this versatile vegetable.

Mesclun Salad with Chive Dressing

This light green salad uses the baby lettuce mixture now available in many greengrocers. You can mix your own. Tear large leaves into bite-size pieces.

250 g (8 oz) mesclun (mixed baby greens), rinsed and dried
1 tablespoon fresh lemon or lime juice
Salt to taste, preferably flaky Maldon salt
Freshly ground pepper to taste
2 tablespoons olive oil, preferably extra virgin
3 tablespoons snipped fresh chives

Toss the mesclun lightly in a salad bowl. In a small bowl, whisk together the lemon or lime juice, the salt, pepper and the oil (added in a slow stream while whisking), until the dressing is emulsified. Whisk in the chives, drizzle the dressing over the mesclun, and toss the salad well. Serves 4.

Stir-Fried Greens with Oyster Sauce

A plate of mixed vegetables (choose the ones you like) is a good addition to an Asian meal or with regular grills or barbecues.

500 g (1 lb) greens: spinach, snow peas (mangetout), Chinese
*   cabbage (Pe-Tsai), snow pea shoots*
2 tablespoons vegetable oil
6 garlic cloves, chopped
1/4 cup fresh coriander (Chinese parsley) leaves
1 tablespoon Thai fish sauce (nam pla)
2 tablespoons oyster sauce
1 tablespoon cornflour (cornstarch) mixed with 1/4 cup
*   (2 1/4 fl oz) water*
1 tablespoon chopped fresh coriander leaves

Wash the vegetables. Cut leafy greens into 5 cm (2 in) pieces, string snow peas, cut broccoli into thin slices. Heat the oil in a wok over high heat and add the garlic. Stir-fry for 30 seconds, then add the greens, including the coriander leaves, and the fish sauce, oyster sauce and cornflour-water mixture. Stir-fry for 3–5 minutes more. Transfer to a serving dish, sprinkle with coriander leaves, and serve hot. Serves 4.

Warm Spring Vegetable Salad

Warm salads of lightly cooked very fresh spring vegetables are a treat. Serve as a first course or as an accompaniment to grilled meat or poultry.

4 white spring onions
2 teaspoons olive oil
8 asparagus spears
About 125 g (4 oz) green beans
1 red capsicum (sweet pepper), seeded
1/2 ripe avocado
DRESSING
1 tablespoon malt vinegar
1 tablespoon Dijon mustard
1 tablespoon lemon juice
Salt and pepper to taste
2–3 tablespoons olive oil
2–3 tablespoons walnut oil

Trim the spring onions, keeping about 2 cm (³/₄ in) of the green part attached. Cut each onion into thirds or quarters lengthwise, depending on size. Heat the oil in a pan and gently cook the onions until softened but still with some firmness to them. Set aside. Trim the asparagus and top and tail the beans, then drop them together into boiling water for about 3 minutes. Drain, cut each into three or four long diagonal slices. Shred the capsicum finely and drop it into boiling water for a minute or so. Drain thoroughly.

Just before serving, warm all the vegetables lightly in the pan with the spring onions. Slice the avocado and add it to the vegetables. Arrange on plates and spoon the dressing over.

Dressing. Put the vinegar, mustard, lemon juice, salt and pepper in a bowl and whisk together. Gradually add the oils, whisking all the time, to form a thickish emulsion. Serves 4.

Som Tom

An exotic Thai vegetable salad, sweet and hot. Dried shrimp and fish sauce are available from Asian markets and health food shops. Serve as a first course or a light lunch.

¹/₂ *Chinese cabbage (Pe-Tsai), shredded*

1 cucumber, peeled and cut into fingers

1 pawpaw (papaya), peeled, seeded and sliced

250 g (8 oz) dried shrimp, soaked and drained, or 500 g (1 lb)
    fresh prawns, shelled

125 g (4 oz) tiny tom (cherry) tomatoes, halved

2 tablespoons roasted macadamia nuts or peanuts
    (groundnuts), chopped

DRESSING

2 tablespoons Thai fish sauce (nam pla)

1 tablespoon brown sugar

1 tablespoon chopped green shallot (spring onion, scallion)

3 tablespoons lime or lemon juice

¹/₂ *teaspoon freshly ground black pepper*

¹/₂–1 *teaspoon chopped fresh chilli or ground chilli powder*

2 garlic cloves, chopped

Make a bed of the shredded cabbage on a serving platter. Arrange the cucumber and pawpaw around the edge, put the shrimp or prawns in the centre, and arrange tomatoes around.

Make the dressing in a jar with a tight-fitting lid: combine the fish sauce, brown sugar, shallot and citrus juice, cover and shake well until the sugar dissolves. Add the pepper, chilli and garlic and shake again. Sprinkle the dressing over the salad and top with nuts and tomatoes. Serves 4–6.

Olive oil is the queen of salad oils and is available in grades from extra virgin, with exquisite flavour, to extra light, ideal for cooking. For salads, oil is sharpened with vinegar or lemon juice.

Bananas with Fresh Passionfruit Sauce

A simple dessert with wonderful fresh tropical flavours. Choose firm bananas for cooking and take care not to overcook them or they will be impossible to turn.

4 bananas
¼ cup (1½ oz) brown sugar
¼ cup (2¼ fl oz) rum or orange juice
1 teaspoon ground ginger
A pinch of salt
6 passionfruit (purple granadillas)
¼ cup (2¼ fl oz) water
2 tablespoons sugar
45 g (1½ oz) butter

*P*eel and cut the bananas in halves, lengthwise. In a shallow dish combine the sugar, half the rum or all the orange juice, and the ginger and salt. Stir well and add the banana halves.

Halve the passionfruit and scoop the flesh into a small bowl. In a small pan heat the water and sugar together until the sugar is dissolved and a light syrup is formed. Stir the syrup into the passionfruit pulp.

Melt half the butter in a sauté pan or chafing dish. Add the bananas, cut sides down, and the accompanying juices. Cook over a gentle heat for 5 minutes. Add the remaining rum and let it ignite. Shake the pan until the flames subside, then swirl in the remaining butter. Arrange the bananas on serving plates and spoon the juices, then the passionfruit sauce over.

Ricotta Desserts

*C*ottage cheese or the Italian ricotta is wonderful for low-fat diets. It can be used in salads or spread on bread, and it is the base for a number of delicious desserts. Buy it in small quantities as you need it, as it doesn't keep as long as a matured cheese. Combined with low-fat yoghurt or orange juice and blended until smooth, it is really delicious. Try the following:

Mix 4 tablespoons of ricotta with 2 teaspoons of honey, and serve with a ripe pear or sliced fruit in season and a few pecans or walnuts.

Flavour ricotta with lemon juice, grated lemon rind and a little sugar to taste, and serve with strawberries.

Remove the core from a thick slice of a sweet, ripe pineapple, and spoon ricotta in the centre.

Halve peaches or apricots, fill the centres with ricotta, and sprinkle with finely chopped almonds or a few pomegranate seeds.

Serve ricotta mixed with slices of pawpaw (papaya), rockmelon (cantaloupe), kiwi fruit, tamarillos (tree tomatoes) and strawberries, decorated with nuts and lemon wedges.

Stone dark, juicy cherries, mix with ricotta, and pile into bowls.

Combine 185 g (6 oz) of ricotta with 3 tablespoons of ground almonds, 2 tablespoons of chopped mixed peel, $\frac{1}{3}$ cup (3 oz) of sugar, the grated rind of 1 small lemon, a few drops of vanilla and 2 tablespoons of mixed raisins and sultanas (golden raisins). Serve with fruits or in small pots topped with toasted slivered almonds.

The poetic pomegranate came to us from Persia. Its deep pink seeds are used in salads and also make that marvellous flavouring, grenadine.

Fragole con Ricotta

If possible, use ricotta that has been delivered that day. The puréed strawberries can be spooned over any fresh fruit in season

> *2 punnets ripe strawberries*
> *4 tablespoons pine nuts*
> *375 g (12 oz) fresh ricotta*

Hull the strawberries and slice them. Place half in a food processor with the pine nuts and process until a purée is formed. The pine nuts thicken the purée slightly. Arrange wedges of ricotta on dessert plates with the remaining sliced strawberries. Spoon the purée over the strawberries and ricotta, and serve. Serves 6.

Oranges and Dates with Pine Nuts

Oranges combine beautifully with dates, as anyone who has made an orange and date cake will know.

> *4 navel oranges*
> *6–8 pitted dates, fresh if available*
> *2 tablespoons rum or 2 teaspoons orange flower water*
> *3 tablespoons toasted pine nuts*
> *A fine dusting of ground cinnamon*

Peel the oranges carefully, removing all the pith. Cut them into medium slices and arrange in a glass serving bowl. Slice the dates finely, spread them over the oranges, and sprinkle with the rum or orange flower water. Cover tightly and leave to macerate for at least an hour. To serve, sprinkle with the toasted pine nuts and dust lightly with ground cinnamon. Serves 6.

Strawberries à la Ritz, pure ambrosia as a mixture of ripe and luscious strawberries together with raspberries and orange segments. A red berry purée lightly flavoured with orange liqueur is folded through the fruits.

Strawberries à la Ritz

> *250 g (8 oz) ripe strawberries, gently washed and hulled*
> *250 g (8 oz) raspberries*
> *2 oranges, peeled and cut into segments*
> *1 tablespoon sugar*
> *2 tablespoons orange-flavoured liqueur (optional)*

Place two-thirds of the strawberries and raspberries in a glass serving bowl with the orange segments. Sprinkle with 1 tablespoon sugar. Whirl the remaining strawberries and raspberries and sugar in an electric blender, or mash with a fork and then force through a sieve. If using liqueur, add to the purée. Fold the sauce through the fruit. Chill, covered, until serving time. Serve with a sweet biscuit, such as Shortbread Sablés (page 327) or Madeleines (page 331). Serves 6–8.

Index

Page numbers in italics indicate illustrations

aigroissade *298*, 299
aïoli *190*, 191
almond, cream and pear tart
  346
  and prune tart *345*, 346, *347*
apples, baked 344; with mint 37
  cake, German 333
apricot and lamb pilaf 380
artichokes, braised 100, *101*
  clamart *8–9*, 98, *99*
  Crécy 100
  dressing 148
  frittata 60
  à la Grecque 100
arugula (rocket) 138
  carpaccio with, and artichoke
    dressing 148, *149*
asparagus 29, 102–4
  with lemon *102*, 103
  prosciutto au gratin 103
avocado, and chicken salad 156,
  157
  with goat cheese and smoked
    salmon en ficelle 63, *63*
  in guacamole 193

bacon, lettuce and tomato
  sandwich (BLT) 54
banana, date cake 334, *335*
  with passionfruit sauce 392
baps 320
basil 28, *29*, 43; sauce 187
bay leaf 28–29
bean sprouts, preparation 307
beans, borlotti, with roast lamb
  236
beans, dried
  haricot bean soup 78
  Tuscan, with sage 300, *301*
beans, green, with herb crumb
  topping 36
  Provençale 104
béchamel sauce 182
beef, appearance of 14
  in carpaccio with arugula and
    artichoke dressing 148, *149*
  in coconut 232
  fillet of, with Italian green
    sauce 222, *223*
  Niçoise 220, *221*
  meatballs in spinach and
    orange sauce 228
  medallions with dill sauce 223
  patties Cordon Bleu 229, *229*
  pepper steak, pan-grilled *224*,
    225

salad, with cumin vinaigrette
  226, *226*
  Korean 152, *153*
  Thai hot 227
stock 66, *67*
beetroot (beets), in borsch 73
  and endive salad 142, *143*
  with orange 105
beurre blanc 182
bisque, prawn 90
blueberry bran muffins *16–17*, 25
borsch 73
bouquet garni 32, *90*
brandy snaps 326
brawn 231
bread and butter pudding with
  whisky 344
breadcrumbs, making 362
bread: baps 320
  olive quick 337
  spoon *158–59*, 161
brioche, dough 320
  fruit loaf *321*, 323
broccoli 106
bruschetta 49, *51*
Brussels sprouts 106
  purée of 107
bucatini with pesto *15*
butter sauce 206; white 182
butternut squash with cumin 384

cabbage 11, 107
  Alsacienne 107
  leaves, stuffed *164*, 165
  steamed, Chinese style 108
Caesar salad *140*, 141
cakes and pastries (*see also*
  pastry)
  almond cream and pear tart
    346
  apple cake, German 333
  banana date cake 334, *335*
  blueberry bran muffins *16–17*,
    25
  brandy snaps 326
  brioche fruit loaf *321*, 323
  cheese biscuits 328, *329*
  chocolate roulade 354
  citrus tart 348
  fruit tarts, fresh 340, *340*
  le gannat *322*, 323
  gâteau de Pithiviers 338, *339*
  gougères bourguignonnes 325
  griddle cakes *22*, 23
  hazelnut crescents 326
  lemon shortbreads 332

lemon tea ring 332
  madeleines *318–19*, 331, *331*
  orange cake 332; Linda's 324
  orange and semolina cake,
    Greek 336, *337*
  orange pecan muffins *16–17*,
    24
  plum soufflé tart 341
  prune and almond tart *345*,
    346, *347*
  shortbread sablés 327
  teacake, Spanish 334
calamari, *see* squid
capers, capsicums with 109
  with chicken breasts 281
caponata Siciliana 135
capsicums (sweet peppers) 108–9,
  109, *388*
  Italian, with capers 109
  roasted, and tomato tians 388
  salad 166, *175*
  stuffed 162
caramel oranges 11, *342–43*,
  359, *359*
cardamom Bavarian cream 355
carpaccio with arugula and
  artichoke dressing 148, *149*
carrots 110, *110*
  soup, cream of 84, *85*
  Vichy 110
cauliflower, Mexican style 111
  Parmigiana 112
cheese, biscuits 328, *329*
  cream, sweet, with fresh fruits
    363
  goat's, avocado and smoked
    salmon en ficelle 63, *63*
  baked 362
  tomatoes and 27
  fresh, herbed *30*, 31
  and herbs in oil 42, *43*
  garlic 31
  herbed 35
  and spinach gnocchi 314, *315*
chervil and potato soup 72
chicken 13, 272–87
  and avocado salad 156, *157*
  barbecued, Thai *272*, 273
  Basque 282, *282*
  breasts, with capers and lemon
    281
  poached 283
  steamed 374
  coriander 374, *375*
  with garlic 273
  gingered, on skewers 379

green peppercorn 280, *280*
grilled, lemon *268–69*, 278
  with mustard sauce 274
  with orange 277
  salad, with balsamic vinegar *386*, 387
  spiced 276, *276*
  Thai 376
lemon pepper 284
marinade for 36
mustard, in yoghurt 380
in plum sauce 283
Provençalc 34
and rice soup 382, 383
roast chicken fantasia *3*, 270, *270, 271*
roasted, French 275
saltimbocca 278, *279*
soup, whole *64–65*, 78
stock 68, 275
tonnato 285, *285*
white cooked 373
chicken liver, warm mushroom and spinach salad 286, *286*
chicken livers and mushrooms 287
chickpeas (garbanzo beans) in aigroissade 299
chillies (chilli peppers) 306
Chinese parsley, *see* coriander
chives 30–31, 43
  dressing 389
chocolate roulade 354
citrus tart 348
clams, with fettuccine 304
  sauce 311
coconut, beef in 232
coriander, chicken 374, *375*
  chutney 187
  soup, spiced 72
coulis, berry 353
court-bouillon 196
couscous with vegetables *178*, 179
cream cheese mould with fresh fruits 363
cresses 12
croques monsieur 57
croutons 74
crudités 141–42, *190*
cucumbers, Lebanese 155
cumin, butternut squash with 384
curried red lentil soup 83
curry, mixed vegetable 173
  mung bean dhal 172
  prawn and pineapple 214

dates, and oranges with pine nuts 394
desserts 342–63
  almond cream and pear tart 346
  apples, baked 344

bananas with fresh passionfruit sauce 392
bread and butter pudding with whisky 344
caramel oranges *11*, *342–43*, 359, *359*
cardamom Bavarian cream 355
chocolate roulade 354
citrus tart 348
demerara meringues *350*, 351–52
fragole con ricotta 393
goat's cheese, baked 362
ice-cream Alexander 360
lemon parfait 360, *361*
mango in lime syrup 358
orange jellies 358
oranges and dates with pine nuts 394
pavlova, rolled 352
peaches, baked stuffed 349, *349*
pears, baked, in red wine 356
  in citrus sauce 356, *357*
prune and almond tart 346, *347*
ricotta, baked 362
strawberries à la Ritz 394
sweet cream cheese mould with fresh fruits 363
dhal, mung bean 172
dill sauce 223, 245
dough, *see* pastry
drinks, pep 18
duckling, with ginger and pears 288
  roast, with green peppercorn sauce 290

eggs, in peas and egg drop soup 76
  ranch-style *48*, 49
  scrambled, and smoked salmon 61
eggplant (aubergine) 114
  in caponata Siciliana 135
  in escalivada 146, *146*
  grilled 114
  and baby squash 133
  mousse *51*, 58
  Parmigiana *96–97*, 115
  stuffed 162
endive and beetroot salad 142, *143*
Esau's soup 169
escabeche of tongue 233
escalivada 146, *146*
escalopes of veal 260–62, *261*

fattoush 155
fennel, in lamb stuffing 234, *235*
fines herbes 32; with fish 199

fish (*see also the names of fish and shellfish*) 13–14, 194–217
  florentine 200
  grilled (broiled) 196, *197*
  poached 196
  raw fish salad 215
  sautéed fish meunière 199
  steaks with orange *198*, 199
  steamed fillets with ginger and sesame oil 204
  steamed fish coriander 202, *203*
  stew, Mediterranean *208*, 209
  stock 68
flamiche, leek *294*, 296, *297*
flan case (shell) 294
fragole con ricotta 393
frittata, artichoke 60
fritters, sweet corn 21
fruit, for breakfast 18, *19*
  tarts, fresh 340, *340*

garbanzo beans, *see* chickpeas
garlic, to smash 108
  cheese 31
  with chicken 273
gâteau de Pithiviers 338, *339*
gazpacho Andaluz 95
ginger, with duckling and pears 288
  mayonnaise 62
  sauce, fresh 374
  with steamed fish 204
  with steamed scallions 216
  with trout 207
gingered chicken/scallops on skewers *378*, 379
gnocchi, with butter and cheese 316
  Parisian, au gratin *312*, 313
  semolina 170, *170*
  spinach and cheese 314
gougères bourguignonnes 325
gravlax 205, *205*
green sauce *184–85*, 186, 222
griddle cakes *22*, 23
guacamole *192*, 193
guavas 327

haricot bean soup 78
harissa sauce *178*, 179
hazelnut crescents 326
herbs 12–13, 26–43, *34, 40*, 127; *see also individual names*
  bread 32
  oils 33, *33*
  quiche 295
  vinegars 33, *33*
hollandaise sauce 183
hot and sour soup 92
huevos rancheros *48*, 49

ice-cream Alexander 360

jellies, orange 358

kebabs, orange lamb 370, *371*
khichri 174

lamb, aillade 238
    appearance of 14
    and apricot pilaf 380, *381*
    butterflied leg 238, *239*
    chops, in caper sauce 242
        with dill sauce 244
    cutlets, devilled 242
    leg stuffed with fennel,
        mushrooms and bacon 234,
        235
    loin, pan-roasted, with fresh
        coriander chutney 370, *372*
    mini topside roast *12, 368*,
        369
    navarin, with baby vegetables
        246, 247
    orange kebabs, 370, *371*
    rack, parsleyed 240, *241*
    roast, with borlotti beans and
        tomatoes 236
        with mustard and peppercorn
        crust 237
    stew with green olives 245
    stir-fried, in pancakes 243
leeks, braised 115
    filo pie 299
    flamiche *294*, 296, *297*
    Niçoise 116, *117*
le gannat *322*, 323
lemon, butter 199
    chicken *268-69*, 278
    and lentil soup 92, *93*
    parfait 360, *361*
    pepper chicken 284
    rice 177
    shortbreads 328
    soup, Greek 91
    tea ring 332
lemon thyme 41
lentil, and lemon soup 92, *93*
    soup, curried red 83
lettuce, cups, stir-fried pork in
    377, *377*
    mixed, and nasturtium salad 154
lime syrup 358
lunch roll 28

madeleines *318-19*, 331, *331*
maître d'hôtel butter 40
mango, in lime syrup 358
marjoram 35-36
mayonnaise, *see* salad dressings
meat, potted *230*, 231
    storing of 14
    testing for doneness 370

meatballs, Persian, in spinach and
    orange sauce 228
meringues, demerara 351-52
    with chestnut and chocolate
    350, 351
    with passionfruit sauce 352
mesclun, and radicchio salad 138,
    139
    salad with chive dressing 389
mint 36-37, *37*, 43
    baked apples with 37
    butter 37
    tea 37
Monte Cristos 55
mornay sauce 182
muesli *16-17*, 20
muffins, blueberry bran and
    orange pecan *16-17*, 24, 25
muffuletta 52, *53*
mullet, red, barbecued *194-95*,
    200
mung bean dhal 172
mushrooms 116-20
    with chicken livers 287
    with chicken liver and spinach
    salad 286, *286*
    creamed 25
    grilled 120, *120*
    in lamb stuffing 234, *235*
    Lyonnaise *118*, 119
    sauce 172
    soup 86, *86*
mussels, preparation of 214
    in Pernod cream 87
    and potato salad 310
    with prawns and fettuccine 303
    with sauce poulette 212
mustard, chicken in yoghurt 380
    cream sauce 263
    and dill sauce 186

nasturtiums, in salad 154, *154*
noodles, fried Hokkien 307

oils, herb 33, *33*
olive quick bread 337
onions, 121, *244*
orange, butter 265
    cake 332; Linda's 324
    caramel *11, 342-43*, 359, *359*
    with grilled chicken 277
    and dates with pine nuts 394
    with fish steaks *198*, 199
    jellies 358
    lamb kebabs 370, *371*
    pecan muffins *16-17*, 24
    salad, Spanish 147
    and semolina cake 336, *337*
    and tomato soup *80*, 81
ox tongue, marinated 233
oyster, sauce 374
    soup Rockefeller 84

pancakes, Chinese, stir-fried lamb
    in 243
    spicy pork in 255
Parmesan twists 58, *59*
parsley 38
    butter 40
    fried 40
    sandwiches 38
parsnip soup, spiced 79
passionfruit sauce 352, 392
pasta dishes
    capellini with wine and clam
    sauce 311
    fettucine, with creamy tomato
    sauce 302
        with mussels and prawns in
        tomato sauce *292-93*, 303
        nero and saffron with clams
        304, *305*
    fusilli with smoked trout salad
    308, 309
    salad, green 302
        summer 168, *168*
    tagliatelle all'Amatriciana 306
    with uncooked tomato sauce
    304
pastry
    baking 'blind' 346
    basic yeast dough 46
    brioche dough *294*, 320
    shortcrust *294*; rich 345
pavlova, rolled 352
peaches, Italian baked stuffed
    349, *349*
pears *11*
    almond cream and pear tart
    346
    baked, in red wine 356, *357*
    in citrus sauce 356, *357*
    with duckling and ginger 288
    and watercress salad 144, *145*
peas 121-22
    and egg drop soup 76
    French style 122, *123*
    vegetable spaghetti with 385
pepper steak, pan-grilled *224*,
    225
peppercorns, green 280
    with chicken 280, *280*
    sauce 281, 291
pesto 187; bucatini with *15*
pilaf, lamb and apricot 380, *381*
    saffron 176
pissaladière *44-45*, 47
pitta bread, in fattoush 115
    herbed pittas 59
pizzas, French baton 56, *56*
    with fresh tomatoes 46
plum soufflé tart 341
po' boys 57
polenta, basic thick 166
    baked in tomato sauce 167

pork, appearance of 14
  Chinese spicy, in pancakes 255
  chops, with lemon and sage
      252, *253*
    marinated 42
    Rosmarin *250*, 251
  fillet piccata 254, *254*
  roast, with garlic 259
    herb crusted loin 252
    Thai 248, *249*
  salad, Thai 155
  schnitzel 258, *258*
  shredded, and noodles in broth
      256
    with peppers 257
  stir-fried, in lettuce cups 377,
      377
  Thai pork fried with garlic 257
potage bonne femme 74, *75*
potage Parmentier 74
potatoes 122–27
  baked stuffed 126
  cakes 196, *197*
  and chervil soup 72
  creamy mashed 125
  and mussel salad 310
  fish 127
  new, with basil 126
    with sun-dried tomato *124*,
      125
  salad 144
  sauté 127
potted meat 231
poultry 13, 268–91; *see also*
      individual names
prawns (shrimp) 91, *201*
  bisque 90
  and pineapple curry 214
  soup, Thai 91
  with mussels and fettuccine
      303
prosciutto, asparagus 103
prune and almond tart *345*, 346,
      347
pumpkin and saffron soup 76, 77
pumpkin-stuffed cabbage leaves
      164, 165

quail Portuguese 288, *289*
quiche, herb 295
  savoury 294
  spinach 295

radicchio and mesclun salad 138,
      139
rémoulade sauce *180–81*, 191
rendang daging 232
rhubarb, poached 18, *19*
rice, boiled, 72
  and chicken soup 382, *383*
  lemon 177
  Portuguese 287

ricotta, baked, savoury 174
  sweet 362
  desserts *364–65*, 392
  fragole con ricotta 393
rillettes of smoked salmon 62
risotto with tomatoes and basil
      167
rouille 209
roulade, chocolate 354
  herbed spinach 171

saffron, pilaf 176
  and pumpkin soup 76, 77
sage 40–41
  cheese 41
  and onion tart 41
  with cannellini beans 300
salad dressings
  aïoli 191
  chive 389
  mayonnaise *180–81*, *190*, 191
    garlic 191
    ginger 62
    yoghurt 193
  vinaigrette (French dressing),
      15, 188, *189*
    cumin 226, *226*
    green herb 220
    hot 188
salad greens 12, 138
salads 11–12, 136–57
  avocado and chicken 156, *157*
  beef, Korean 152, *153*
    Thai hot 227
  beetroot and endive 142, *143*
  butternut squash with cumin
      384
  Caesar *140*, 141
  capsicum 166, *175*
  carpaccio with arugula and
      artichoke dressing 148, *149*
  crudités 141
  escalivada 146
  fattoush 155
  grilled chicken, with balsamic
      vinegar *386*, 387
  green pasta 302
  lettuce, mixed, and nasturtium
      154
  mesclun, with chive dressing
      389
  mesclun and radicchio 138,
      139
  mussel and potato 310
  orange, Spanish 147
  pear and watercress 144, 145
  pork, Thai 155
  potato 144
  raw fish 215
  Som Tom 390
  summer pasta 168, *168*
  tomato 147

warm chicken liver, mushroom
      and spinach 286, *286*
  seafood *150*, 151
  spring vegetable 390
salmon, fillets, poached, with
      butter sauce 206, *206*
  marinated (gravlax) 205, *205*
  smoked, with goat cheese and
      avocado en ficelle 63, *63*
    open sandwiches 62, *63*
    rillettes of 62
    with scrambled egg 61
  soup 88, *89*
  steaks, grilled 204
  tartare with ginger mayonnaise
      on pumpernickel 61
sandwiches, *see* snacks
sardines, barbecued 200
  grilled 211
sauces 14–15, 180–93
  aïoli 191
  béchamel 182
  beurre blanc 182
  butter 206
  caper 243
  clam 311
  dill 223, 245
  ginger, fresh 374
  green *184–85*, 186, 222, *223*
  green peppercorn 281, 291
  guacamole 193
  harissa *178*, 179
  hollandaise 183
  Madeira cream 267
  mornay 182, 314
  mushroom 172
  mustard 274
  mustard cream 263
  mustard and dill 186
  oyster 374
  passionfruit 392
  pesto 187
  poulette 214
  rémoulade *180–81*, 191
  rouille 209
  tomato, chunky, and basil 184
    creamy 303
    fresh 184, *185*
    uncooked 304
  white butter 182
scallops *201*
  en brochette 215
  gingered, on skewers *378*, 379
  steamed, with ginger and spring
      onions 216, *217*
scaloppine, veal, with sherry
      vinegar 262
scampi *201*
seafood (*see also individual*
      names)
  salad, warm *150*, 151
semolina gnocchi 170, *170*

sesame cheese straws 330
shellfish (*see also names of shellfish*) 7, *202*
  bisque 90
shortbread sablés 327
shortbreads, lemon 328
snacks *29*, 44–63
  artichoke frittata 60
  bruschetta 49, *51*
  croques monsieur 57
  egg, scrambled, and smoked salmon 61
  eggplant mousse *51*, 58
  goat cheese, avocado and smoked salmon en ficelle 63, *63*
  huevos rancheros *48*, 49
  lunch roll 28
  muffuletta 52, *53*
  Parmesan twists 58, *59*
  pissaladière *44–45*, 47
  pittas, herbed 59
  pizzas, French baton 56, *56*
    with fresh tomatoes 46
  po' boys 57
  rillettes of smoked salmon 62
  salmon tartare with ginger mayonnaise on pumpernickel 61
  sandwiches
    bacon, lettuce and tomato 54
    croques monsieur 57
    Monte Cristos 55
    parsley 38
    smoked salmon open 62, *63*
  tapénade 50, *51*
  tomato Crostini 54
sorrel soup, cream of 82
soups (*see also* stock) 64–95
  borsch 73
  Brussels sprouts, purée of 107
  carrot, cream of 84, *85*
  chicken, whole *64–65*, 78
  chicken and rice 382, *383*
  coriander, spiced 72
  Esau's 169
  gazpacho Andaluz 95
  haricot bean 78
  hot and sour 92
  lemon, Greek 91
  lentil, curried 83
    and lemon 92, *93*
  mushroom, cream of 86, *86*
  mussels in Pernod cream 87
  oyster, Rockefeller 84
  parsnip, spiced 79
  peas and egg drop 76
  potage bonne femme 74, *75*
  potage Parmentier 74
  potato and chervil 72
  prawn, Thai 91
  prawn bisque 90

pumpkin and saffron 76, 77
salmon, fresh 88, *89*
sorrel, cream of 82
sweet corn 82
tomato, and orange *80*, 81
  roasted, and basil 366, *367*
vichyssoise 74
zuppa di stracciatella *94*, 95
zuppa di verdura *70*, 71
spinach, and cheese gnocchi 314, *315*
  in chicken liver and warm mushroom salad 286, *286*
  creamed, Tiffany 128
  and orange sauce with meatballs 228
  quiche 295
  roulade, herbed 171
  washing and cooking 128
spoon bread *158–59*, 161
squash, baby, and grilled eggplant 133
  butternut, with cumin 384
squid, baked stuffed 212, *213*
  cleaning and preparing 211
  with tomato and peas 210, *210*
stir-fried greens with oyster sauce 389
stock, beef 66, *67*
  chicken 68, 275
  duck 291
  fish 68
  vegetable 69
strawberries, à la Ritz 394
  with ricotta 393
sweet corn 112–13
  Creole 113, *113*
  fritters 21
  soup 82

tapénade 50, *51*
tarts, *see* cakes and pastries
teacake, Spanish 334
Thai: barbecued chicken *272*, 273
  grilled chicken 376
  hot beef salad 227
  pork roast 248, *249*
  pork salad 155
  prawn soup 91
thyme 41–42
tomatoes 55, 128–31, *306*, *388*
  with basil *29*
  cherry, pan-fried 366
  Crostini 54
  and goat's cheese 27
  in gazpacho 95
  Hassler *129*, 130
  with mixed herbs 34
  and orange soup *80*, 81
  pizza with 46

Provençale 38, *39*
  with risotto and basil 167
  roasted, and basil soup 366, *367*
  and roasted capsicum tians 388
  salad *29*, 147
  sauce, *see* sauces
  stuffed 162
trout with ginger 207
tuna, in green pasta salad 302
turnips, steamed with 131
Tuscan beans with sage 300, *301*

veal, appearance of 14
  birds with anchovies 263, *263*
  with black olives *218–19*, 266
  chops, grilled, with orange butter 265
    with Madeira cream sauce 267
  escalopes 260–62, *261*
    with mustard cream sauce 262
    with sherry vinegar 262
  Wiener schnitzel 264
vegetable spaghetti with fresh peas 385
vegetable stock 69
vegetables 10–11, 96–136; *see also names of vegetables*
  grilled 225
    vegetable platter 136, *137*
    sauté of ratatouille vegetables 134, *134*
  steamed 384
  stuffed, Mediterranean-style 161, *163*
  vegetable chilli bowl *158–59*, 160
  curry, mixed 173
vichyssoise 74
vinaigrette (French dressing) 15, 188, *189*
  cumin 226, *226*
  green herb 220
  hot 188
vine leaves, stuffed 162
vinegars 15

watercress and pear salad 144, *145*
weights and measures 6
Wiener schnitzel 264

yoghurt, fruits with 18
  mayonnaise 193
  mustard chicken in 380

zucchini (courgettes) 131–32, *131*
zuppa di stracciatella *94*, 95
  di verdura *70*, 71